D1393997

Photo: *Robert Turnbull, Columbus, Ohio*

GILBERT RYLE

19th August, 1900 to 6th October, 1976
President, 1945–46

PROCEEDINGS OF

THE
ARISTOTELIAN
SOCIETY

New Series—Vol. LXXVII

CONTAINING THE
PAPERS READ BEFORE
THE SOCIETY DURING
THE NINETY-EIGHTH
SESSION 1976/77

Published by
The Compton Press Ltd.
in association with The Aristotelian Society

First published 1977 by
The Compton Press Ltd.
The Old Brewery,
Tisbury, Wilts.

ISBN 0-900193-06-9

ISSN 0066-7374

Printed in England by
The Compton Press Ltd.,
The Old Brewery,
Tisbury, Wilts.

CONTENTS

ERRATA

page 54 lines 11–12:   *delete* exceptions *insert* exception
"   91 line 16:   *delete* mark *insert* remark
"   101 " 27:   *delete* comma *insert* full stop
"   156 " 14:   The formula in (1c) should read:

$$\overline{\overline{\mathrm{D}}}\ \mathop{\mathrm{k}}_{\mathrm{N}} f$$

"   217 " 4 from foot: *delete* superficial
"   222 " 14:   *delete* emphasis *insert* emphasise
"   226 " 3 from foot: *delete* It *insert* I
"   238 " 9:   *delete* hieratocracy *insert* hierocracy
"   245 note 8 line 4:   *delete* look *insert* looked
"   246 final line: for *in* read *on*

NOTE TO PAPER VII
Self-Knowledge and Intention
by Roger Scruton

The author draws attention to the connexion between his argument and papers by S. Shoemaker ("Self-knowledge and Self-awareness", *Journal of Philosophy*, 1968), G. J. Hopkins, ("Wittgenstein and Physicalism", *P.A.S.*, 1975–6), and, above all, M. J. Budd ("Materialism and Immaterialism", *P.A.S.*, 1969–70), whose important unpublished work on sensations contains much that is relevant to the argument in Section I.

I*—The Presidential Address

IDEALISM AND REALISM: AN OLD CONTROVERSY RENEWED

by D. M. MacKinnon

In his recent writings on the philosophy of logic, Michael Dummett has insisted that the dispute between idealism and realism is the central issue of metaphysics. Although it is always dangerous to refer to philosophical cruces as if they were contests between hypostatized abstractions, there is no doubt at all that Dummett is referring to issues of central importance. Moreover, they are issues which continually recur in new forms, even in forms startlingly unlike previous, even supposedly classical formulations. Thus problems raised by the apparently inescapable implications of part of Wittgenstein's later philosophy, especially his philosophy of mathematics, are a very long way from the sorts of question that beginners in philosophy first encounter in the study of Berkeley. Yet several writers on Wittgenstein have found it profitable and illuminating to trace analogies between his thinking and that of Kant, who devoted a celebrated passage in the Analytic of Principles to refuting what he called "idealism", encountered in "dogmatic" form in Berkeley, and in "problematic" form in Descartes. Kant's refutation is interesting in itself; but in his work it is a necessary part of his subtle and strenuous effort to have the best of both worlds, to hold together a view which treated learning about the world as a finding, with one that regarded such learning as a constructive act. It is partly in response to this dual claim that the analogy between his work and that of Wittgenstein is to be found, and far though Berkeley may be from Wittgenstein, it is worth remembering that it was by reference to Berkeley that in part at least Kant

* Meeting of the Aristotelian Society at 5/7, Tavistock Place, London, W.C.1, on Monday, 11th October, 1976 at 7.30 p.m.

defined his own position, and that the position of a man sensitive as Wittgenstein was to the pull of hardly reconcilable
considerations.

Do we invent, or do we discover? If we are at all sensitive to
etymology, we may suspect that this is no genuine dichotomy;
for the sense of the Latin *invenire* lingers in the title of the
ancient feast of the Invention of the Cross, commemorating
Helena's alleged finding of the instrument of Christ's execution. The inventor achieves, and by achieving discloses possibilities. The frontier between inventing and discovering does
not coincide with that between "knowing how" and "knowing
that"; rather it suggests that there are important areas of
border dispute between these allegedly contrasted opposites.
I learn unguessed secrets by manipulating a situation to bend
its potentialities to the purposes of my enquiry. Collingwood
pointed out how often causal enquiries were practically determined;[1] the identification of one feature in a situation rather
than another, as the cause of difficulties that confront us, is
determined by that feature's amenability to practical treatment. Thus a motorist will blame his difficulties on the state
of his brakes, rather than on the gradient of "Rest-and-be-
Thankful" or Porlock Hill; this because his brakes are, within
limits, under his own control; (if he is no expert, he can seek
technical assistance when they are clearly out of order); whereas he can do nothing about the gradient of the hill. Again if
a D.I.Y. enthusiast blows up his bungalow, and nearly kills his
wife, his two children, and himself, we find the cause in his
belief that he could effectively service his gas-fired central
heating installation himself, and not on the properties of
natural gas. In both these cases, attribution of cause is expressive of selectivity, conditioned by interest and available skills.

Our knowledge of the world about us is directed, and enlarged and advanced by our concerns, and it assumes the kinds
of form that it takes partly by reason of its permeation by such
interests. We are part of the world, and when we hold it at a
distance from ourselves, as we do when we seek to enlarge our
understanding of its order, the very act of doing so constrains
the world to assume a different look from the one it has when
we are living, breathing, eating, what you will. Yet when we
recall the extent to which we are unquestionably part of the

natural world, we find that we can do no other than acknowledge the authority of the objective. The world is as it is, and not as we might want it. We can surmount the hill, and keep ourselves and our families alive by having our brakes mended, or by admitting that gas-fired installations demand the skill of the professional. Yet it is because hills are as they are, and natural gas as it is, that we must adjust in the way in which we have to. It is the way in which things are that sets us the problem of practical adjustment, and certainly we often learn sharp lessons concerning their order through the defeat of early initiatives and of unreflective interference.

Again, when we turn to consider the most significant and powerful styles of conceptual innovation, we certainly find our horizons enlarged, it may be by the resources of more powerful sorts of mathematics or by such developments as electron-microscopy and sheer virtuosity in their exploitation. But there remain horizons. There are conceptual constants which make possible the assimilation of the most novel advances, either in suggestion of theoretical order, or in manipulative technique. Yet it was Kant who, with an unexampled delicacy and subtlety of intellectual perception, insisted that these constants were *our* constants, and that where that *our* is concerned, it is most difficult to draw the line between what is imposed from the side of the subject, and what from that of the material with which the subject has to do. If these constants are expressive of the form of the world, they are so expressive as realizing the inescapable limits of our understanding.

The term *anthropocentric* is not infrequently used to characterize the point of view that insists on the relativity of most, if not all, forms of conceptual order to the human experient. Kant's doctrine was anthropocentric in so far as he argued that the objective world from which the subject differentiated himself and by so doing achieved self-consciousness, was, in respect of its most pervasive structural order, expressive of the way in which that subject necessarily came to terms with what was thrust at him. What we called our world, we had assimilated by imposing on the matter of sensation, a shape that we could only confidently affirm to characterize it within the limits of our experience.

The constants of spatial location, and of temporal date, of substantial permanence, and of causal determination, interwoven one with another as they are, are constants of a human world. Yet there is nothing arbitrary in our use of them. Indeed it is on the ground of his totally uncritical attachment to the fundamental laws of Newtonian physics that Kant has been most frequently charged with lapse into the sort of dogmatism he disliked in others. His own vaunted apparatus of "transcendental proof", ingenious though its conception may be, does not in the end (we are told) deliver him from bondage to the illusions that the cosmology he knew was of final authority, and that the sorts of natural law that he was concerned to insist to be of universal scope,[2] were alone admissible as patterns of change *etc.* Such dogmatism (illustrated *e.g.*, by his belief that he has proved *a priori* the "law of the conservation of mass") is at least evidence of the extent to which any suggestion that conceptual order was a matter of arbitrary choice was inimical to Kant. If he regarded the experiential constants he sought so painfully to extract and to vindicate (at his most profound, differentiating them by rarefied abstraction from the fundamental laws of classical physics) as expressive of the characteristic styles of the human experient, they were significant not as belonging in any sense to the inner life of the subject, but in the constitution of his world. It was as conditions of objectivity that their sense lay.

"How are objects of experience possible?" To ask such a question is to direct attention away from the sort of consideration that would encourage a man to treat intellectual activity as if it were a prolonged essay in imaginative or inventive ingenuity. Certainly imaginative boldness, conceptual as well as experimental innovation, are both alike indispensable. Indeed if one moves from study of nature to that of human history, or indeed human behaviour, the extent to which advance of understanding depends on the fusion of careful study of available material with the kind of intuitive perception which may succeed in unlocking the secrets of complex situations of seemingly impenetrable density cannot be denied. Any slavish adherence to supposedly secure, itemised atoms of alleged certainty without the inevitable risk that must accompany an essay in constructive understanding dooms the adherent to the sort of safe success, wherein security is purchased at the cost of fundamental advances both in insight and practical mastery.

In his book—*The Logic of Modern Physics*—Professor P. W. Bridgman summarized Einstein's analysis of the concept of simultaneity by claiming that he was insisting that the statement that two events are simultaneous was equivalent to the statement that two events satisfy the conditions required for us to pronounce them simultaneous. In other words, simultaneity is reduced to terms of the criterion or criteria for the application of the concept, and two events are properly judged simultaneous when we judge ourselves justified in so regarding them. The standard or standards by reference to which we think ourselves thus justified are of our own devising. What we mean when we claim two events to be simultaneous is not that the statement that they are simultaneous accords with the facts, but that the use of the concept of simultaneity in respect of their occurrence is justified.

But what of the principles by which it is justified? And what is involved in the attempt to formulate them? If we approach the analysis of the concept of truth by way of examples of proposition to which the application of the picture-theory is not *prima facie* implausible, we come to think of questions concerning acceptability or inacceptability as settleable by comparison of proposition and fact in a way analogous to that in which *e.g.*, the features of an "identikit" picture may be compared with those of the man the police believe likely to be able to help them with their enquiries. What is more important we are sure that the question whether or not one proposition is true or false can be settled independently of the question whether or not another proposition is true or false. Thus the question whether or not there is a thunderstorm in Barcelona on July 1st 1976 can be settled without reference to the question whether or not there is a Spanish treasure-ship sunk in Tobermory Bay in the inner Hebrides. Thus, without committing ourselves to the logical mythology of "atomic propositions" corresponding with "atomic facts", and the implied ontology of ultimate simples, we are enabled to make sense of the view that there are a number of propositions of whose truth in the sense of correspondence we are assured which are genuinely independent one of another.

At this point inevitably we are reminded of controversies concerning the so-called externality or internality of relations to the terms they are said to relate, which were closely interwoven with the arguments between protagonists of the so-called "coherence" theory of truth and those who like Russell and Moore in the first decade of the present century, sought to rehabilitate the classical Aristotelian doctrine of truth as "correspondence".[3] Indeed the thesis that at least some of the relations in which some states of affairs in the world stood to other states of affairs left the states of affairs in themselves totally unaffected was an ontological assumption (defended, for instance, by Moore in his very influential paper—*Internal and External Relations*) that was seen to be demanded by any form of correspondence theory.

The coherentist would argue in reply to the claims made for the alleged correspondence of structure as well as of features between proposition and fact in the examples taken that the alleged separability of these statements from the continuum of the world of experience was far less clear cut than we might suppose. Thus in the two examples taken assumptions concerning date and location involving quite sophisticated methods of chronology and cartography were in use. Further the frontiers between events (and *fact* in the context of these discussions has been effectively defined as an event or set of events regarded as making a given proposition true or false)[4] are blurred: they cannot be endowed in their individuality with the sort of self-containedness that must be found in them if they are to fulfil the rôle which the referents of true propositions must play.

"It is in the stream of life that an expression has meaning". This remark of Wittgenstein's is often quoted as embodying the fundamental insight underlying a so-called "holistic" theory of meaning. According to this view, to understand what we say when we utter any sort of sentence, we must do justice to its total context in language. If we claim that by knowing what individual language-fragments purport to refer to and therefore by knowing what must be the case if the propositions these fragments frame are to be accounted true, we fail to do justice to the extent that the force and significance of such fragments reside in their total setting. Further it is only in regard to that setting that we know what it is that we are doing when we use this or that sentence. Even such relatively simple factual statements as the two mentioned in illustration above (*viz.,* concerning the weather in Barcelona, and the sunken treasure-ship in Tobermory Bay) cannot be treated as if they were somehow detachable from the whole business of living in which they have their home. The claim that to grasp the meaning of an expression we must attend to the intricacies of its rôle in our language as a whole is clearly bound up with the emphasis on justified assertibility or use as distinct from truth-conditions, that I illustrated above by reference to Bridgman's comment on Einstein's definition of simultaneity. In Wittgenstein's later work, it is arguably in his treatment of problems in the philosophy of mathematics that his emphasis on assertibility as the ground of legitimate use comes full-tide, and with a wealth of examples, concerned now to cure hearers or readers of the illusion that "pure mathematics is the physics of the intelligible realm" and by revealing the special rôles of calculation in advancing knowledge of the details of our world, to throw light on the relation of pure to applied mathematics; now to bring out for the whole theory of necessary truth, the implications of regarding mathematics as invention rather than discovery; now to criticize Russell's work on the foundations of mathematics, he seems to ground every sort of necessity in an arbitrary *fiat* of the subject. Yet what he is doing only begins to become clear when viewed in relation to language as a whole.

The phrase "holistic theory of meaning" may recall the metaphysical slogan of the thoroughgoing coherentists that "nothing is true, but the whole of truth". The palpable absurdity of speaking of the "whole of truth" as true has often been pointed out: but those who, for instance, heard the late Professor Harold Joachim lecture in Oxford as late as the mid-thirties will recall the incantatory quality of his diction as if he would communicate a vision in which the familiar would emerge transformed, but with its many contraditions eliminated (a strict Hegelian would say *aufgehoben*) by this transformation.

Certainly those who champion the "holistic" solution to the problem of meaning are innocent alike of indulgence in absurdity and of invocation of an incommunicable absolute. And again for the most part they eschew the generous ambiguity with which such notions as coherence and system were employed by coherentists enabling them to blur the differences between very different sorts of system and between equally different examples of coherent discourse. Thus we speak of the system of Euclidean geometry, of Leibniz' metaphysical system, of systems of book-classification in libraries, of so-and-so's system for betting on horses, or playing roulette; we characterize a search or investigation as systematic when we intend no more than that it is conducted according to a plan. Again we blame a lecturer for incoherence when we mean that we have been unable to grasp the relations between different phases of his argument, or the design informing the presentation of items that seem in order to have mention almost at random. Further when we acquit a man of the charge of being under the influence of drink on the ground that his speech was coherent, we refer to the fact that his statements were intelligible and consistent both internally and one with another.

In practice we do use the notion of coherence, invested with a certain "openness of texture", in admitting or disallowing the claim of assertions made concerning matters of fact to our acceptance, or at least to our consideration. Thus in the claim recently made that the recovery from a terminal cancer of the intestines of a Glasgow dock labourer named Fegan was miraculous (effected allegedly by the intercession of a 17th century Jesuit martyr, James Ogilvie, who was executed for refusing to acknowledge the supremacy in matters ecclesiastical in Scotland of James VI), the general practitioner, who was attending Fegan in what he confidently expected to be the last stages of a lengthy illness, while admitting such surprise that he momentarily questioned his diagnosis (he was not, I suspect, speaking seriously), disallowed the possibility that the sufficient and necessary condition of his patient's recovery should be found in divine intervention (whether or not elicited by the Jesuit's prayers, those prayers having themselves been as a matter of fact invoked by a group, including Fegan's wife and parish priest.) Even if the G.P. could be accused of a metaphysically and theologically unsophisticated attitude to the relations of primary to secondary causality, we can hardly deny the good sense he showed in seeking to explain Fegan's recovery naturalistically. A specialist indeed suggested that in this very remarkable recovery, there was possibly a paradigmatic, certainly a highly dramatic, instance of the spontaneous regression of a cancer: of such regressions there are now a sufficient number for their occurrence to constitute a phenomenon urgently requiring investigation, not least to find ways in which such regressions might be effectively induced. Such characterization is not explanatory: Fegan's recovery has been tentatively identified, and (it may be) the concept through which it has been so identified enlarged. One might even say that its significance has been defined, and that, in a way that at once banishes substitution of self-indulgent mystery-mongering for understanding while at the same time emphasising fields in respect of which explanatory concepts are not available, but must be sought.

This example illustrates the extent to which in a properly sophisticated every-day use of the notion of coherence, a balance is struck between insistence on the fluidity of any sort of confidently embraced conceptual system and refusal to disallow the relative authority of certain experiential constants. Yet these constants, often conceived much more loosely than through a quasi-Kantian "transcendental deduction", are never by the coherentist invested with any sort of inviolability, whether by appeal to alleged rational intuition or to a supposedly unchallengeable common sense. It is certainly the case that for the coherentist this fluidity (if I may continue the metaphor) belongs to the waters of a river or ocean whose pattern is ultimately both stable, all-embracing and all-reconciling. But the analogies between the coherentist's attitude and the principle implicit in the attitude of those who subscribe to a "holistic" theory of meaning is worth exploring; and it is arguable that both agree in a determination, if not to abandon, at least radically to depreciate concern with what is or is not the case in the sense in which such concern is affirmed as central by those who identify truth fundamentally with correspondence: this though they realize the need for the utmost sophistication in analysis of that correspondence.

If truth, however, is identified with correspondence with fact, it should be clearly recognized that correspondence is to be regarded as the "focal meaning" of the term—truth. That is, we most certainly do use the term "truth" when it would be a sheer mistake to suppose that we could substitute for it "correspondence with fact". For instance, if we claim that one physical theory has displaced another, and are not content with analysing that displacement in terms of greater conceptual economy, comprehensiveness, simplicity, even aesthetic quality, but wish to insist on a more secure purchase-hold on what is the case, we immediately recognize the inadequacy of the notion of correspondence to convey the advance achieved. Again,[5] if we allow that it makes sense to speak of truth in connexion with a system of non-Euclidean geometry, it is obvious that here truth must be analysed in terms of the internal coherence between axioms, postulates, theorems, *etc.* It is as if the spread of the notion of truth enables the notion to comprehend relationships between propositions that seem to have little or nothing to do with its "focal" sense.

So indeed in the classical instance of forms of being in Aristotle, *sterēsis* or deprivation may be thought to have nothing significantly in common with substance. And again, to develop an example used by Professor J. L. Austin,[6] forms of Fascist polity may be noticed that cannot be regarded as inspirationally derivative from the political ideas and enterprises of Benito Mussolini (for instance that of Charles Maurras and l'Action Française which antedates by a considerable period, the preparation of the so-called "March on Rome"), but which are none the less, properly classified as Fascist by reference to the paradigm of Mussolini's movement. The conceptual unity is established through the tracing of the relationships to the "focal" realization; we may say that sometimes it is the positing of the "focal" case, as distributing its sense *kat' analogian*[7] through the quasi-derivative realizations, that enables us to group together what otherwise might fall apart.

The issue with which this paper is concerned can now be restated in terms of the extent to which we allow the notion of truth in the sense of correspondence to pervade and control the way in which we understand our thinking to relate to what is the case. Or must we see our coming to terms with our world as something that is pervaded less by bringing our thought into submission to what is the case than by continually adjusting and revising standards of the acceptable of which we are in the last resort ourselves the authors?

It is a commonplace to claim for the so-called "anti-realism", inspired by Brouwer's rejection of the "law of excluded middle" that it does justice to the very many propositions of which it is impossible for us to say decisively whether they be true or false. Admission or rejection is a matter for our own decision. And what may be claimed in respect of universal propositions or unrestricted generality must also be said where very many, if not all, the most important, indeed exciting things we say about the past are concerned. It is not simply that where, for instance, the study of such a period as XVIIth century English history is concerned, characteristically Marxist assumptions serve to direct the attention of historians, already cognizant of the variety of source-materials available, to tracts of that material they have hitherto neglected; nor is it also simply a matter of setting the constitutional and religious conflicts of the age of the Civil War in the context of contemporary economic conflicts and changes, and seeking to understand the former by reference to the latter. Rather it is a sense that no frontiers can easily be set to the corrigibility of historical judgments, and that revolutions of perspective at least as great as the one mentioned may occur, altering our most elementary sense of what it is to come to terms with the past as historians.

To one concerned with questions in the philosophy of theology to-day these issues are necessarily raised very sharply where the question of the so-called "essence of Christianity" is concerned. It has been a commonplace to insist that if truth or indeed falsity is to be claimed for Christianity, this claim demands that certain statements shall be defensibly made concerning the life and teaching of its alleged founder. Thus Bertrand Russell insisted that the claims made for the supreme moral excellence of Jesus fell to the ground in view of the fact that he is represented in the Gospels as threatening everlasting torment to those whose behaviour failed to conform with the standards he proclaimed, or indeed refused to adhere to him. Similarly others have been moved to a very different judgment from Russell's by the way in which (from their reading of the Gospel narratives) Jesus is represented as going to his death, disdaining any and every sort of violent intervention to attempt to extricate him from his predicament, praying for the executive agents of his brutal execution, indeed by his whole endurance, expressing in deed the inwardness of the reply to his flatterer, which so much impressed Kant: "Why callest thou me good? One only is good: namely God".

Yet it is very often insisted to-day that Russell and the believer whose attitudes I have contrasted with his are alike guilty of the same errors both in supposing that from the Gospels (and other New Testament writings) it is possible to extract a portrait of the so-called "founder of Christianity", and also in supposing that if it were so, the features discernible in such a portrait would be of fundamental importance to the question whether or not Christianity is true or false. The question whether or not such a portrait can be extracted from the New Testament writings is a highly technical question, involving, in particular, an answer to the question not whether or not the Gospels are biographies (in the sense in which *e.g.*, Xenophon's *Memorabilia Socratis*, Plutarch's *Lives*, Suetonius' *Lives of the Caesars* etc. may be so regarded) but whether or not they may be judged in any sense properly biographical in character, whatever other purposes, even other primary purposes, they may have served. There is, however, no doubt at all that the very genuine difficulties involved in treating the Gospels as biographical sources have proved very congenial to those who would argue the total or near-total irrelevance of the historical reconstruction of the likeness of Jesus of Nazareth to the question of the truth or falsity of Christianity. Indeed they would argue that when we come to see Gospel-writing as an episode or a set of episodes in the development of the Christian movement, we will come to see that it is that movement to which we may (if we choose) adhere which gave the Gospels their significance, and in which indeed in their contemporary use they continue to find significance. Their sense resides not in what they purport to describe as having happened, but in the uses to which they may be put.[8] We should not seek to conceive what it is that they say in order to decide whether or not it is the case, but rather to find them acceptable by constraining them to translation into terms of our own situation.

It is claimed for such an attitude that it acknowledges both the corrigibility of any and every historical reconstruction of the past, and at the same time, by emphasising the priority of questions of use over reference in determining whether or not certain alleged vehicles of meaning may still be given free currency, it allows significant sources to continue to exercise a special authority. But in all this we make ourselves and the laws concerning what may be permissibly said, which we are for ever fashioning and refashioning, the ultimate arbiters.

Yet the distinction between historical reconstruction and historical fiction remains. The past may be something that we regard ourselves as continually refashioning. But there are irreversible advances in historical understanding. Yet certainly such advances are necessarily limited in scope to the human scene; for historical work (unless one regards geology, evolutionary biology, and cosmology as historical in character) is necessarily and innocently anthropocentric. It is a sheer mistake to infer from the proposition that many disputed questions are to-day incapable of settlement and likely to remain so, that no questions here are capable of decisive settlement. For there are constants which help to define the area of the problematic.

Yet what of the more deeply pervasive anthropocentrism mentioned at the outset of this paper? Have we not in the end to reckon with the extent to which standards which are necessarily human standards, pervade and determine the very structural constants through which we seek to let that which is the case have its way with us? Is not the very concept of the world whose order is as it is and not as we would have it, a concept framed in terms of our seeking to distinguish the world from ourselves and thereby to enter more deeply on the irreducible uniqueness of our self-hood? It may be that as a result of empirical investigation whether cosmological or directed to the close study of animal behaviour and communication (*e.g.*, among dolphins) some of the constants which we employ (*e.g.*, time, space, communication itself) will be delivered from part of their anthropocentric taint. Yet the idealist's claim that we decide what questions are answerable or how questions should be understood that they may be made answerable, continues to infect our confidence that we know what must be the case if this or that proposition is to be accounted true, even if we shall never ourselves be able to determine whether or not it is so. In knowing the truth-conditions of a statement, do we or do we not leave behind or disregard built-in limitations of our human condition? It is as if at this point another question began to emerge: namely, what limitations we may suppose one day likely or conceivably to be overcome, and what we must accept as built-in to the very possibility of asking whether or not something is the case? It may well be that a part at least of the enquiry traditionally named 'ontology' is concerned to lay hold of the latter and to give an account of them as comprehensive and as free of counter-intuitive paradox as possible. It may indeed also emerge here that the very discontent with idealism, to which reference has often been made in this paper, is expressive of a recurrent sense that to abandon concern with what is the case, and to allow all that one can justify oneself in accepting in the sense in which one can render it acceptable, is to convert awareness of anthropocentrism from a problem into a solution, or rather into a recipe for dissolving a multitude of problems. Yet through continual worrying at these problems, some insight may be won, even though that insight be very different in nature and content from what we might anticipate.

NOTES

[1] *P.A.S.*, 1937-8, pp. 85-112.

[2] I am not forgetting his great interest in teleological explanation, especially in biology.

[3] In his valuable article on the correspondence theory of truth, contributed to the *Encyclopaedia of Philosophy* (edited by Professor Paul Edwards), the late Dr. A. N. Prior rightly emphasised the permanent value of this early 20th century discussion as a contribution to the philosophy of logic.

[4] *e.g.*, by Professor John Wisdom in his series of articles in *Mind* on *Logical Constructions*, and by Professor H. H. Price.

[5] I am much indebted here to discussions with the late Dr. Friedrich Waismann.

[6] In his essay—"The Meaning of a word"—in *Philosophical Papers* (O.U.P.).

[7] Mediæval students of Aristotle spoke of such predication as "analogy of attribution", and some, for instance Cajetan, in his *de Analogia Nominum*, depreciated its importance in metaphysics vis-à-vis "analogy of proper proportionality".

[8] These uses may, of course, differ profoundly from one Gospel to another. Indeed in answering the question—What is a Gospel?—we may find a classical illustration of four works grouped together by reason of analogy, or "family resemblance".

II*—SCRUTON AND WRIGHT ON ANTI-REALISM *ETC.*

by P. F. Strawson

Both symposiasts agree that a theory of meaning for a language should also be a theory of understanding, *i.e.*, it should yield an account of what a speaker's understanding of the language consists in. They both refer to truth-theories, of a kind familiarly advocated: theories which implicitly represent the speaker's understanding of the declarative sentences of the language as consisting in knowing, in effect, under what conditions those sentences would be true [or: under what conditions utterance of those sentences would yield truth], irrespective of whether it could be *conclusively* ascertained that those conditions held or did not hold. Mr. Scruton is inclined to say that such a theory could be correct as far as it went, but would not be complete or adequate; that it would require *supplementation* by an account, which might be more grateful to the verificationist ear, of the criteria which an understanding speaker would use for the application of certain predicates of the language, *viz.*, those which were treated as primitive by the theory. However, such supplementation, he suggests, would constitute no challenge to the realist framework of the theory.

Mr. Wright suggests that this view of Scruton's shows a misunderstanding of what a truth-theory purports to supply. Such a theory states the satisfaction-conditions of primitive predicates quite explicitly, and indeed it is on this basis that it delivers the truth-conditions of sentences. So why, Wright enquires, if the truth-theory requires any supplementation at all, should it require supplementation only in the case of primitive predicates? Why not, for example and crucially, in the case of quantifiers too? The enquiry is pertinent, and

---

* This address was delivered by Prof. Strawson on Sunday, 11th July, 1976, as Chairman of the symposium "Truth Conditions and Criteria" by Mr. Roger Scruton and Mr. Crispin Wright during the annual Joint Session of this Society and the Mind Association at the University of Warwick; see *Arist. Soc., Supplementary Volume* L, 1976, pp. 193-245. At the request of members, the address is here presented in the form in which it was originally delivered.

its pertinence leads one to suppose that Wright's suggestion of a misunderstanding on Scruton's part may well be correct. But Wright's own position on the matter of supplementation is also open to question. He seems to think that if a truth-theory delivered an account of what the understanding speaker knows, then such a theory should be in no need of supplementation at all—it would already embody a full account of speaker's understanding. But this is by no means clear. To say what a speaker knows is not of itself to give an account of what his knowing it in practice consists in, of how his knowledge is manifested in his use of the language.

A rational speaker's grasp of his language is *manifested* in, *inter alia*, his responding in certain ways to the recognisable situations with which he is and has been confronted. So much is agreed on all hands, and is part of the reason why the theory of knowledge and the theory of understanding are inseparable. But Mr. Wright seems to take it as evident that the rational speaker's response to such situations can in *no* case be *governed* by a certain kind of conception—a conception of a state of affairs, of a condition of truth, which, for one reason or another, in fact or in principle, is not, or is no longer, or is not for the speaker, accessible to direct observation or memory. But this question—whether the rational speaker's response can be so governed—is just the question at issue; and one has the impression that Mr. Wright quite handsomely begs it. For on this crucial point I do not find that he produces any real argument. He suggests that no one who takes seriously the connexion between meaning and use can dissent from his view. But this is not at all obvious. It *is* obvious enough that, as Wright puts it, "grasp of the sense of a sentence cannot be displayed in *response* to unrecognisable conditions". No truth-theorist needs to dispute this tautology. It is enough for the truth-theorist that the grasp of the sense of a sentence can be displayed in response to *recognisable* conditions—of various sorts: there are those which conclusively establish the truth or falsity of the sentence; there are those which (given our general theory of the world) constitute evidence, more or less good, for or against the truth of the sentence; there are even those which point to the unavoidable absence of evidence either way. The appropriate response varies, of course, from case to case, in the last case being of the form, 'We shall never know whether p or not'. Perhaps Wright objects to this because he thinks we oughtn't to *have* a general theory of the world which extends further, so to speak, than we can see. But this is a matter in which we have no option; and any theory of meaning had better adapt itself to the fact even at the cost of sacrificing a dogma or two.

I have not so far spoken as if it was anything but reasonably clear what the issue between the verificationist or anti-realist and his truth-theoretical opponent amounted to. But in fact I am very hazy about exactly where the actual lines of disagreement are supposed to be drawn. And this point at least must remain *un*clear just so long as it remains unclear where the limits of possible conclusive verification are supposed to fall; unclear just in which cases, and why, what the one party regards as the truth-condition of a sentence is seen by the other as verification-transcendent and therefore as something either wholly dubious or at least as having no rôle to play in the explanation of the speaker's understanding of the sentence. So we need to know *at least* what is to count as falling within the range of "recognisable situations", what is to count as conclusive verification, *whose* capacity in fact or in principle to do the recognising is in question, what importance, if any, to attach to the disjunction "in fact or in principle" and what "in principle" means. My own impression is not that we are in the presence of a single clear-cut issue, but rather that we are in a confused area in which several well-worn philosophical problems are jostling each other as well as a number of new, and perhaps gratuitous, perplexities. Certainly the route *into* the area is relatively new: the new anti-realism starts from certain views on mathematical truth and mathematical discourse and seeks to generalise them to the extent of advancing counterpart views on discourse concerning the natural world. Of mathematics I am quite incompetent to speak. But there is a certain initial air of paradox about this approach; for I suppose that part at least of the appeal of anti-realist views about pure mathematics lay precisely in the *contrast* between the content of that science and the subject-matters of history, geography, natural science and ordinary chat; that it lay precisely in the view that the notion of a realm of facts waiting to be explored, some parts of which might, indeed would, remain undisclosed or be irrecoverably lost sight of, (a matter at best of speculation or uncertain inference)—that any such notion was quite improperly imported into mathematics from its natural home, *viz.*, the natural world.

However, general complaints of unclarity or initial paradox don't advance discussion of any issue very much, so I should like to refer to one or two particular cases. I take first the ancient case of the sentence 'John is in pain', spoken of John by another. Mr. Wright, if I have understood him correctly, attributes to his opponent the view that the sentence (or statement) has a truth-condition which, from the speaker's point of view, is necessarily verification-transcendent, but which nevertheless governs the speaker's use of the sentence. The speaker's knowledge of these truth-conditions, on this view, constitutes his grasp of its meaning. What is Mr. Wright's alternative view of the relation of truth-condition to meaning in this case? There seem to be three possibilities:

(1) The sentence has no *truth-condition* at all; it is just a right thing to say in a certain range of circumstances, and knowing its meaning is practical knowledge of what those circumstances are.

(2) The sentence has truth-conditions, and knowing its meaning is practical knowledge of these; but its truth-conditions (at least for everyone except John) are nothing other than the disjunction of the circumstances aforementioned.

(3) The sentence has a truth-condition, but this has nothing to do with its meaning (at least for anyone except perhaps John); anyone else can understand the sentence without knowing what its truth-condition is.

I have arranged the possibilities in order of decreasing attractiveness. The last has the consequence that someone could have a complete grasp of the meaning of what he said without knowing what he was saying, *i.e.*, asserting—an unappealing thought. The second amounts to a behaviourist, or some other variety of physicalistic, reductionism—with perhaps the additional feature that the predicate 'in pain' has a different sense in the mouth of a self-ascriber from that which it has in the mouth an other-ascriber. The first—which denies that the sentence has a truth-condition at all—is the least unattractive; but it has the unsatisfactory feature that it leaves one with no account of what the speaker, in uttering the sentence, is actually doing. It is really no good simply saying that he is making an "assertoric use" of the sentence when it has just been denied that there is anything he actually asserts in uttering it. Something different, or at least something further, must be said. Thus, for example, Ramsey, when he denied the propositional status of variable hypotheticals (open generalisations), was ready with an alternative account: they are not judgments, he said, but rules for judging. They could be adopted or rejected, but not, strictly speaking, asserted or denied. Or Mackie, who denies truth-value to conditionals, at least in their core meaning, offers an account of what one is doing in uttering them. It is not my purpose here either to endorse or to criticise such accounts. The point is that *some* alternative account of what the speaker is doing in saying 'John is in pain' must also be forthcoming if the sentence is denied a truth-value; and the truth is that no remotely plausible account is, in this case, available. Indeed the correct and only plausible account of the whole matter is precisely the one which Wright rejects. It *is* part of what it is now fashionable to call our general *theory* of the world that we regard other people as subject to roughly the same range of sensations as we are painfully or joyously or indifferently aware of in ourselves; and it is in no way contrary to reason to regard ourselves—as in any case we cannot help doing—as justified in certain circumstances in ascribing to John a particular state of feeling which we cannot in the nature of the case experience ourselves, and his being in which is therefore, if such is the standard invoked, necessarily verification-transcendent. The seas of argument may wash for ever around these rocks of truth; but the rocks are not worn away.

I consider another kind of case—the case of statements about the past, a past remote enough to be beyond the reach of the memory of anyone now living. An example would be: 'Lord Anglesey had his leg shot off at Wellington's side' or 'Charles Stuart walked bareheaded to his place of execution'. On the day in question, or the next day, such a sentence may be uttered by someone on the strength of observation or re-membered observation of an occurrence or series of occur-rences which the sentence itself describes and which can fairly be identified, at least for such a speaker, as fulfilling its truth-condition. For us the situation is different. We not only were not, but, given the dates of our births, are in principle debar-red from having been, in a position to make any such observa-tion. If we assert such a sentence, it has to be on the strength of the historical evidence. Exactly the same question arises for the anti-realist in this case as in the case of 'John is in pain': *i.e.*, what is the relation, as far as *we* are concerned, between truth-condition and meaning. The same range of answers is available as before: no truth-condition at all, truth-condition absorbed into evidence or truth-condition irrelevant to mean-ing. But the point most worth emphasising in this case is that whichever answer is chosen has the consequence that the sen-tence in our mouths has a different *meaning* from that which it has in the mouths of those who were in fact or in principle—though I confess to being unclear as to what principle—in a position to recognise that condition as obtaining which the sentence appears to describe. I think this conclusion about difference of meaning—indeed difference of kind of meaning—must be unacceptable. And in particular it must be un-acceptable to anyone who rightly cherishes the doctrine that the meaning of a sentence is determined by the meanings of its constituents and the way in which they are combined in the sentence. For he will surely be reluctant to locate an *am-biguity* anywhere either in the constituents or in the construc-tion of these sentences (at least as uttered by any Englishman). I have taken an example from the relatively recent past; but it would be a matter of no great difficulty, especially if we dwell upon the point about the relation between sentence-meaning and sentence-composition, to mount an argument carrying a truth-condition conception of meaning as far back in the past as you please.

I should like to consider some other and more difficult kinds of example, but it would take time and I fear I should exceed a chairman's licence if I did so. The general point I have wanted to make is this. The conception of verification-transcendent truth-conditions—at least in one or another of the relatively stringent senses of 'verification-transcendent' which Wright's anti-realist seems to favour—this conception, and its link with that of meaning, is an essential part of a general view of the world which is in no way contrary to reason and to which we are in any case inescapably committed. This does not mean for one moment that we have to sacrifice any of the real gains secured to us in the past under the banner of a more modest verificationism. In particular, it does not mean that any *concepts,* or pretended concepts, plain or fancy, for which it is claimed that they have, or might have, application *in* the world, are immune from empiricist criticism. Nor does it mean that we are committed in advance to saying, of every type of sentence which is declarative in form and introduces no dubious concept, that the meaning of any sentence of the type is wholly, or even in part, a matter of truth-conditions, strictly understood. The notions of truth, assertion and fact have areas of unproblematic application which are a good deal more comprehensive than Wright's anti-realist seems prepared to allow; but it does not follow that these areas are simply co-extensive with the range of use of declarative sentences. Where the application of these notions *is* problematic, it is certainly our business to show how this is so and how the use of the types of sentence concerned is related to that of statements which are unproblematically true or false. But we have to do this in detail, case by case and bearing in mind all the time the general framework of our thought. Few things are more implausible that the idea that we can be rapidly forced into a wholesale revision *either* of our metaphysics *or* of our logic by a dogmatic interpretation of the observation, in itself irreproachable, that our understanding of a language is manifested only in our use of it.

III*—EMPIRICO-REALISM AND CONTINGENT TRUTHS

by Guy Stock

I

I assume that any theory of truth should allow room for the idea that a truth is true in virtue of representing some object as it is. Likewise, I assume that any account of knowledge should portray knowledge as involving agreement, and error as involving disagreement with its object.

One kind of general inquiry into the nature of truth [1] which seems to me possible would consist in taking a particular conception of a truth consistent with the foregoing assumptions and attempting to see how it requires and is required by other conceptions within the context of a representational account of thought and language. For example, we might take a conception of a proposition which allows for the possibility of unconditional contingent truths and falsehoods. Or, in contrast, we might take the conception of a proposition which only allows for the possibility of a proposition having truth conditions, and therefore being a truth or a falsehood, within an already accepted system of logically interrelated propositions constituting a body of knowledge. We might take either of these conceptions and examine how it is connected with others in philosophical logic like those of sense, reference, negation, contingency and necessity; or how it is connected with ideas that shade off into epistemology like those concerning the nature and possibility of basic propositions, the distinction between immediate experience and thought, and the nature of the distinction which is to be drawn between the *a posteriori* and the *a priori*; or, yet again, how it is connected with ideas that shade off even further into metaphysics like those in regard to the nature of the knowing subject, pluralism and monism, the nature of space and time, and so on.

* Meeting of the Aristotelian Society at 5/7, Tavistock Place, London, W.C.1, on Monday, 25th October 1976, at 7.30 p.m.

I want to concentrate on the former conception of a proposition and to examine, in particular, the conception of immediate experience or sensation with which it is connected within the context of empiricism. I shall argue that an empiricism which wishes to allow for unconditional contingent truths and falsehoods requires an account of immediate experience or sensation which is unintelligible. I shall label the kind of theory under attack "empirico-realist".

However at this point I must hasten to emphasize that it would be a complete mistake to construe my attack on empirico-realism as in any sense an attack on the value or methods of empirical science as it is presently practised. Perhaps I can underline this point by reference to the history of philosophy. Both Leibniz, a realist, and Bradley, an idealist, rejected an empiricist epistemology. But the theories of both equally make it inconceivable that human beings should be able to discover the laws of nature which govern the behaviour of particular things in this world in any other way than by sense perception and the systematic methods of controlled observation that have proved successful in our practice of empirical science. What I say, in this respect and others, is intended to be in the tradition of Leibniz and Bradley.

II

I shall begin by introducing a "theoretical schema". This schema will beg some philosophical questions but not, I hope, those I wish to discuss.

I shall take the notion of a *thought* as fundamental and regard a proposition primarily[2] as an expression in language of what a person thinks to be the case.

Neither thoughts nor propositions will be conceived as *third realm*[3] objects. They will not therefore be conceived as objects having an ontological status which, on the one hand, is to be contrasted with that of *mental* objects and, on the other hand, with that of *physical* objects. Thus neither thoughts nor propositions will be construed as entities which possess truth values independently of consciousness and language. Nor will they be taken to be capable of becoming the objects of propositional attitudes assumed by people from time to time.

A thought, nevertheless, will be taken to be independent of any particular language and of any particular person in so far as the same thought can be expressed by synonymous sentences from different languages, and the thought expressed by the use of a given sentence can be understood by different persons. If the same thought is expressed by different people, or by the same person at different times, we can allow that the same proposition is uttered even if the sentences used are not only different tokens but also different types.

According to this schema any thought will be capable of verbal expression. However it will be open for a person to have indefinitely many thoughts which he in fact never formulates verbally even to himself. Moreover it will be left open for a person to have thoughts which, for example, through linguistic incompetence he does not, or even cannot, formulate verbally. However, if a person cannot formulate verbally his thought even to himself then he will not be able to be conscious of himself as having had that thought.

A proposition, in being the perceptible expression of what somebody thinks to be the case, will have a spatio-temporal aspect. A person will construct a proposition in space and time by taking words which have established meanings in a given language and by combining them in such a way as to produce what will count as an indicative sentence of that language.[4] The established semantic and syntactical conventions of the language will place constraints on how words can be combined with one another so as to form sentences. Only if such constraints are adhered to can a particular sequence of words from a given language constitute something which is acceptable as a sentence to users of the language and thus be capable of being understood by them as an expression of what somebody thinks to be the case.

A proposition will *present*[5] a state of affairs as obtaining in regard to some object[6] which is known or could be known. Any proposition will be either true or false, and it will be true if and only if the state of affairs it presents as obtaining in regard to its object in fact obtains.

The state of affairs that a proposition presents as obtaining will be its *sense*. The sense of a given proposition constructed in a particular language will be a function of the meanings

its constituent words have as a result of the established semantic and syntactical conventions of the language, and the order
in which the words are combined in the context of the proposition in question.

Within this theoretical schema no room is allowed for the
idea of a thought's being identifiable independently of the
proposition which could express it. Hence knowledge of a
person's thought (even one's own) is portrayed as having a different status from knowing something to obtain in regard to an
object which might conceivably not have obtained in regard
to that very object. Thoughts are not, therefore, to be conceived as objects of knowledge related by a special mode of
cognition ("inner sense") only to the person whose thoughts
they are. To know what a person thinks, even in one's own
case, is to know the propositions, and hence to know the truth
conditions of propositions in some language, which would
express what the person thinks to be the case.[7]

Finally the schema will involve what might be called a
"representational" account of perception. In any sense perception a state of affairs will appear to a person as obtaining in
regard to some object and thus, for any perception, a proposition could be constructed which would express it. This being
so a perception will be portrayed as being a species of thought
—albeit, perhaps, a rather special one.

This theoretical schema, thus far developed, I take to be
largely neutral as to the nature of contingent truths and immediate experience and, consequently, largely neutral as to
the precise ways in which certain centrally important logical
and epistemological distinctions are to be drawn.

It is open to further development along empirico-realist
lines so as to incorporate (i) a conception of a proposition
which allows for the possibility of unconditional truths and
falsehoods in regard to objects of perceptual knowledge and
(ii) a conception of immediate experience (or sensation) as a
relation occurring between a person and the particular existents of which he can have perceptual knowledge, which constitutes the source of all genuine knowledge of reality, and
which allows knowledge of contingent truths to be marked off
theoretically as absolutely distinct from knowledge of necessary truths.

But the schema is equally open to development along idealist lines so as to incorporate (i) a conception of a proposition which excludes the possibility of a proposition possessing truth conditions, and hence a truth value, in logical isolation from some system of logically interrelated propositions which as a whole can be known to be more or less true than competing systems presently available, and (ii) a non-relational account of immediate experience[8] which does not allow empirical knowledge to be marked off theoretically in terms of its source as absolutely distinct from other kinds of knowledge and, consequently, which can provide no theoretical justification for portraying our empirical knowledge of this world as constituting the only genuine knowledge a person can have of reality.

I want to examine how far development of the schema along lines which are at once distinctively realist and distinctively empiricist is intelligible.

III

Using the terminology developed in the previous section I can say that I take realism to portray the reality[9] to which thought and language relates as a *universe*[10] consisting of indefinitely, perhaps infinitely, many objects in regard to each of which indefinitely, perhaps infinitely, many states of affairs obtain. Moreover a distinctively realist account of the relation of thought and language to reality I take to be such as to demand that any and every state of affairs that actually obtains in regard to any object, or might possibly have obtained, could in principle be represented by some proposition. Both the contingently existing universe and what does not exist but might possibly have existed is thus conceived to be in principle totally representable in thought and language.

This thesis of total representability can be illustrated by reference to the history of philosophy. For example, it can be seen as involved in Carnap's conception of a universal language.[11] Carnap characterizes (in the formal mode) a universal language as a language into which every sentence can be translated or, alternatively, (in the material mode) as a language which can describe every state of affairs. Thus the conception of such an ideal language we can take to be that of a language into which every sentence, both the true ones and the false ones, could be translated; or alternatively, that of a language which would enable its possessor to construct propositions presenting not only the states of affairs that actually obtain in regard to objects but also those that do not but could have obtained.

The same thesis can also be seen to be involved in a non-empiricist realism, like Leibniz's, which takes the concept of an omniscient being to be logically possible. An omniscient being is conceived not only to have knowledge of everything that exists but also to be capable of thinking everything the existence of which is merely possible. He is portrayed as being, so to speak, the possessor of a language into which every sentence could be translated. He can thus construct propositions which present the infinity of possibilities open to reality and, in being omniscient, apprehends the truth values of those propositions *sub specie aeternitatis*.

This thesis of total representability by propositions I take to indicate an essential feature of a realist conception of the nature of reality. The opposite side of the same realist coin can then be taken to be a thesis about the nature of language. It is the thesis that propositions in general possess determinateness of sense. This thesis I take to involve the claim that no state of affairs that obtains in regard to any given object could not have obtained, and no state of affairs that does not obtain in regard to any given object could have obtained, without the truth value of some proposition constructible by the possessor of an ideal language being opposite from what it is.

But, we can now ask, what precisely will the requirement that propositions in general possess determinateness of sense demand of the nature of propositions?

Perhaps we can begin to see what it demands by examining how propositions, at least apparently, might fail to meet the requirement.

Any complex proposition which is a conjunction of propositions will apparently fail to meet it. For example, if the conjunction "p and q" happened to be false, reality could have been other than it is in at least two describable ways without the truth value of the proposition in question being opposite from what it is. Likewise with any proposition which is a disjunction of propositions. For example, if "p or q" were true reality could have been other than it is in at least two describable ways without its truth value being opposite. So we can say of such conjunctive and disjunctive propositions that they are apparently "ambiguous in their truth conditions"[12] and thus, at least apparently, lack determinateness of sense.

However the existence of such propositions is not in itself sufficient evidence to show that propositions constructible in language do not in general possess determinateness of sense. This is so since if, in the context of a theory, all propositions could be portrayed as translatable into an ideal language and the truth conditions of all complex propositions constructible in the ideal language could be portrayed as being representable by non-complex propositions which were unambiguous in their truth conditions, then that theory would have succeeded in showing how the propositions of language in general could possess determinateness of sense.

But if such a theory could be maintained what, we can inquire, would be demanded of the non-complex propositions constructible in an ideal language and postulated as capable of representing the truth conditions of all complex contingent propositions?

If the postulated propositions were to be of subject predicate form, and we assume "ϕa" to be a putative elementary proposition, then it is clear that if "ϕa" were to be unambiguous in its truth conditions no account of how the name "a" in that context succeeded in referring to an object would be possible in terms of the idea of its being shorthand for a description or descriptions contingently true of some one object.

Similarly, no possible predicate of an elementary proposition could be portrayed as being such that its meaning could be analysed in terms of a conjunctive or disjunctive statement of conditions for its application since any proposition containing such a predicate would again be ambiguous in its truth conditions. The possible predicates of the elementary propositions constructible in an ideal language would have to be classically unanalysable or "simple".

Moreover it is apparent that the logical behaviour of the possible predicates of elementary propositions could not be analogous to that of ordinary language predicates capable of ascribing properties which are subject to continuous variation in degree as, for example, colours are. This can be shown in the following way.

Given a language L_1 containing a colour predicate "ϕ" it will always be theoretically possible for there to be a language L_2 containing colour predicates "ϕ'" and "ϕ''" such that "ϕ" could be true of O if and only if either "ϕ'" or "ϕ''" was true of it. But if this is so the proposition "ϕa", for example, will be ambiguous in its truth conditions since its truth would be compatible with a in fact being either ϕ' or ϕ''. In so far as colour is subject to continuous variation in degree this argument could be repeated indefinitely in regard to any proposition containing any possible colour predicate.

Further any predicate ascribing a given degree of some property subject to continuous variation in degree will have to be construed as logically contrary to any other predicate capable of ascribing a different degree of the same property. Hence any proposition ascribing a certain degree of such a property will be ambiguous in its truth conditions in that, if it happened to be false, its falsity would be compatible with the object's being other than it is with respect to the property in question in an infinite number of in principle describable ways without the truth value of the proposition in question being opposite from what it is.

From these considerations perhaps we can see more clearly what will be demanded of the elementary propositions constructible in an ideal language if they are to be unambiguous in their truth conditions. We can say if "ϕa" is to be unambiguous in its truth conditions it must be such that (i) if it were true, its truth would not be conditional on any other contingent state of affairs obtaining in regard to a or anything else, nor on any contingent state of affairs not obtaining in regard to a or anything else, but simply and solely on a's in fact being ϕ. And (ii) if it were false, its falsity would not be conditional on any contingent state of affairs obtaining in regard to a or anything else, nor on any other contingent state of affairs not obtaining in regard to a or anything else, but simply and solely on a's not in fact being ϕ.[13]

So in the context of a theory with an empiricist epistemology the truth of the elementary proposition "ϕa" would be portrayed as depending simply on the state of affairs which could only be ascribed by the unanalysable predicate "ψ" (or some synonymous predicate from another language) happening to obtain in perceptible fact in regard to a particular object given in sensation, namely, a. The falsity of "ψa" would be portrayed as depending simply on the state of affairs which could only be ascribed by the unanalysable predicate "ψ" (or some synonymous predicate from another language) happening not to obtain in perceptible fact in regard to a particular object given in sensation, namely a.

Thus the proposition "ϕa" would be an unconditional contingent truth: the proposition "ψa" an unconditional contingent falsehood. Further if[14] the truth conditions of all the complex empirical propositions constructible in an ideal language could be represented by such unconditional truths and falsehoods then any empirical truth whatsoever would have been portrayed as *simply* true and any falsehood as *simply* false.

Moreover, since nothing could follow from the obtaining or not of the state of affairs presented by "ϕa" as to the obtaining or not of any other state of affairs in regard to a or any other object which could be given in sensation, the kind of proposition required to be possible by the realist demand for determinateness of sense fits happily with the kind required by the empiricist demand that there be no logical connexions in fact. If the truth conditions of our ordinary propositions about material objects and suchlike, which patently are logically related to one another, could be taken in principle to be representable by means of strictly atomic propositions then all the logical relations between our ordinary empirical propositions could be taken to be merely a consequence of the truth-functional composition of logically independent propositions presenting states of affairs as obtaining in regard to particular objects given in sensation.

IV

Now it is obvious that in our ordinary languages we cannot construct contingent propositions that come remotely near to meeting the conditions required if a proposition is to be unambiguous in its truth conditions. However it is important to realize that the empirico-realist argument I have outlined

does not attempt to establish the existence of atomic propositions as a class of propositions which cannot in fact be doubted
and of which, if our attentions were drawn to them, we could
become explicitly conscious as epistemologically basic. Rather
it is an argument which aims at, and I think succeeds in,
establishing what must be the case in regard to the foundations
of our empirical knowledge of reality if empirical knowledge
in general is to be such as to be expressible in a language the
propositions of which possess determinateness of sense.[15]

Construed in this way the argument cannot conceivably be
refuted by indicating that we cannot in fact give examples of
the kind of epistemologically basic, atomic propositions required to be possible. The empirico-realist can blandly claim
that it is merely a matter of contingent, but nevertheless in-
eluctable, psychological fact that human beings cannot become explicitly conscious of the atomic propositions that
would express the foundations of their empirical beliefs true
and false of reality.

However, on the other hand, if the conception of an epistemologically basic atomic proposition and the empiricist idea
of sensation that goes along with it could be shown to be unintelligible then the empiricist version of realism which requires their possibility would necessarily collapse.

With this in mind I want to try to see precisely what is involved in the empiricist conception of immediate experience
in sensation. I will attempt to do this by characterizing an
alternative conception of immediate experience which is in
instructive ways incompatible with an empiricist epistemological schema. This alternative conception of immediate experience is a "non-relational" one and it can be conveniently
illustrated by reference to Leibniz's epistemology.

According to the Leibnizian schema, what is known *a posteriori* by us is the same as what is known *a priori* by God:
namely, reality in all its infinity. Our perception of what
exists is not to be distinguished from God's either by reference to its special source in sensation or by reference to the
extent of its object. It is distinguished simply by the confusion
which, in a different degree for each, attends the perception
of every subject except that of the omniscient one. Accordingly a self-conscious being's possession of the empirical knowledge which he can express by means of propositions is

portrayed simply as a matter of his being to a certain degree clear about, and self-reflectively aware of, what is represented more or less confusedly in the perception of every finite substance.[16]

Morover the appearance of reality, in the temporally successive sense-perceptions of self-conscious creatures, as a spatio-temporally ordered system of objects in which each of our bodies has a unique position is itself portrayed as being a function of the uniquely different degree of confusion which attends the perception of each created substance. To God, whose perception is attended by no degree of confusion, reality does not appear as a spatio-temporally extended system, with some parts closer to him than others, and consequently is not knowable by him *a posteriori*. The omniscient being apprehends things *a priori* as they are in reality: spatio-temporally unextended.

It follows that the theoretical notion of perception internal to Leibniz's epistemology is not to be construed as any kind of relation that could be thought to occur or not occur between existents. Our having empirical knowledge of relations that can be thought to occur or not occur between existents is portrayed simply as being to some degree clear about what is represented more or less confusedly in the perception of every creature. However it is important to see that in embracing this epistemology Leibniz is not involved in denying that by doing empirical science we can get to know all sorts of relations which must in fact hold between material objects at present spatially close to us and our central nervous systems if we are to be able to see, hear, touch, taste, smell or be aware of them kinaesthetically. What Leibniz rejects is the intelligibility of the idea of sensation postulated within the context of an epistemological theory as a cognitive relation contingently occurring between existents.

With or without commitment to Leibniz's realism and pluralism it is possible to give a theoretical account of *immediate experience* and its relation to self-conscious thought along the lines of the Leibnizian schema. Self-conscious thought in general, and empirical knowledge in particular, can be portrayed theoretically as a representation in propositional form of what is implicit (unselfconsciously and even unconsciously) in immediate experience. On such an account immediate experience is not construed as any kind of relation that can be thought to hold or not hold between existents of which we can have empirical knowledge, any more than Leibniz's theoretical notion of perception is to be so construed. Nor *a fortiori* is immediate experience itself to be construed as any kind of object representable truly or falsely in propositions. Propositions express thoughts which represent with some degree of clarity what is implicit in immediate experience, namely, reality.

We can now ask: how precisely does such an account of immediate experience differ in its consequences from the relational account of immediate experience in sensation offered by empiricism?

Given a non-relational account of immediate experience there is no theoretical room for the logical possibility of the thought that nothing might have existed.[17] The logical possibility of this thought can only arise given a theoretical conception of immediate experience or sensation as itself a contingent (or external) relation occurring between a person and the particular existents of which he can have perceptual knowledge. For the empiricist *ex hypothesi* sensation must occur as a necessary condition of perception of objects but equally *ex hypothesi* sensation is taken to be a contingent relation occurring between a person and the objects of his perceptual knowledge.

The sense in which in the context of an empirico-realist epistemology sensation is construed to be a contingent relation can be illustrated by referring again to our realist fiction—the possessor of an ideal language. Given that the possessor of an ideal language perceives that ϕa, in so far as sensation is construed theoretically as a contingent relation, it is possible for him to construct the general proposition "$(x) (\sim\phi x)$", which is contingently false, and so for every possible predicate of an elementary proposition. Even though we in practice can only suppose of some object we know in fact to exist that it might not have existed by supposing other things existing in the world to have been different nevertheless, according to empirico-realism, it would be in principle possible to suppose that every contingent proposition that could be constructed might have been false. In so far as sensation is construed as a contingent relation *ex hypothesi* it is logically possible to suppose that nothing might have existed to be given in sensation.

On the other hand in the context of a theory which embodies a non-relational account of immediate experience and in which thought, and hence knowledge of all kinds, is portrayed as a more or less clear representation of what is implicit in immediate experience, no theoretical room is left for the logical possibility of the thought that nothing might have existed to be known. In the context of such a theory any particular object of knowledge can be taken to be contingent if and only if, in the light of what is known of the system in which the object exists, it is possible to make suppositions which would have necessitated the non-existence of the thing as it is known. There is thus no room in theory or practice for a truth or a falsehood which is contingent and yet unconditional. Correspondingly there can be no merely positive propositions, nor no account of negation given which portrays negation as an operation which merely excludes something from being the case.

Moreover, given a non-relational account of immediate experience, identification of a particular object is logically possible only by means of descriptions believed or known to be true of it. Without the idea of sensation as a non-conceptual yet cognitive relation with existent particulars there is no room for logically proper names of particulars and, consequently, no room for the possibility of a proposition expressing knowledge of a particular which is known but not known by means of an identifying description.

V

Now can we really make sense of the empiricist idea of sensation as a non-conceptual cognitive relation holding contingently, but as a necessary condition, between a person and the particulars he can pèrceive?

For a start, a theory which embodies it must rule out the possibility of a kind of theory of meaning which philosophers who regard themselves as empiricists are often inclined to give.[18] This can be seen to be so in the following way.

If S, the possessor of an ideal language, could for any and every possible true elementary proposition "ϕa" construct a general proposition "$(x)\,(\sim\!\phi x)$" which was contingently false then what S knows in knowing the meanings of the predicate expressions of his language could not be portrayed theoretically as being logically dependent on the existence of any object or combination of objects the existence of which is contingent. If it were there would be something the existence of which was *ex hypothesi* contingent but in regard to which the possessor of an ideal language could not conceive that it might not have existed.

Moreover, given the conception of an ideal language, the consistent empirico-realist must say the same of the ordinary language user as he says of the theoretically possible possessor of an ideal language. As a matter of fact a person in learning language comes to know and believe an indefinite multiplicity of contingent truths about the actual world. However what he knows in knowing the truth conditions of the contingent propositions which could express his knowledge and beliefs cannot be portrayed in the context of an empirico-realist theory as being logically dependent on the existence of any object or combination of objects which the possessor of an ideal language could conceive not to exist, *i.e.*, on any contingent fact about the world.

However if this is so the empirico-realist could give no theoretical account of what it is a person knows in knowing the truth conditions of contingent propositions which portrayed that knowledge as a matter of knowing (implicitly or explicitly) any facts that obtain in regard to contingent existents. He could not, therefore, give a theoretical account of the knowledge that a language user has in knowing how to construct and understand the senses of propositions which portrayed it as a know-how in principle describable in terms of the person's knowledge of facts. For example he could not portray it as knowledge gained inductively as a result of the person having perceived conjunctions between features ("utterances" and "situations") frequently conjoined in his perceptual environment.

So in the classic Russellian version of logical atomism S's grasp of the meanings of the possible predicates of atomic propositions, and hence the ability of any language user to understand the senses of contingent propositions, is portrayed theoretically as dependent on an *a priori* mode of immediate experience of abstract universals the non-being of which is inconceivable. Acquaintance with such universals is taken to be a necessary condition of (i) the ability to perceive *a posteriori* states of affairs that in fact obtain in regard to particulars immediately experienced in sensation and of (ii) the ability to think what might be the case or not the case in regard to existents quite independently of anything that is known in fact to obtain or not obtain. Thus we can say, on this Russellian account, a being with a faculty of thought but no sensibility would have been a logical possibility,[19] although the elementary sentences such a being could construct would be general and their truth values would necessarily remain unknown to him.

Of course the consistent empirico-realist might be happy to give up the kind of empiricist theory of meaning in question. But then we can still ask: is there any evidence which he could appeal to in support of his theoretical conception of sensation as a contingent relation?

I hope it is obvious by now that it is not a matter for dispute that what a person can see *etc.* at any given moment of time depends on certain spatial relations holding between his receptors and the things he can presently perceive, and it is a contingent matter that these relations in fact obtain as they do. Nor is it open to dispute that, for example, it is a contingent matter that evolution resulted in beings like ourselves with central nervous systems and sense organs who are able to perceive things going on in and around their bodies each moment of their waking life.

The philosophical question at issue is: are we in describing these things as contingent saying any more than that, in the light of our empirical knowledge of this world, we can make supposals that would have necessitated the facts being otherwise than we know them, or currently believe them, to be?

In other words the question is a question about the concept of contingency and the concept of empirical knowledge and such a question is not to be answered by appeal to examples agreed to be contingent empirical facts. Nor is it to be answered, to my mind, by treating cognition as Quine does "from within our own evolving theory of a cognized world" (*Word and Object* p. 235). It is not, I think, answerable independently of reference to some more or less systematic theory like that I have characterized as empirico-realism, or like that offered by Leibniz or, yet again, Bradley.

Further it is not a matter for dispute that a person's ability to perceive things in space presently located appropriately to his sense organs is to be seen as playing a fundamental rôle in his ability to think and communicate about particular objects which might or might not exist in the actual world presently beyond the range of his sense organs. It plays a fundamental rôle since a person's ability to identify particular things as occupying positions in the spatio-temporal series that contains his body enables him to eliminate the logical possibility of ambiguity in reference which necessarily infects empirical descriptions when those descriptions are not accompaniable by an expression indicating a position in a given spatio-temporal series—for example, *this* one.

Such an account, thus far, is acceptable to both the empirico-realist and a philosopher who rejects a relational account of immediate experience.[20]

However the empirico-realist cannot portray the material objects which at any given moment of his waking life a person can perceive around his body, and pick out by means of egocentric demonstratives, as nameable particulars given in sensation. A person's ability to identify linguistically a particular material object patently depends on his knowing truths about the object. So any proposition expressing a person's knowledge of a demonstratively indicated particular will be ambiguous in its truth conditions. Thus the empirico-realist is compelled to portray propositions about material objects, even if the propositions are superficially non-complex, as being in principle subject to logical analysis. Correspondingly he will be compelled to portray any material object as a "logical construction" which can be known to exist only by perception of properties, relational and otherwise, of particulars immediately experienced in senstation.

But what theoretical characterization can the empirico-realist give of these particulars which he takes to be the genuine objects of immediate experience in sensation? If such an object is not to be thought of as the kind of thing that can occupy a space for a period of time, and yet sensation is construed to be a relation occurring between things in space and time, presumably the existence of an object of sensation must be conceived to be confined to a point in space and to the instant of its being immediately experienced.

In principle there is no logical difficulty in the idea of a relation occurring at an instant of time between things in space the existence of which is confined to that instant. No doubt, for example, the physiologist knows many such relations which must hold between events inside and outside a person's head at any given instant of time during a period throughout which a person is perceiving some material object appropriately located relative to his sense organs. But appeals to analogies which make use of the idea of something occurring at an instant during a temporally extended process of which we have empirical knowledge cannot make intelligible, still less justify, the idea of sensation postulated within an epistemological theory as a relation which supposedly provides the source of all the genuine knowledge a person has of spatio-temporally extended reality.

Moreover even if, for purposes of argument, we accept the idea of sensation as an instantaneous relation with instantaneous existents at points in space, what is the empirico-realist to say about a person's cognition of Space and Time in which the relation of sensation is supposed instantaneously to occur?

Space and Time themselves can hardly be construed as particular existents immediately experienced in sensation since this would require Space and Time to be spatio-temporally locatable. However, on the other hand, if Space and Time are to be construed as providing principles of individuation for particulars known by description then a person's cognition of Space and Time themselves cannot be taken to be "via concepts" since the concept of a spatio-temporal series does not rule out the logical possibility of a multiplicity of spatio-temporally unrelated series.

Alternatively, as a last resort no doubt, an explicitly Kantian move might be attempted. It might be argued that the nature of human sensibility happens in fact to be such that things given to us in sensation appear as spatio-temporally related in a single series. However if the spatio-temporality of things is portrayed simply as a consequence of the "forms" of human sensibility the things given in sensation themselves could not be portrayed as being the kinds of thing that human beings can know to exist at particular positions in Space and Time and perceive to have empirical properties. It would follow then that sensation itself could not be portrayed as a relation in the occurring spatio-temporal series between things instantaneous or otherwise. Hence sensation originally postulated as a relation occurring between a person and the objects of his knowledge cannot conceivably perform that role once Space and Time themselves are taken to be mere forms of sensibility.

VI

To sum up. I have been concerned with a kind of theory of the relation of thought and language to reality which

(i) aims to allow for the idea of unconditional contingent truths and falsehoods and
(ii) employs a theoretical conception of sensation as an immediate cognitive relation which must occur between a person and the existents of which he can have perceptual knowledge and which portrays perception, in virtue of its involving sensation, as providing the only source of genuine knowledge we can have of reality.

Such an empirico-realism, I have attempted to argue, requires a logical atomism and a conception of sensation which is unintelligible.

Of course not many philosophers now would want to defend any form of logical atomism. However many are inclined, in a more or less vague sense, to regard themselves as empiricists and realists as opposed to being of an idealist persuasion. Even more are inclined, for better or worse reasons, to draw limits to "genuine" knowledge along traditional empiricist lines.

It seems to me, therefore, that raising the kind of issue I've raised can be justified by an appeal to two kinds of reason:

(i) For a philosopher to make a decision as to the meanings of a whole range of technical, logical and epistemological concepts commonly employed in philosophy is, implicitly or explicitly, to take a stand in regard to the sort of issue I've discussed. The grounds for such decisions should be made explicit.

And (ii) a philosophical justification of a view as to the possibility or impossibility of, for example, religious and moral knowledge, or a philosophical justification of a view about the nature of history and the sciences, cannot be achieved by arguments which are logically independent of the philosopher's conception of the nature of knowledge and truth in general. For the philosopher the more general question must be settled first.

John Anderson[21] argued that a philosopher ought to be self-conscious about the implications of being a realist and empiricist as opposed to being an idealist or rationalist. I think he was certainly right in this. But in regard to the truth I'm bound to conclude he was wrong.[22]

NOTES

[1] This inquiry, as I undertake it, I take to be in substance the dispute in the history of philosophy between the correspondence and coherence theories of truth.

[2] This qualification is intended to indicate that subsequently for various reasons it will be necessary to widen this characterization, e.g., to allow as propositions a person's utterances which through dishonesty or linguistic incompetence fail to express what he really thinks to be the case; or to allow (as in Logical Atomism) for the idea of a proposition as a theoretical requirement.

[3] Cf. Frege "The Thought"—Mind 1956; G. E. Moore "The Nature of Judgment"—Mind 1899; and more recently Sir Karl Popper Objective Knowledge chap. 3.

[4] A language, in this context, might be taken to be just a very narrow dialect within a natural language or even a code the rules of which have been established by, and are only known by, the person who uses it. The problem of how precisely one distinguishes one language from another is not relevant here. The point is that a language must have rules which are established in advance and independently of any given act which could count as an act in accordance or not in accordance with them.

[5] I want to reserve "asserts" to describe something a person does in constructing a proposition. Thus a person can on occasion assert what he doesn't think to be the case; he can do this because the proposition he utters presents what it does in virtue of the objectively established conventions of the language.

⁶ The category of thing that can be an object or state of affairs is intended to be left wide open.

⁷ A proposition can fail to express what a person thinks, or express what he thinks more or less inaccurately. But the relation a proposition has to the thought it expresses accurately is not to be confused with the relation it has to an object in regard to which it presents truly a state of affairs as obtaining.

⁸ *Cf.* F. H. Bradley "Our Knowledge of Immediate Experience" *Essays on Truth and Reality* chap. VI.

⁹ Or, if we are dealing with a "partial" realist, ". . . the segment of reality in regard to which it is maintained that a realist account of the relation of language to reality is appropriate as . . .".

¹⁰ More precisely I should have said ". . . as *simply* a universe . . ." since the idealist would agree that reality is a universe or, better, an indefinite multiplicity of knowable universes. However, according to a distinctively idealist schema language and thought is such that in principle the nature of reality is never totally representable.

¹¹ R. Carnap *The Unity of Science* (trans. Max Black) p. 42.

¹² G. E. M. Anscombe *An Introduction to Wittgenstein's Tractacus* p. 47.

¹³ It is open at this point to somebody, who wanted to avoid the atomism I'm trying to commit the realist to, to argue that there is another way consistent with empiricism and realism of portraying the contingent propositions of language as in general possessing determinateness of sense. If someone came up with such an account I should have to examine it *ad hominem*.

¹⁴ I have no general argument to support an "only if". But I am not clear how else the concept of a contingent truth that was simply true, and a contingent falsehood that was simply false, could be characterized if it were to be characterized in a way which was distinctly realist. *Cf.* J. L. Mackie *Truth Paradox and Probability* chap. 2 gives a characterization of truths that are simply true and known by sensation; but in that context, at least, he does not give an account of sensation.

¹⁵ The structure of the argument I have described has obvious affinities to that of Wittgenstein's *Tractatus*; although, of course, Wittgenstein rejects the kind of empiricist epistemology which requires sensation to be a cognitive relation occurring between a subject and an object.

¹⁶ *Cf.* Kant *Critique of Pure Reason* B61/B62.

¹⁷ *Cf.* the Idealist version of the ontological argument.

¹⁸ *Cf.* Bernard Harrison *Meaning and Structure* chap. 1: the kind of theory of meaning Harrison locates in Price and Quine is what I have in mind.

¹⁹ The concept of a creature with a faculty of thought but no sensibility would, for Leibniz, be impossible. God has no sensibility but that is not to lack a faculty: it is to apprehend everything perspicuously.

²⁰ *Cf.* F. H. Bradley *Essays on Truth and Reality* chap. XVI; B. Russell *Logic and Knowledge* (ed. R. C. Marsh) "On the nature of Acquaintance" pp. 127 ff.

²¹ John Anderson *Studies in Empirical Philosophy* chap. 1 "Empiricism".

²² I thank the members of the philosophy departments of Aberdeen, Stirling and Mannheim Universities for discussing earlier versions of this paper. In particular I'm in debt to Michael Partridge for unfailing generosity in sharing his thoughts on these topics. Also I would express gratitude to the German Academic Exchange and the British Academy for financial help which enabled me to spend a term at Mannheim University and work on what results here.

IV*—WHY SHOULD I BE JUST?

by D. R. Fisher[1]

The aim of this paper is to attempt to answer the question 'Why should I be just?'

At the beginning of Book V of the *Nicomachean Ethics*, Aristotle distinguishes two senses of justice: a broad sense in which justice is equated with 'righteousness' and comprehends a wide range of morally good behaviour; and a narrower sense itself subdivided into two which Aristotle calls 'distributive' and 'corrective' justice. The sense of 'just' for which I propose to seek an answer to the question 'Why should I be just?' corresponds to the former broader sense. In this meaning acting justly is basically not harming others and thus includes, for example, abstention from murder, rape, theft, and lying. As thus conceived justice can perhaps be regarded as the cornerstone of morality. The problem thus becomes 'Why should I not harm others even when it may appear in my interest to do so?'

It is, I take it, a logically necessary truth that if A has reason to ϕ, considers ϕ-ing is the thing for him to do, then A must in some sense want to ϕ. For if he doesn't want to ϕ, why should he regard it as the thing to do? He may, of course, not want to ϕ for its own sake but as a means to something else which he wants. In so far however as 'He who wills the end wills the means' it is appropriate even in this case to say that he wants to ϕ. The acceptance of this logical truth does not however commit one to egoism (not all wants are self-centred) nor to psychological hedonism since it is certainly not true to say that A necessarily looks forward with pleasure to everything which in this minimal sense of 'wanting' he wants to do. (I shall argue these points at more length later.) The sense of 'wanting' with which I am here concerned is, I believe, that discussed by Miss Anscombe where she claims that 'the primitive sign of wanting is trying to get.'[2]

If it is logically true that if A has reason to ϕ, A must regard ϕ-ing as conducive either directly or indirectly to the

---

* Meeting of the Aristotelian Society at 5/7, Tavistock Place, London, W.C.1, on Monday, 8th November 1976, at 7.30 p.m.

attainment of his wants, it would also seem to follow that if one
is to give A a reason to ϕ, one must show that ϕ-ing is thus connected with the attainment of his wants. Of course, on particular occasions, in giving A a reason to ϕ, one may not refer
to desires. One may, for example, urge A to do X because it
would promote his future happiness and one may say that this
is the reason for doing X. In such a case, however, it must be
assumed that A wants to promote his future happiness—for
if he did not, why should he do X? Indeed, if he subscribed to
some self-denying ascetic sect, the fact that X promoted his
future happiness might give him reason not to do X. Similarly,
if it is assumed that one's audience wants to do what is just, to
point out that to do X is just, may provide him with a sufficient
reason to do X. If, however, one cannot assume that one's
audience does thus already accept the value of acting justly,
then it will not provide a sufficient reason for doing X, simply
to say that doing X is just. If I am therefore to provide A with
a reason to do X, I must be able to show that doing X is either
directly what A wants or else indirectly is a necessary means to
the attainment of what A wants.

There is, I hope, nothing mysterious about this contention
and it is, I believe, at least part of what Hume meant in his
discussion in Part III of the *Treatise on Human Nature* where
he maintains that reason alone cannot move a man to act but
that passion (*i.e.*, desires/wants) is the mover. It is also, I believe, part of what Aristotle was arguing in his somewhat obscure discussion in the *Nicomachean Ethics* and elsewhere
about the central rôle of the practical syllogism in practical
reasoning. The practical syllogism is a form of reasoning which
moves from a statement of wants/desires via a middle premiss
focusing the want statement on the present situation either by
a statement of perceptual insight or a statement of the necessary means of achieving these wants, to the conclusion that a
certain action should be performed. An unAristotelian example of such a syllogism would be:

I want to catch the 8.25 train to Waterloo
(the want statement).
Unless I run, I will not reach the train on time
(the statement of a necessary means of achieving this want).
Therefore I must run.

For those who believe that normative statements cannot be derived from purely factual premises, this piece of rather obvious reasoning is perhaps surprising. It is not however to anybody who—like myself—habitually lies in bed too long in the morning. Moreover although it is neither an example of strictly deductive nor inductive logic it is—as again I know from bitter experience—a perfectly valid piece of reasoning.

If therefore we are to show why I should act justly, we must be able to show that acting justly is either what I want or else conduces indirectly to the attainment of my wants/aims. If I cannot show that acting justly does thus conduce to the attainment of my wants, then I shall have been unable to show that it is rational for me to act justly. This statement of what I believe is the central question in ethics has been somewhat overlooked in much recent moral philosophy, although this neglect has been a relatively modern phenomenon—certainly the question why should I be just was a central question in much of Plato's writing in the 4th century B.C., as indeed it was the central question which the author of the Book of Job sought to answer—albeit in somewhat different terms—in the same century in a different part of the Mediterranean area.

The reasons for this recent neglect are no doubt multifarious but perhaps the following two factors played a significant part. Firstly acting justly—as we have defined it—is obviously to the benefit of others. Unless therefore an agent happened to want to benefit others, it was perhaps regarded as a doomed venture to show that acting justly might also satisfy the wants of an agent who didn't share such altruistic feelings. In this sense, recent moral philosophers have therefore—as Philippa Foot pointed out in her article on "Moral Beliefs" in 1958[3]—unconsciously accepted Thrasymachus' contention in Book I of the *Republic* that injustice is more profitable than justice. The second consideration was that if—*per impossibile*—you could show that justice was more profitable than injustice, you would thereby perform a grave disservice to morality by reducing it to mere expediency from which it had been assiduously distinguished by Protestant moralists—notably, of course, Kant with his absolute distinction between the categorical imperatives of morality and the hypothetical imperatives of other practical reasoning. Moreover in so far as this late Protestant theory of morality has been encapsulated into ordinary language, some recent linguistic philosophers have even sought to establish—by their examination of the use of moral terms in ordinary language—that such a theory was somehow 'logically true'. They have thus neglected to notice the fact that whilst ordinary language may reflect a particular theory or world-view, this hardly establishes that this theory is 'eternally true'. Whilst I shall return later to the question of the need to distinguish morality from expediency, my basic answer to both these considerations is that unless you can show that acting justly does lead—albeit indirectly—to the attainment of the agent's wants, then you cannot claim that morality has a rational foundation and the conclusion that morality is fundamentally irrational is surely more horrendous than the offence which any blurring of the distinction between morality and expediency may occasion the Victorian moral sentiment.

Why then should I act justly? Why should I forgo harming others? How does acting justly/forgoing harming others conduce to the attainment of my wants or ends?

Let us first consider an easy case. If A wants to promote or at least respect the good or welfare of others, then A obviously has a reason to act justly. This is, as I have said, an easy case and it will not satisfy us since it is, of course, a merely contingent fact as to whether people feel such altruistic motives. Equally however we should not discount such altruism since it does exist and is perhaps more common than some hard-headed philosophers would suppose. Nor is it—as some of these philosophers have maintained—merely a disguised form of self-interest. There is a valid distinction between the pursuit of desires aimed at my own pleasure/well-being and those aimed at promoting the well-being or pleasure of others. Of course it is true that if A wants to help B, then helping B satisfies A's desires. It may also be generally true that the satisfaction of desires is intrinsically pleasant (although a curious child who desires to find out what a naked flame feels like may find the satisfaction of this desire not very pleasant). It does not however follow that if A wants to help B, what A *really* wants is the pleasure that comes from satisfying this desire. Satisfaction presupposes a desire and a desire presupposes an object. But the satisfaction of the desire cannot itself be the object of that same desire—for otherwise we are left with the merely empty desire to satisfy our desire—but what do we desire? One might, of course, have a higher-order desire to satisfy one's desires—or, better, as many of one's desires as it was practicable to satisfy (since they may not all be compatible)—but whether or not one has such a higher-order desire is a contingent and not a necessary fact. Altruism is thus both a real phenomenon and a logically respectable one. Since however not everyone is altruistic, it does not solve our problem.

A second case, which again does not solve our problem but is perhaps worth consideration, is that of the agent with religious beliefs. He may accept Thrasymachus' argument that at least in this life the unjust prosper and that injustice is more profitable than justice. He believes, however, that in the life to come this situation is reversed and that the just are amply compensated for such profits of injustice as they forwent in this transitory vale of tears. A man with such beliefs clearly has reason to act justly. I regret however that the ontological presuppositions of this example are too extravagant to satisfy most philosophers today. I must therefore move on to the real problem.

And this is how in a secular morality to convince the purely self-centred man that he should act justly. Why should the man who lacks the altruism of my first example or the religious beliefs of my second, why should he forgo harming others when it appears profitable to do harm? How can we show such a man that acting justly does conduce to the attainment of his wants? Since *ex hypothesi* we have assumed he does not want to help others, this reduces the problem to that of showing that acting justly is really in his own interest—the only motivation we can confidently assume him to possess.

This was, of course, the problem which Plato attempted to answer in the *Republic* by refuting the claims of Thrasymachus and Glaucon that injustice is more profitable than justice. Plato's own solution of this problem has not, however, found general acceptance and can be faulted on a number of grounds. Not the least of these is that—as David Sachs pointed out in an interesting article in 1963[4]—the definition of justice which Plato finally adopts seems to bear little intrinsic relation to the sense of justice which Thrasymachus and Glaucon themselves used and in which sense they had asked Socrates to show that justice was more profitable than injustice. With Plato's own account of justice I am not however here concerned. What I am more concerned with is the account of justice which Plato puts into the mouth of Glaucon at the beginning of Book 2 of the *Republic* when the latter attempts to restate the argument that injustice is more profitable than justice (an argument which Glaucon, in fact, disclaims, despite his eloquent presentation of it). Glaucon is there made to argue that:

"Our natural instinct is to inflict wrong or injury and to avoid suffering it, but the disadvantages of suffering it exceed the advantages of inflicting it; after a taste of both, therefore, men decide that, as they can't have the ha'pence without the kicks, they had better make a compact with each other and avoid both. They accordingly proceed to make laws and mutual agreements, and what the law lays down they call lawful and right. This is the origin and nature of justice. It lies between what is most desirable, to do wrong and avoid punishment, and what is most undesirable, to suffer wrong without redress; justice and right lie between these two and are accepted not as being good in themselves, but as having a relative value due to our inability to do wrong. For anyone who had the power to do wrong and called himself a man would never make any such agreement with anyone—he would be mad if he did."[5]

Plato does not attempt a detailed refutation of this account of justice but he clearly regards its inadequacy to lie in the alleged consequences set out by Glaucon in the last sentence of the passage just quoted. If men only act justly so that they secure the benefit of not being harmed by others, then if they could by some other means secure the latter benefit they would have no reason to act justly and thus forgo the benefit of harming others when it is in their interest to do so. Glaucon proceeds to describe just such a case. Gyges had discovered a magical bezel ring by turning which he could disappear and then by turning it the other way reappear whenever he wished. Since by virtue of his possession of the magical ring, Gyges could get away with injustice with impunity, he clearly had no reason to enter into any 'social contract'—he could secure the benefits of never being harmed by others, whilst still enjoying the advantages of harming them. And this, of course, is precisely what Gyges did. As soon as he had discovered the magical properties of the ring "he managed to get himself included in the party that was to report to the king, and when he arrived seduced the queen and with her help attacked and murdered the king and seized the throne".[6]

For Plato the fact that on Glaucon's account of justice it is impossible to answer the question—at least for a Gyges—why should I be just, undermines Glaucon's argument and this is why the remaining eight books of the *Republic* are devoted to developing an alternative account of justice. I propose to argue that, on the contrary, Glaucon's account of justice is substantially correct and that the fact that on this account, it is not possible to persuade a Gyges to act justly far from being the weakness of the argument is one of its strengths since this limitation of the argument correctly represents the position of actual moral reasoning. The paradoxical nature of this latter remark will, I hope, disappear shortly.

In order to establish this, it is necessary first to expand Glaucon's rather bald account and, in particular, to make explicit the assumptions upon which the argument rests. To help do this, I shall develop and explore some suggestions contained in Professor von Wright's chapter on 'Justice' in his book *The Varieties of Goodness*.[7]

First, then, let us consider the evaluation of goods which Glaucon makes. "Our natural instinct," Glaucon says, "is to inflict wrong or injury . . . but the disadvantages of suffering it exceed the advantages of inflicting it." What is however "most desirable [is] to do wrong and avoid punishment," whilst what is "most undesirable [is] to suffer wrong without redress."

To facilitate the argument let us call these goods:

The good of never being harmed by others $= G_1$
The good of sometimes harming others $\quad = G_2$
The good of never being harmed by others
and sometimes harming them (*i.e.*, $G_1 + G_2$) $= G_3$

Thus according to Glaucon, G_1 is a greater good than G_2 but G_3 is a greater good than G_1 (since $G_3 = G_1 + G_2$ this is, of course, true by definition). The worst position is to secure neither G_1 nor G_2.

An initial objection to Glaucon's account might be that this is a rather cynical view of human nature. As I have just argued, people do have altruistic feelings, they do seek to promote or respect the welfare of others and it is simply not true of everyone that their "natural instinct is to inflict wrong or injury." This is, I believe, certainly true but does not undermine Glaucon's argument. Since it is a contingent fact as to whether people experience such finer feelings, it is necessary to discount them if we are to construct an argument that will appeal to everybody. The only motivation we can therefore assume people to have is that of seeking their own self-interest. In so far as harming others may appear to promote this self-interest, it is reasonable to assume that people will seek to do so. Whilst Glaucon's statement is perhaps rather extravagantly expressed (since it does completely ignore altruism), for the purposes of this argument this cynical assumption about human motivation is perfectly legitimate.

The crucial assumption which Glaucon derives from his account of men's relative evaluation of goods is:

A1 Never being harmed by others is a greater good than sometimes harming them.

Whilst there may be exceptions to this assumption—which I shall consider later—it does seem to be true 'by and large and for the most part'—as Aristotle might say. Whilst murder might sometimes be to my advantage, not being murdered is clearly even more so. Stealing from others may sometimes be to my profit, but the security of knowing that others will not steal from me is surely an even greater good. Moreover even Gyges would not dispute this evaluation—although he would, of course, deny that it was necessary to forgo the lesser good of sometimes harming others in order to secure this greater good.

Glaucon's basic argument is that men's recognition of the truth of A1 provides them with the motivation to act justly. Although men's natural instinct is to harm each other when it is in their interest to do so, they soon discover that if they do this, they, in turn suffer harm. But since never being harmed by others (G_1) is a greater good than that of sometimes harming others (G_2), they realize that it is in their interest to forgo G_2 if this is the only way of securing G_1. Ideally, however, according to Glaucon they would naturally prefer to secure both goods for themselves *i.e.*, G3.

Glaucon's argument here is a little elliptical since he does not spell out exactly why men have to forgo G2 in order to secure G1 nor why they do not all seek G3. The argument, in fact, depends upon two further assumptions which Glaucon does not make explicit:

A2 Men are approximate equals by nature
A3 Men can join together to cooperate[8]

Following von Wright let us imagine a society of three men *x*, *y* and *z*. According to Glaucon *x*, *y* and *z* would naturally seek to harm each other whenever it was in their interest to do so. But if each of them pursues such a policy, each will, in turn, suffer harm—unless, of course, he is so much stronger than the others that he can resist their harming him, whilst still harming them. This latter eventuality is however ruled out by A2 and A3. Both of these assumptions do again seem true—at least 'by and large and for the most part.' Men do share similar powers and abilities and where there are inequalities they can be minimized in virtue of A3. Thus even if *x* is stronger than *y*, it is unlikely that he will be stronger than both *y* and *z*. If *x* pursues a policy of harming others whenever it is in his interest to do so, *y* and *z* who will both suffer the effects of this policy will have an interest in joining forces to retaliate against *x*. Thus even if *x* is strong enough to prevent *y* taking retaliatory action against him, he will not be strong enough to prevent both *y* and *z* from doing so. Despite the inequalities of nature, *x* will thus not succeed in harming others with impunity, and if each of them does follow a policy of harming others whenever it is in his interest to do so, each of them will sooner or later find that he suffers harm in turn. Whilst in this 'state of nature' they thus secure G2, they lose the greater good G1 of never being harmed by others.

If however they each forgo G2, they will secure G1. Since G1 is a greater good than G2, they therefore have an interest in reaching mutual agreement to forgo harming each other so that they in turn will never be harmed. Let us therefore suppose that *x*, *y* and *z* conclude such an agreement. As Glaucon notes, this arrangement is, in a sense, a second best since ideally they would prefer—if it were possible—to secure both goods for themselves *i.e.*, G_3. It is however impossible—as we have seen—for all three of them to achieve this. Indeed it is impossible for two of them to do so—for suppose that y and z refuse to forgo harming others, whilst x does fulfil the the agreement to abstain from harming others. y may therefore harm both z and x, and z may harm both y and x. Thus whereas y and z may secure G_2 (the good of harming others) neither of them will secure G_1 (the good of never being harmed), whilst the poor gullible fool x will obtain neither G_1 nor G_2. But since $G_3 = G_1 + G_2$ and no one secures both G_1 and G_2, no one secures G_3. However whilst it is impossible (given A_2 and A_3) for all of them or even two of them to secure G_3, it is logically possible for one of them to do so. Suppose x and y fulfil their agreement to abstain from harm, but z does not do so, z will then get the benefit of never being harmed (G_1) plus the benefit (G_2) of sometimes harming others. But, of course, if z does this then x and y lose the benefit of never being harmed. They are thus paying the price (abstaining from harming others) but are not securing in return the benefit of never being harmed. And, as Glaucon notes, "what is most undesirable [is] to suffer wrong without redress." It is thus very much in their interest to prevent z from his parasitic action. In virtue of A_2 and A_3 even if z is stronger than x or y, he is unlikely to be stronger than both. If therefore x and y join together against z they can persuade him—through fear of punishment—to pay his due and forgo harming others. In short—despite the logical possibility of such parasitic action—in virtue of A_2 and A_3, it is still in z's interest to act justly. Moreover—as von Wright notes—this same mechanism of normative pressure can be applied whoever tries to play the rogue and seeks to add to the benefits of other people's justice, the benefits of injustice: if it is x, y and z can combine against him, if y then x and z.

Given therefore the three assumptions *viz*:

A1 Never being harmed by others is a greater good than sometimes harming others

A2 Men are approximate equals by nature

A3 Men can join together to cooperate,

it is possible to show that in this simplified society of three it is in the interests of each of them to act justly even if we discount all altruistic or other-regarding motives. Granted these assumptions, this argument seems valid. The problem is now therefore to examine these assumptions further and in doing so, to see how we can dispose of the apparent counter-example of Gyges. We shall need also to consider whether this theoretically simplified society of three bears any relation to the society in which we actually live.

That these assumptions are true for most people is, I think, not an extravagant claim. It is important to emphasize also that A_2 and A_3 do not deny that there may be inequalities of nature or that men may be aware of these—on the contrary, it is because they are aware that this may be so, that men are motivated to join together to minimize such inequalities. These assumptions do not therefore presuppose the convenient 'veil of ignorance' which Professor Rawls exploits in his interesting recent attempt to demonstrate that it would be rational for men in a state of nature to choose his two principles of 'Justice as Fairness'. In what he calls the 'original position' Rawls assumes that "no one knows his place in society, his class position or social status, nor does anyone know his future in the distribution of rational assets and abilities, his intelligence, strength and the like . . . or even their conception of the good or their special psychological insights."[9] By drawing this 'veil of ignorance' over the original position, Rawls makes his task too easy—since he excludes from consideration precisely those factors which his two principles of justice also exclude, it comes as no surprise therefore that he succeeds in demonstrating that men in his original position would choose such principles. His argument is thus, in effect, circular. Moreover by exploiting this 'veil of ignorance', Rawls also risks making his argument irrelevant to the actual pressures of moral discourse. As I have stated the problem of this paper it is to seek to convince a man who does know all the facts about his powers, abilities and position that none the less it is in his interest to act justly. It is, after all, little use when seeking to persuade a miner to moderate his pay claim to ask him to imagine himself in a state of nature where he was unaware of the power which his union could exert.

Given, therefore, that for most people these three assumptions are true, it can be shown that for most people it is in their interest to act justly and moreover—since they will not secure the benefits of justice unless others also act justly—it is in the interests of the majority to ensure by the mechanism of normative pressure which we have examined, that as far as possible everyone does act justly. I have, however, carefully only claimed that they are true of most people since it is obviously possible to construct counter-examples. The problem is whether these exceptions undermine the whole argument.

Let us consider A2 and A3 together. The obvious exceptions to these is Gyges with his magical ring (or to update the example we might think of 'Doctor No' with his personal secret nuclear weapon). The possession of a magical ring clearly renders Gyges unequal with his fellows (and thus breaches A2) and A3 is no use since men cannot combine together successfully against Gyges to persuade him to act justly since, whenever he is in a tight corner, he can simply turn his magical ring and disappear. It might be tempting to discount such examples because of the fanciful stage settings which they require (magical rings, nuclear weapons). This would however be a mistake since such unbridgeable inequalities do not appear at all fanciful if we elevate the argument from the realm of individuals to that of relations between states—it is not difficult to think of examples of states that are so powerful that their neighbours cannot combine together against them.

It is, of course, possible to argue that although it might appear in Gyges' interest to act unjustly, this would not be in his 'real interest' in view of the extreme insecurity and isolation that he would have to endure in order to carry out his life of perfect injustice. Plato, for example, uses such considerations to show that the 'Tyrannical Man' of Book 9 of the *Republic* would really be extremely unhappy—"friend of neither god nor man."[10] Such considerations have some force (and may even have some application to international affairs—nations do, after all, like individuals need friends and allies). It is however simply not possible to rule out by logic that Gyges—even if he looked at the problem completely rationally—might not still choose to act unjustly.

The problem thus is whether the possibility of a Gyges undermines the whole argument. The answer is, I believe, that it does not. If it is accepted—as I think it must be—that if someone is to be given a reason to act justly, then acting justly must be shown to somehow conduce to the attainment of his wants/ends—then if we discount—as we must since we cannot guarantee their applicability—altruistic or religious motives, the only way that we can show that it is rational to act justly is to show that it is in his self-interest to do so. Given the truth of A1–A3 of the vast majority of people, it is possible to show that for most people it is in their interest to act justly. In so far however as these assumptions do not hold true of Gyges, then he has no reason to act justly and indeed, has no reason to subscribe to the moral code of his fellows. His magical ring and assumed lack of any altruistic or other-regarding motives set him apart from his fellows outside the moral community to which they belong. The fact that it is not possible to persuade Gyges to act justly does not however invalidate the attempt to show that morality can be based on self-interest, since this limitation of the power of moral argument does appear to correctly represent the limitations of moral reasoning in the real world. A small powerless country like Czechoslovakia did not have at her disposal any convincing rational argument to dissuade Russia from invading her in 1968, as soon as it became clear that NATO would not intervene in such circumstances. This is not to deny the injustice of Russia's action but merely to point to the painful truth that given the circumstances of 1968 and the international balance of power then prevailing, it was very difficult to dissuade Russia from committing such injustice by means of rational argument. This might have been possible if one could have counted on Russia's possessing the international counterpart of altruistic feelings—respect for the territorial sovereignty and integrity of other countries. Unfortunately, however, Russia did not at the time experience such feelings towards Czechoslovakia, or at any rate not sufficiently strongly to outweigh the advantages she considered would be gained by using force to ensure Czechoslovakia's firm adherence to the policies of the Warsaw Pact. Given this and the fact that Russia correctly calculated that neither NATO nor the UN would risk a confrontation with Russia over Czechoslovakia, it is difficult to say that her action was not rational.

If altruism is discounted, the justification of morality

depends upon certain assumptions about human beings and if
and when these assumptions do not hold true, it must be
recognised that it is not possible to persuade those for whom
they are not true to act morally. Since however these assumptions hold true of most people, it is in the interests of the
majority to act justly and, moreover, it is in the interests of the
majority to seek to ensure that these assumptions hold
true as far as possible of everybody so that everybody has
a reason to act justly. For unless the moral community
embraces everybody, the majority will not secure the full
benefit of their own just actions. If it can be shown that
somebody might possess the tremendous advantages of a
Gyges, then it is in the interests of the rest of us to try to prevent this. Indeed this can be argued to be one of the prime
justifications of democracy. It may have very obvious weak-
nesses but it does at least ensure that the majority have the
means to get rid, without violent revolution, of any individual who attempts to seize excessive political power and thus
put himself in a position of such gross inequality with his
fellows that they can no longer persuade him to act justly.
Democracy thus provides the institutional means for prevent-
ing someone from placing himself—like Plato's 'Tyrannical
Man' of Book IX of the *Republic*—outside the moral community.

Similarly in the international situation, after the invasion
of Czechoslovakia it was often said that we should never allow
such an event to happen again. The way however to achieve
this would be to change the international balance of power
so that it would be true of states—as of individuals—that they
were approximately equals (A_2) and such inequalities as
existed could be minimized by cooperative action (A_3). If
these assumptions held true of all states, then by parity of
reasoning with the argument for individuals, it would be in
the interests of all states to act justly. The justification of an
institution such as the United Nations is that it does endeavour to achieve this by providing the institutional means
whereby a sufficient number of nations can cooperate together
to check the otherwise irresistible power of a particular nation
and thus minimize the inequalities of nature. The UN has
not, of course, been very successful at doing this largely

because it has proved so difficult to get a number of different nations ever to agree in time upon the appropriate course of action. In principle, however, it is only by changing the international balance of power by institutions such as the UN that one can guarantee that the force of moral argument will apply to the dealings between nations.

Having examined assumptions A2 and A3, let us now turn back to the initial assumption A1:

> Never being harmed by others is a greater good than sometimes harming them.

I have maintained that this assumption is also by and large true, although it is again not possible to rule out by logic that in particular circumstances, particular people's evaluations may differ from those of the majority. A trivial example would be that of the masochist. I say trivial since, in fact, the extent to which the masochist's wants and needs differ from other men's is very limited. He may like being whipped by a leather-booted buxom blonde but he would not really choose to have all his possessions stolen or to be murdered.[11] Even the masochist would therefore accept the general validity of A1.

A more interesting case would perhaps be that of the Great Train Robbers. It could be argued that it might be in the interests of one of the Train Robbers to be imprisoned for a number of years, if at the end of his sentence he could still enjoy the untold wealth he stole. It would not be my choice but it cannot be excluded by logic that it might be his. To this extent he might therefore not subscribe to A3. Since however it is in the interests of the majority to prevent such crimes, just as it is—as we have seen—in the majority's interest to try to devise institutional structures that will minimize such gross inequalities of nature as might invalidate A2 and A3, so it is in their interest to try to ensure that A1—which holds true for most people—holds true for everyone. This might therefore be an argument for increasing the severity of punishments to ensure that it is never in the interests of the criminal to serve time if only he can later reap the stored benefits of his crime. Once again we must recognize that moral reasoning relates to practical states of affairs which are not static but can be changed. Our society is not perfect and the possibility of a criminal's not accepting A1, may reveal an imperfection in our legal system that needs to be remedied.

Further, we must consider the more general difficulty that our society is unquestionably bigger than the society of three which we earlier envisaged. Do the arguments which appeared valid for a society of three, also apply to our society? The main problem is that whereas it was very easy to suppose in the society of three that one of them would not be able to get away with his injustice because the normative pressure which the other two could exert was so all-pervading, it is notoriously true that in our society the right arm of the law does not reach everywhere—people do get away with their crimes.

Whilst this is true, it would not therefore follow that it would be rational for anyone to adopt as a policy of life that of always harming others whenever it appeared in his interest so to do. Anyone who adopted such a policy of 'perfect injustice' would—unless he were a Gyges—inevitably be caught and punished. The more worrying case is that of the man who adopts a policy of acting unjustly only occasionally. If he is skilful and cunning and chooses his occasion carefully, he might be able to get away with it and if so, it might be rational for him to attempt to do so. Again, I cannot exclude this possibility by logic. I could, indeed, show—by the argument deployed earlier—that it would be impossible for everyone or even most people to attempt thus to add to the profits of others' justice, the profits of their own injustice since if most people tried to do this, they would clearly lose the benefit of never being harmed by others. Parasitic action by a few is however logically possible.

If someone were to consider whether to adopt such a course of action, he would, of course, have to consider not only the chances of successfully getting away with his crime but also the likelihood that if caught the punishment might outweigh the benefits of the crime and this could well tip the balance of calculations against committing the crime. In our imperfect society it cannot be ruled out *a priori* that for a particular person in a particular set of circumstances it might be rational for him to commit a crime. Once again, however, this would suggest that since it is in the interests of the majority to prevent this happening, it may be in the interests of the majority to strengthen the crime-detection mechanisms so as to ensure that as few people as possible do succeed in getting away with their crimes. If the chances of getting away with a crime are not sufficient to outweigh the risk of being caught and punished, it would, of course, cease to be rational for anyone to commit a crime. However, whilst in theory it would be possible to strengthen the powers of the police to ensure that an absolute minimum of crimes remains undetected, it would not necessarily follow that we should choose to do this. Such a police state might have the obvious advantage that it was never rational for a criminal to commit a crime (unless he were Gyges) but this advantage would have to be weighed against the loss of personal liberty such a system would entail. Basing morality on self-interest does not magically guarantee a simple answer to every moral question since our interests may clearly conflict and difficult calculations may still be necessary to decide where the balance of advantage lies. In the event we may therefore consider it to be more in our interest to tolerate a few criminals getting away with their crimes than to suffer the personal inconvenience and restrictions of liberty that a significant strengthening of police powers may involve.

I hope therefore that I have satisfactorily shown that justice can be founded upon self-interest and that justice can be shown to be more profitable than injustice. I have however admitted that such arguments may not work in circumstances where the assumptions on which moral reasoning are based do not hold true. Far from regarding the admission of the possibility of a Gyges as refuting the argument, this is, I believe, one of its strengths since in real life this is precisely where the limits of reason to persuade self-centred people to act justly are in fact reached. Men adopt a moral code because —given the truth of assumptions A1–A3—this is the only way they can secure the greater good of never being harmed by others. If any of these assumptions do not however hold true of a particular person, then such a person does indeed have no reason (assuming he is not altruistic) to join the moral community. But since these assumptions unquestionably hold true for most of us in most circumstances, it is in our interest to act justly and it is, moreover, in our interest to ensure that as far as possible these assumptions hold true of everybody so that everybody has reason to subscribe to the moral code. It is in our interest to ensure that a Gyges cannot exist. We need therefore constantly to examine our institutions—both national and international—to ensure that they are so framed as to validate, as far as is possible and desirable, the assumptions upon which morality is based so that it is in the interests of everyone to act justly. This view of morality not only therefore enables us to demonstrate that it is reasonable to act justly but also provides a valuable critical standpoint from which to examine the way in which society is organized.

Finally, however, I promised earlier to revert to the problem of whether it is satisfactory to base morality upon self-interest. My basic reply to this objection is first, to repeat what I said earlier—that I see no alternative to some such form of argument if morality is to be given a rational foundation given the fundamental position which the wants and desires of the agent must take in any rational form of practical reasoning and given that it is a merely contingent fact as to whether the agent may want to respect or promote the welfare of others. That morality is fundamentally irrational is a pessimistic conclusion which I see no reason to accept.

Secondly, I would dispute that this argument does destroy the distinction between morality and expediency. Morality can be founded on self-interest but it is enlightened long-term self-interest and the claims of morality as conceived in this paper may still conflict with shorter-term considerations. The problem of *akrasia—video meliora proboque deteriora sequor* —can therefore still arise. Even though I accept that it is in my interest to forgo harming others in order to secure the greater benefit of never being harmed by them, I may still be tempted by short-term considerations to forget my longer-term interest. Indeed it is this possibility of a conflict of interests that introduces the 'anankic' element into moral reasoning. Because morality may involve performing actions which in themselves I would not choose to do, I may have to be persuaded to do them by the argument that since I want to secure the greater good of never being harmed and unless I forgo harming others I will not secure this, therefore I 'ought' to forgo harming others. The basic form of moral reasoning is thus no different from that of the practical syllogism which we considered earlier which moved from a statement of my wants *via* a middle premiss stating a necessary means of achieving these wants to the conclusion that I must therefore perform an action (running for a train) which I would not of itself choose to do. The only difference is that in moral reasoning the word 'ought' rather than 'must' usually appears in English but this does not seem to reveal a fundamental difference. 'Ought' can, after all, occur in non-moral practical syllogisms, and in Greek, for example, there is no verbal distinction between 'ought' and 'must'—the same words '*dei*' and '*chrē*' are used for both.

Thirdly, those who argue that to base morality upon self-interest undermines morality are not always consistent in their argument. After all, virtues such as temperance and prudence are surely based on enlightened self-interest and yet it is seldom disputed that these are moral virtues.

Finally one must recall that the aim of this paper has been to show that morality can be based on self-interest so that one could convince the self-centred secular realist—who denied all feelings for others—that he should none the less act justly. I am not therefore denying the importance of altruism and the 'love of others as oneself'—indeed I consider they occupy a very important position in morality. Such beautiful concepts could not however be relied upon for the purposes of convincing the hard-headed realist since we knew in advance that he would not experience such feelings or be swayed by such considerations.

NOTES

[1] I am grateful to Professor D. D. Raphael who kindly read and criticized an earlier draft of this paper. I have also benefited from discussion of this topic with Dr. A. R. Colclough.

[2] G. E. M. Anscombe *Intention* Sect. 36.

[3] *Proceedings of the Aristotelian Society* Vol. 59 (1958-9) pp. 83-104.

[4] *Philosophical Review* LXXII (1963) pp. 141-58.

[5] Book II of *Republic* Sect. 359. Quotation is from H. D. P. Lee's translation (Penguin Classics) pp. 89-90.

[6] *Ibidem* Sect. 360; p. 91 of Lee's translation.

[7] Chapter X *The Varieties of Goodness*, by G. H. von Wright.

[8] For these assumptions see also von Wright *ibidem*.

[9] p. 12 J. Rawls *A Theory of Justice*.

[10] *Republic* Sect. 580.

[11] Indeed in so far as the masochist welcomes such flagellation he presumably does not regard it as 'being harmed' and hence as in any way inconsistent with the general truth of A1.

V*—THEORIES OF TRUTH

by Paul Foulkes

I

What is truth? When jesting Pilate, having asked that question, failed to stay proceedings until an answer was found, he acted like the ruthless procurator reported by historians. In ignoring his own rhetorical query, however, he showed good sense: for it has no answer. We shall examine why not, and why, nevertheless, many think that they can find one. The various views adopted reflect the different concerns that shelter under this one heading.

The words 'true', and its correlative 'false', do indeed have simple meanings that readily commend themselves even to the untutored: to say that things are as they are is to give a manifest or true account, to say that they are as they are not is to give a deceptive or false account. There is nothing new in that: it is what the Eleatic stranger tells Theaetetus (*Sophist*, 263b). Nothing that is more to the point has been said on this topic since.

Nevertheless, some further reflections seem appropriate, or these remarks would have been briefer.

II

To begin with: there may be those who wish to call the foregoing definition a theory. In a loose sense of the term this is quite common and harmless. Why such a definition should be so named is another matter, for we do not normally refer to definitions in this way: a dictionary is not a catalogue of theories, but the issue is incidental. Clearly, there is a use for the word 'true'. What concerns us here is something else, namely, whether there can be a recipe or prior guarantee for truth.

---

* Meeting of the Aristotelian Society at 5/7, Tavistock Place, London, W.C.1, on Monday, 22nd November, 1976 at 7.30 p.m.

At first sight, it looks as though deductive inference is an obvious instance. Not so, however. Valid deductive inference preserves truth if we have true premisses, but it will not help us to attain it if we have not. We shall return to this point later.

A more serious problem arises when the foregoing definition is described as the correspondence theory of truth, a description that has often and justly been criticized. We do indeed speak of true statements as corresponding to the facts, but here the metaphor is not quite so harmless. For in saying this we do at least imply that there are two ranges and a relation that holds between their respective members. On one side we have facts, on the other statements, and the relation of correspondence holds between a fact and a true statement, while it does not hold between a fact and a false statement. This clearly will not do, for various reasons. Take first the ranges. It seems doubtful if one could set out all possible statements in some specifiable order, but let us assume for the sake of argument that something like it could be achieved. There would then still be the problem of setting out the facts on the other side. The trouble is that there does not seem to be any independent principle of individuation by means of which we might pick out facts and arrange them in some order. For what we normally do is precisely to pick out facts by means of statements. For each fact there are then two statements, one true, to which it corresponds, the other false, to which it fails to correspond. This is simply circular.

There is worse to come, however. On the correspondence view, if anybody wants to assert that the relation does hold, he risks sliding into a regress. For making the assertion would introduce a second-order correspondence. The first-order correspondence will either hold or not hold. Any question of its holding, if answered in the affirmative, amounts to the statement that the statement 'the correspondence holds' is true. That, if truth is correspondence, will introduce the second-order correspondence, and so on indefinitely.

Other awkward questions remain: what, for instance, do false statements correspond to? Not, of course, to facts. Neither to non-facts, for there are none. Notice that on the present view it is improper to speak of facts as true, or as false: truth or falsehood belongs to, or is identified with, the holding or not holding of the relation of correspondence. People do of course use the phrase 'true facts', or dismiss as false something that they do call facts; but this is short-hand for something else. If somebody reveals the true facts of a case, he is thereby implying that what others had paraded as facts were not facts but errors (or perhaps lies, if the intention had been to deceive). The true facts then are simply the facts, while facts dismissed as false are allegations of fact that are now considered as false statements (as not corresponding to the facts).

It is readily seen from this example how easy it is to slide into identifying a true statement with the fact that it states. One might be tempted to solve the original problem by adopting this identification instead of the correspondence relation as an account of truth, but this will not work either: exactly the same difficulties arise as before. We should be led into a regress of identifications and there would be nothing with which to identify false statements.

Closely connected with the correspondence theory is the question of how we assess whether we have given a better or worse account of some situation that we wish to capture in a report or description. The report will of course be in words, and therefore raises the whole question of how words mean; or, if this is felt to be too speculative a question, how they are used. This general question is, however, not our main concern here. Given that somebody has set down a written report, how is he to judge that it is adequate? Certainly such a judgment must involve a rehearsal of features observed and a checking of them against the written record. However, as before, it is not in any very useful sense a correspondence that one is chceking. There is here the additional difficulty that the report, of its very nature, must have a sequential structure of its own which the facts reported on may lack. Quite apart from that complication, the report will have to be selective: it will pick out what in the special circumstances is regarded as important, in an order that seems to give the account the sequence felt to be appropriate in the context. There is no such thing as a complete or exhaustive account. Its limits are set in each instance by the conditions of the case, and for that no general formal prescriptions can be specified. An adequate report must certainly include what is important, but these features are not available as a standing group that an account could preferentially reflect.

What may be asked in either of these cases is this: when we assess whether a statement is true or false, or an account adequate or not, what is the character of this assessment? Is it in its turn a further statement at a higher level, a second-order consideration? If it were, then, on a correspondence theory of truth, we should at once fall back into the regress that we noticed earlier. That theory, however, is not a necessary condition for the regress to occur, any formula that seeks to explicate truth as the fulfilment of some condition would be equally susceptible. For we could always ask the question whether that condition was fulfilled or not. Unless, therefore, at some stage the regress were stopped by fiat, by insisting that beyond a certain level the question may not be asked, we should have to answer an infinity of questions in order to settle the single question with which we began. This would be somewhat discouraging. It would also be completely arbitrary. We must therefore nip the regress in the bud: it is the first step that counts.

We should therefore have to say that the assessment is in some sense direct. While this raises more problems than it settles, we can at least give up trying to seek correspondences, in any literal sense, between words and things; but neither should we try to climb through a hierarchy of levels, as though the higher we went the greater the overview of the terrain. More needs to be said on this, but not here.

III

Another widely held view is that the truth of a statement consists in its hanging together with other statements. This coherence theory of truth comes in a number of different though related varieties. The first goes back to the idealist notion that all truths hang together and make up a whole, whose articulation requires the rehearsal of all the constituent truths. On this view anything less than the whole truth, or rather the truth of the whole, is an untruth. It is not an attractive view. Since we have to make our discoveries piecemeal and in stages, we should on this theory be condemned to perpetual and pervasive ignorance. This plainly will not do. We must indeed always allow that we know little, but it is still something. Besides, even if we recognize that we shall never be omniscient, we constantly extend our grasp of the world, albeit in desperately small steps. The idealist view of truth is thus simply wrong.

Oddly enough, vestiges of this view survive in some rather unexpected quarters. Some logicians currently use the word 'implies' in a sense according to which any truth implies any other truth. This way of talking does not accord well with what the innocent user of language tends to expect. Perhaps so much the worse for common sense but in that case we should have to admit that this kind of technical vocabulary is a natural adjunct to idealist metaphysics. This only by way of parenthesis.

An approach related to this makes truth a feature of a system of statements. There are two variants to this theory, one weak and the other strong. In a weak sense of coherence, a statement p coheres with a system s, if p is not incompatible with s; that is, s does not entail not-p. In a strong sense, a statement p coheres with a system s, if not-p is incompatible with s; that is, s entails p. This way of looking at truth tends to be favoured by those who are interested in formal systems of the kind we meet in mathematics. The difference between the two variants is of some importance in the development of such systems.

In the weak case the system s does not discriminate between p and not-p. Either may therefore be adopted as part of a new system that remains consistent. This is the sort of case we meet in geometry, when we either adopt or reject Euclid's parallel axiom and thereby create two systems, which are accordingly called Euclidean and non-Euclidean respectively. Since neither the parallel axiom nor its contradictory is entailed by the remaining axioms, we must choose either one or the other as part of our system, so that at this stage geometrical theory divides into two self-consistent branches. These branches are of course mutually inconsistent, since they respectively contain one each of a pair of contradictory statements.

In the strong case the system s picks out one or the other of

p and its contradictory, although at a given stage of enquiry in the field we may not know which. This is the situation that confronts us for example in arithmetic when we have to establish or refute a conjecture. There must have been a time, probably early in the fifth century B.C., when Greek mathematicians did not yet know whether there was a greatest prime number or not. Who first discovered that there was not is not known, but when Euclid nearly two centuries later gave a proof to this effect, the matter was settled. Perhaps we should not say that it was put beyond doubt, since anyone who comes to this field for the first time may well have qualms. However, this can be met by showing him the proof. If after that he is still dissatisfied, he must be given up as a hopeless case. Unless, that is, the ground of his doubt is of a more radical kind and he wishes to raise general critical objections to the deductive procedure that is being used. In that case we are concerned with a different problem, which must be settled before we can address ourselves to the kind of issue we are discussing here.

Not all conjectures of this type are resolved as easily as the one just described, although even that must have been difficult enough in its time. Take for example the question whether or not there are infinitely many primes that can be expressed as the sum of one plus the square of an integer (primes such as 17, 37, 101). Two hundred years ago, Euler thought there were, but could not prove it and the problem remains unsolved to this day. In cases such as these, however, we do not have the beginning of two branches: the basic principles of arithmetic leave no loopholes that might allow such problems to escape solution, even if they have so far not been solved. Mathematicians do not develop two arithmetics, one Eulerian and the other non-Eulerian, according to which way the solution of the problem might go. Likewise for other such unsolved conjectures.

These examples are as such incidental to our purpose, but they do show why the coherence theory is attractive to those who handle abstract systems. As an account of truth, however, it is suspect. We have already suggested one reason that directly concerns the strong version, namely that a valid inference does not establish its own premises. Thus coherence is here at best truth contingent on other truths. In the case of weak coherence, what can be said about compatibility is that true statements can never be incompatible with each other, while false statements, or false and true statements, may or may not be incompatible with each other. Compatibility relations do not tell us anything about truth and falsehood as regards each statement involved. Formal systems are thus not primarily concerned with truth and falsehood, but with consistency and valid inference. In this sense they do indeed cohere, each as a structure in itself, although different systems obviously need not cohere with each other, as indeed they cannot if they bring together a pair of contradictory statements. In dealing with one set of facts we therefore cannot, at one and the same time, use two systems that are incompatible with each other.

IV

If the coherence theory has special attractions for those who wield abstract formal systems, the historian thinks along quite different lines. Here we meet a theory that might be called poietic, namely, the formula of Vico, that the truth is that which is made. On this view, since history is pre-eminently of man's own making, that is what he can be said to come to know best. He can of course know mathematics, too, since he has created it, but it is a shadowy kind of knowledge belonging to the realm of the abstract, whereas history is something fully real, in our world. Therefore genuine certainty is to be had above all of history. That, very briefly, is Vico's message. It emphasizes an aspect of truth familiar to every teacher: in order to know, one must do more than read or listen. One must, as the phrase goes, make knowledge one's own, by recreating it through active performance. For example, to gain a full grasp of a theorem, one must be able to reconstruct the proof, and acquire the skill of applying it in the appropriate circumstances.

If no more than this were meant, one might agree with Vico. Certainly our active participation can help us to attain a better grasp of what is true, and what we ourselves create has for us a kind of immediate certainty. Moreover, his formula breaks a connexion between the true and the good, which we have inherited from the Greeks. If the truth is linked with action, this latter may be good or bad. We therefore can then acknowledge more readily the active existence of evil, whereas on the classical view it was regarded as purely negative and passive, as the lack of good.

Nevertheless, as a general principle, the formula fails. For if one identifies truth with action, then any practice whatever will have truth on its side: we could no longer distinguish between actions as regards truth, and action will indeed become the only truth. This leads to a form of extreme existentialist complacency: any of my actions will be justified as true by the mere circumstance that it is mine. This puts us squarely beyond good and evil, which is perhaps a little too far for a theory of truth to go. Of course it is we who are pressing the theory too far, but it is in terms of consequences not bargained for that theories are to be amended.

A close relative to Vico's view is the pragmatic theory of truth put forward by William James, who sees truth as that which has fruitful consequences. This, too, has some sense in it, but becomes untenable if taken seriously on its own terms. What the pragmatic theory points to is the way we go about solving the problems we meet in our everyday lives. Whatever helps us to resolve difficulties is to that extent useful and these are the truths that we seek in trying to remove obstacles. However, if we identify truth with that which has useful consequences, then one and the same thing may be both true and not true. Take a situation where there is a conflict of interests between two people: what is useful to one may be harmful, or at least not useful, to the other. The item in question is then true for the former and not so for the latter. The notion of true-for-somebody is suspect on other grounds as well, but in any case since interests may change, we are left with a totally elusive concept. Moreover, how is one to judge such an issue if one's own interests are not involved? The whole theory breaks down. A champion of pragmatism might perhaps object that nobody ever judges anything without some involvement of his interests; but even if that were true (useful to whom?), how could the pragmatist know it and assert it as true? The recipe evidently fails.

Another time-honoured approach to this problem is what

might be called the oracular theory of truth. This is the view that truth is what some particular person says, either at all times or under certain special circumstances: the deliverances of wise men, or the occasional pronouncements of indifferent men from special points of vantage, *ex cathedra* as it were. In all such cases it is pertinent to ask who told them and how did he know? More searchingly still, we may enquire whether what they say is true because they say it, or whether they say it because it is true. This is an old and famous problem. The outcome is that a reference back to an authority merely shifts the question to a different place and the dispensation will be reliable only if the authority is: if we take the latter on trust, then we simply cease to ask. A variant of this theory seeks the truth in certain special records or sacred books, which come in various sizes and colours. The same strictures apply as above.

We shall say nothing about truth in formalized languages, for we are here not concerned with semantic paradoxes, nor with the problem of formalizing the concept of truth. Besides, the attendant notion of a hierarchy of languages brings with it difficulties of its own that belong to a different area.

V

What, it may be asked, is the motive for seeking to establish theories of truth at all? Briefly, it seems to be this: to secure guaranteed objects of knowledge. We constantly seek to extend our knowledge, or at least to assert that we have it, by laying claims to truth for our opinions. If we could find a method for establishing truths beyond doubt, then we should have an unfailing device for gaining knowledge. It is the quest for certainty that inspires the search for truth guarantees. One way of doing this which does not directly concern us here is simply to invent a set of elementary theoretical truth carriers out of which one then attempts to construct experiences that are recorded as true statements. The other is to seek truth in some test, comparison or procedure that might be carried out at the level of experience. It is these attempts that we have met in the various theories here discussed.

There are, however, no such certifying procedures. We have to fight our own human ignorance as best we may and try to gain knowledge by constant exercise of critical vigilance. In this we do indeed discriminate between ways of proceeding. Thus, even if there is no certainty, we shall make more headway if we follow rational principles of enquiry rather than float adrift on a sea of wishful thinking. As we said earlier, if we strive after knowledge, we must make it our own. It is not given to us to see the whole at once and together. If it were, enquiry would be superfluous. Such a state is certainly not attainable by us, and whether by some other intelligence must remain a mystery. Meanwhile we shall have to battle on amidst uncertainty.

VI*—GUILT AND SHAME AS MORAL CONCEPTS

by Anthony O'Hear

1. *Guilt and Feelings of Guilt*

A man is said to be guilty when he has broken some law or code by which he is bound, as a result of which he incurs a liability to punishment. Guilt itself is like a burden or a pollution which can be removed only by undergoing the appropriate punishment or by being forgiven by the appropriate authority. Looked at in this way, guilt is something objectively present once transgression has taken place (although one may be presumed innocent until *proved* guilty, policemen complain that far too many guilty men are free), whether or not the offender feels any guilt or not. A genuine offender against either a legal or a moral code may not have internalised any respect for the code and so be unrepentant, while someone who feels guilt may actually have done nothing forbidden, although he must, where his guilt is rational, in some sense or other, believe that he has, or, where it is not rational, have feelings of unease appropriate to such a belief.

The logic of guilt in the legal situation straightforwardly involves the notions of a broken law, a relevant authority and consequent liability to punishment.[1] These features are also present in the Judaeo-Christian ethic, in which law, authority and punishment are all prominent, and morality itself has a legalistic face. Moral guilt here has the same structure as legal guilt, the main difference being that the intimate relationship between the authority and the subject, according to which the authority knows everything about the subject and his intentions, means that what counts is the judgment delivered *in foro interno*. When the authority and his judgments are internalised in this way, it is natural that guilt feelings should have taken the centre of the stage to the extent that people have come to think of guilt itself as an emotion.[2]

* Meeting of the Aristotelian Society at 5/7, Tavistock Place, London, W.C.1, on Monday 6th December, 1976, at 7.30 p.m.

The parallel between legal and moral guilt is striking in
the Judaeo-Christian case. This leads naturally to asking
whether, whenever we might speak of guilt outside a legal
context, such parallels can be drawn, with a view to establishing whether the same concept is being used in each case, or
whether we have examples of accidents of usage without philosophical interest. In his paper "The Sense of Justice",[3] John
Rawls describes three stages in the development of a genuinely
moral sense of guilt. The first stage is what he calls authority
guilt. This is felt by children when they disobey the commands
of their parents. It is part of the love and trust that a child has
for its parents that, having no independent standards of its
own, it should accept the precepts of its parents and so be
liable to feelings of guilt if it breaks them. Now clearly, authority guilt shares with legal and 'Judaeo-Christian' guilt the
central elements of an authority, its commands and punishments. Indeed, some would argue that all later guilt feelings
have their origins in early fears of breaking parental prohibi-
tions, with society or God playing the parental rôle; though
this is not part of what I want to defend, it underlines the continuity between authority guilt and the other cases we have
considered.

Rawls' second stage is association guilt. This arises from
group participation in joint activities, such as games or social
institutions. On breaking mutual bonds, one will be prone to
feelings of association guilt, which means that one will show a
willingness to admit what one has done, accept reproofs and
penalties and seek reinstatement. There is a clear similarity
between association guilt and legal guilt, the group here being
the authority imposing its laws and punishments. Guilt feelings will be natural enough because the participants presumably desire both membership and the well-being of the group
and will dislike whatever tends to harm these ends.

Rawls' final stage is called principle guilt. This is where we
feel guilty not because we are injuring those we have particular bonds with (such as parents or chosen associates), but
because the love and trust of our parents and the co-operative
feelings to our associates are extended to others in accordance
with the principles of justice, in such a way that we feel guilty
about acting against the spirit of existing just institutions or

about resisting reforms required to set up new institutions required by the principles of justice. According to Rawls, not only are guilt feelings based on the principles of justice the only completely moral guilt feelings (because they are based on moral principles, rather than one's feelings for particular individuals), but someone who lacks a sense of justice (and hence has no liability to such feelings) "lacks certain fundamental attitudes and capacities included under the notion of humanity."[4]

The question which arises here is whether accepting the principles of justice necessarily leads to a liability to feelings sufficiently like the other types of guilt feelings to be included in the same class. Two factors initially confuse the issue. First, the talk of just institutions already suggests a quasi-legal perspective. Some of what might count as unjust here (*e.g.*, cheating a business partner) might be forbidden by a law one feels bound by and so, for that reason, produce guilt feelings. Secondly, one might, as a Christian for example, feel bound by a divine command to help those in need, and so feel guilty at not contributing to famine relief. But, in a case where a man does not see himself as being under any prescription to be just, and he is not acting illegally, what reason is there to call his feelings of regret at hurting someone feelings of guilt, rather than feelings of sympathetic sorrow, or shame, for example? It is not easy to get a clear view of the issues here because, as Miss Anscombe has pointed out, people do still tend to conceive themselves to be under positive prescriptions to be moral, even though they no longer think of morality in legalistic terms, as was the case when it was seen as being God's law. This legalistic way of thinking of morality, when continued in abstraction from its background of law leads, she argues, inevitably to confusion. Transposing something she says on this point, we might say that where there is no law or judge, the notion of guilt may retain its psychological effect, but not its meaning.[5] On this point, H. D. Lewis has also pointed out that the notion of guilt depends for its sense on the idea that one is bound by a categorical imperative, and that as a result, the classical Greek philosophers had little consciousness of guilt because, for them moral evil was seen not as a wilful violation of the moral law, but as a functional disorder, not unlike aesthetic, intellectual or physical shortcomings.[6] Certainly there is something parochial in Rawls' insistence on the connexion between the sense of justice and guilt. Our original question on the connexion between legal and other types of guilt thus broadens into the question as to whether there can be ethical systems without our emphasis on guilt.

2. *Shame: Its Objects and Logic*

In contrast with guilt, shame is not a notion whose central connotations are legal or moral. Although we can feel shame at doing something illegal or immoral, we can equally easily be ashamed of a bad piece of work, or of a social gaffe, or of saying something foolish, or of failing in a supererogatory ideal. Nor, in these cases, need our intentions or our ability to have done better be particularly relevant to our shame, whereas with guilt, in legal as well as in moral contexts, questions of intention and ability are relevant to determining the nature and extent of the offence. (Cases of strict liability may provide an exception here, but in a case where there has been no negligence, the sense in which someone strictly liable is said to be guilty appears to be a purely formal, not to say emasculated one.) In addition, while guilt seems normally to involve a transgressive action or attitude, shame can without any problem be felt for a much wider variety of objects: aspects of one's character or taste, elements of one's upbringing, such as one's accent, one's poverty, or one's parentage, even one's physical appearance or disabilities. One can also feel shame at being associated, even involuntarily, with groups whose behaviour one deplores, such as English football supporters abroad, or merely through being present at some degrading or indecent scene, such as a gratuitous act of cruelty.

The reason why shame has such a wide variety of possible objects, so that a man's shame need not be restricted to what is reprehensible or intentional in his conduct, as some philosophical accounts suggest, is because shame is logically dependent on seeing something "dishonouring, ridiculous, or indecorous in one's own conduct or circumstances (or in those of others whose honour or disgrace one regards as one's own)" (*Shorter Oxford English Dictionary*).[7] This explains why shame can be felt as a result of the failings of groups to which one belongs or because of one's inherited social or economic background or appearance. It also suggests that shame need not depend on a fear of public exposure, actual or potential, as is argued by Ruth Benedict, who says that shame "requires an audience or at least a man's fantasy of an audience".[8] Although, as we shall see, there is some truth in the view that shame rather than guilt is the characteristic emotion of the social man, it is quite possible to think of people, such as writers or craftsmen, with high standards of their own, feeling shame just because they have let themselves down (not produced a masterpiece), without thinking of them imagining other craftsmen inspecting and condemning their work.

Not only can shame be felt privately and because of privately held ideals, but feeling shame involves more than being subject to the external sanctions of shame. Just as guilt, as opposed to fear of punishment, is felt only when the authority or law involved is respected internally, so being publicly shamed produces feelings of shame, as opposed to feelings of embarrassment, resentment, rebellion or anger, only when one feels that the public disapproval is in some way in harmony with one's own feelings of how one would like to see oneself. Thus, in Homer, Thersites, although publicly shamed, feels no shame, and is therefore an enemy to Homeric society because his attitude makes it clear that he rejects its values.[9]

Although shame does not then require the background of a real or imaginary audience as Benedict suggests, and although it requires more than the ridicule of an audience to be felt, the example of Thersites suggests that it can play a significant rôle in enforcing the ethic of a society. Some light on this apparent conflict is thrown by Sartre when he says that "I am ashamed of myself *as I appear* to the Other . . . I recognise that I *am* as the Other sees me."[10] Now this is a necessary truth only if I, in my self-judging rôle, can be the Other. What is important here is precisely the idea that in the experience of shame there is a sense in which the individual concerned is playing two rôles, judger and judged. The fantasy of an audience is psychologically neither necessary nor sufficient for shame, but logically, there is obviously a connexion between one's own judgments and those of others. If a judgment is objective, it is in principle acceptable to anyone. As one's own judge, one is, if one is reasonable about it, in principle judging oneself as any reasonable person would.

Of course, not all shame is reasonable in this sense. I may not be judging myself correctly, or against standards anyone else would accept. In such cases, I may well be told that my shame is unreasonable, that I should feel no shame at what is worrying me, and although this may often be said or intended in a conventional comforting way, the fact that it can be said at all depends on the feeling that there should be some similarity between an individual's judgment of his conduct and that of others, which arises from the connexion in judgment between rationality and what is acceptable to any reasonable person. Thus a man might learn that it is unreasonable to feel shame at his physical appearance or birth, or at his failing to produce a masterpiece, and consequently change his standards and cease to feel shame in these areas. On the other hand, a man might learn through the judgments of others, what standards are expected of him, and to see that he ought to feel shame, where previously he had not.

3. Shame, Public and Private

David Richards, whose criticisms of the Benedict view that there is something essentially public about shame I have substantially echoed, claims that the experience of shame involves "the belief of failing to attain one's conception of the self's competence, some self-ideal of excellence".[11] This, I shall now argue, is too narrow, and leads him to underestimate the possibilities of shame as a moral sanction, and consequently to over-estimate the rôle guilt needs to play in morality.

Even allowing Richards a generously broad interpretation of competence, it is unclear that shame at illegitimacy or physical ugliness involves corresponding desires for competences of any sort, but, leaving this aside, Richards' view implies that a man will feel shame just where he fails to reach some ideal he has. Similarly, Helen Lynd defines shame as "a wound to one's self-esteem, a painful feeling or sense of degradation excited by one's previous idea of one's excellence", and Rawls says that in moral shame we feel a diminishment of self resulting from "our disappointment with ourself for failing to live up to our ideals", and that "a person feels ashamed because . . . he has failed to live up to a conception of moral worth which he has set himself to achieve."[12] What Richards, Rawls and Lynd, in stressing the relation between shame and one's ideals, are correctly concerned to do is to present a concept of shame which can operate in independence of the attitudes of others, but in doing so, they overlook the fact that one can perceive through the shame resulting from the disapproval of others whom one respects (or even from merely being confronted with some example of a standard immeasurably higher than one's own), not that one is failing to reach one's own current ideals, but rather that one should adopt new ones. One can, in other words, be shamed into accepting new standards, which would not appear to be possible on the account we are considering. The fact that others judge me in a certain way leads me to judge myself in a new way.

Richards, indeed, in seeing shame in terms of failure to reach ideals one has set oneself (and which may therefore have a degree of choice about them), is uneasy in speaking of shame as the primary experience of a man who fails to meet basic moral demands:

> it is not legitimate either to strive or not to strive, or choose or not to choose, to follow *these* principles, for they define the basic boundary conditions of a decent social life; indeed, the moral principles of obligation and duty define what we are morally at liberty in aspiring after, or opting for. Thus it is to be expected that one who desires to act on such principles typically believes himself to be transgressing basic moral norms, not failing to attain self-ideals, and thus experiences guilt, not shame (though, of course, the latter can be felt, in so far as immorality is regarded as a failure to attain self-ideals, which is quite possible, and not infrequent).[13]

But what is not clear is that only optional self-ideals can provoke shame. If a man saw his basic moral requirements not, as Richards appears to, in terms of quasi-legal boundaries that he had to avoid transgressing,[14] but in terms of the essential desiderata of any decent or honourable life within his society imparted to him through his upbringing in that society, then, what we have so far seen would lead us to expect shame rather than guilt to be his primary negative moral feeling. We are presented with so elevated a picture of the rôle of shame by Aristotle in the *Nichomachean Ethics,* in which obeying the sense of shame is seen as abstaining from the base acts because of their baseness, rather than from a fear of punishment or ridicule, while complete shamelessness implies the lack of an effective conception of the honourable, and as such is something alien to a civilised person.[15]

In societies where ethics is conceived basically in terms of honour, rather than in terms of obedience to a moral law, we do indeed find shame at the centre of the stage. This is so in the *Iliad*, as Professor Dodds has shown,[16] but the *Iliad* presents a problem for the general line of argument presented here, because shame is conceived there exclusively in terms of public loss of face, and this in turn comes about only when one has done something with bad consequences. An example of this is that when Agamemnon steals Achilles' mistress Bryseis for himself, he is in no way ashamed at the injustice of what he has done, nor would anyone have expected him to be, if he had got away with it. Loss of face and the consequent apology come about only when Achilles withdraws in a sulk, as a result of which the Greeks lose a battle. It appears here that shame is completely bound up with public scorn or ridicule, which itself occurs only when some publicly evident bad consequences result from an action. Similarly in J. K. Campbell's study of the Sarakatsani shepherds in Epirus and in Juliet du Boulay's *Portrait of a Greek Mountain Village,*[17] we find contemporary societies in which in practice a man's honour is largely dependent on how he appears to others. Not only does this lead to the acceptance of the practice of inveterate lying to save face, but to an absence of any Aristotelian idea of a man's virtue and nobility being primarily a question of his underlying character.

However, although in Homeric society, and to a lesser degree in the other societies I have mentioned, shame and honour are closely connected to public reputation, this is not because shame requires an audience or the fantasy of an audience, but because, as Dodds remarks, the highest value of those societies is public esteem. This is the ideal to be striven for and cherished (despite Thersites), so that in these societies there is no ground for a distinction between an account of shame in terms of public disapproval and one which separates shame logically from the attitudes of others. But this is not because of the nature of shame, but because of the type of values accepted by the society. Once certain types of conduct or character are seen as valuable in themselves, independently of their appreciation by others, shame too can operate independently of public condemnation or fantasies of public disapproval. In stressing the independence of shame from its external reference of public criticism, I am not, of course, denying that the attitudes of others are initially instrumental in provoking, teaching and reinforcing feelings of shame and in giving us the ideals involved, (this will be particularly evident in the small, close-knit societies of the sort we have been considering), nor that there will be a connexion between what it is reasonable to be ashamed about and what anyone would think dishonourable. But, it is equally true that even though guilt can be felt independently of public condemnation, it is through the experience of offending others such as parents and teachers that guilt is initially learned and that what it is reasonable to feel guilt for is what anyone would condemn. Perhaps even more significant here than these similarities between the relations of shame and guilt to public attitudes is the fact that even in those societies where shame and honour are most closely connected to public appearance and reputation, there must, as Juliet du Boulay points out, also be a personal awareness of honour co-existing with the public sense, to explain why one might care about public judgments in such a way that they provoke shame.[18] This sense of self-respect provides the basis for a less socially dependent concept of honour, in which shame is not tied to fear of exposure, but to a fuller view of personal worth, involving ideals such as those of reliability, fairness, decency and fidelity, as is apparently the case among the Egyptian Bedouin.[19]

If other regarding ideals can be included in a man's sense of his personal honour, then it is surely not the case, as Richards claims, that with shame there is never anyone but oneself to make reparation to in order to overcome one's shame.[20] If one's shame is at having wronged someone else, it may well be necessary to right the wrong in order to restore one's honour. Once again, Richards' advocacy of a narrow concept of shame seems to have blinded him to the possible rôle the concept could play in morality.

4. *Shame and Guilt in Current Moral Thought*

An answer to the question about the sense of justice and liability to guilt now suggests itself. If an unjust action is conceived as a transgression against a moral injunction, it will provoke guilt, while if it is seen as something unworthy of an honourable man, it will provoke shame. Of course, these two ways of looking at it are not mutually exclusive. Nevertheless there are problems for us in either way. Honour is not a notion that features very prominently in our moral thought. In practice, a man's honour has usually been seen in the light of his membership of a particular group, often by contrast to other groups. This has led if not actually to exaggerated concentration on the *machismo* aspect of honour, to a rather wooden and at times inhumane interpretation of one's honour, so that to us a degree of dishonour might well on occasion appear desirable. At the same time, it might be possible to develop a less exclusive sense of honour which was based on one's human nature as such, and which enjoined certain ideals of character and behaviour as belonging to a good man.

Guilt, on the other hand, is very much a live issue among contemporary moralists. The difficulty here is to develop a sense of moral guilt which can do without the elements of law, authority and liability to punishment which characterise guilt in the legal Judaeo-Christian contexts. We have seen that Richards and Rawls think of moral guilt in terms of transgressions against what one ought to do, but it still has to be shown against Miss Anscombe's arguments that the moral 'ought' can do the work required of it outside a law conception of ethics, for how, outside such a conception, can we cash out the idea that we are *bound* by morality?[21] Until this is done, one suspects that much of our talk about feeling guilty about having done wrong amounts to little more than an uneasy sense that one has offended someone, and that bad consequences are likely to ensue on meeting them again.

The Freudian account of guilt, with its talk of the dictates and punishments of the aggressive super-ego, itself an internalisation of childhood authority figures, whatever its psychological plausibility, certainly preserves the logical structure of guilt. It does so, however, at the expense of the rationality of guilt, because it is hardly rational in adult life to feel bound by the authority of one's parents as one did when a child. By contrast, in an attempt to elaborate a sense of guilt not rooted in infantility, Erich Fromm speaks of a man's feeling guilty "for not living up to his own expectations of himself", adding that it is only because of the "patterns of our culture" that it makes little sense to feel guilty for neglecting oneself.[22] If, however, the general line of argument in this paper is correct, then what Fromm is talking about is shame rather than guilt, and missing a conceptual distinction between what is imposed on one by some authority as a law and what is conceived of as an ideal.

Martin Buber, too, attempts to develop a sense of guilt which is neither Freudian nor dependent on the breaking of positive, social, moral or religious laws, but which results from each of us injuring the order of being by an active devotion to the world—"an existential guilt beyond all mere violations of taboos", which occurs "when someone injures an order of the human world".[23] In the light of this, Joseph K. in Kafka's *The Trial* is criticised for his lack of awareness of his existential guilt, precisely for the way he sincerely holds himself to be completely innocent of any crime. It seems that each man is in fact guilty of injuring the order of reality, perhaps just by "attempting to snatch at the world with twenty hands" (as Joseph K. himself puts it)—as if his very existence in the world is seen as a crime. It is fairly clear from what he says that Buber thinks of the order we all injure in terms of a basic natural law, which governs human existence in such a way that one first becomes aware of it just from the unease that results from violating it. Even if the notion of such a law could be expanded and defended, it seems irrational to feel guilty for breaking a law whose very existence one remains unaware of until one has broken it. The existential unease expressed by Kafka in his stories and diaries would seem to be a classic case for a Freudian interpretation, rather than to require the postulation of primal laws governing human existence.

Of course, it might be argued that Buber's notion of a basic natural law and consequent liability to existential guilt could even now be ethically extremely valuable. Similarly, Philip Rieff writes that without a

> sense of true guilt . . . and elaborately cultivated strength of inhibition preventing or punishing transgressive activity, there can be neither aristocracies of the feeling intellect nor democracies of obedience. Guilt, subserving the interdicts, is inseparable from the working of high culture.[24]

Waiving any doubts about the truth of this claim, the problem remains to outline the interdicts involved and to establish the nature of their authority:

> Who are to be our truth-tellers—better, say, our guilt-provokers? I do not know. I am without authority . . .[25]

It is at this point that the difficulties of expounding a coherent notion of guilt severed from actual laws and authorities become critical.

This is not to deny that psychologically moral guilt continues to be a powerful force even outside a generally accepted law conception of ethics. This need not altogether surprise us, accustomed as we are to talk of irrational guilt feelings, in which the subject is unable to point to anything he would regard as an offence as the object, or in which he claims that they are provoked by something he no longer believes is wrong. Commenting on such feelings, Rawls says that we should think of them not as guilt feelings proper, but as "certain sensations and feelings of uneasiness, and the like, which resemble those which he has when he feels guilty".[26]

But this seems to make irrational guilt feelings into unintelligible ones, and to leave it obscure as to why people, on having such feelings, both think of them as guilt feelings and attempt to discover some fault or forbidden desire underlying them. Indeed, in the case where the subject denies that he still believes that what underlies the feeling is wrong, the fact that guilt feelings were experienced even though one's explicit beliefs had changed could indicate that at a deeper level, one's beliefs had not changed as much as one thought. The old authority still has power.

In conclusion, it is possible to speculate that what is now required is a concept other than that of that concept of guilt here analysed, which involves notions of laws, authorities and liabilities to punishment, in order to characterise the way people care about having been unjust, unkind and so on. In a way, it hardly matters whether what might emerge is called guilt or not, so long as we recognise that it will be no nearer to the guilt of Claudius in *Hamlet*, whose offence calls for vengeance and requires remission from an all-knowing heavenly court, before which "there is no shuffling" and which looks for a change of heart before it will pardon, than is this Judaeo-Christian sense of guilt to the infectious, hereditary pollution attaching automatically even to the unintentional breaking of taboos which apparently held sway in archaic Thebes.

NOTES

[1] I say 'straightforwardly' here because it is not clear that in all cases of judgments in international law, those being tried are subject to a relevant authority or liable to any legal punishment, but in such cases it is an open question as to whether the courts properly have jurisdiction over them.

[2] *E.g.*, R. Harré and P. F. Secord, *The Explanation of Social Behaviour* (Oxford, 1972), p. 145.

[3] *Philosophical Review, 60,* 1963, pp. 281-305.

[4] *Loc. cit,* p. 299.

[5] In "Modern Moral Philosophy", *Philosophy, 33,* 1958, pp. 1-20.

[6] In "Guilt and Freedom", in *A modern Introduction to Ethics* (ed. M. K. Munitz), New York, 1958, pp. 400-15.

[7] Aristotle connects shame to voluntary actions (*Eth. Nic.,* 1128 b28) while E. Bedford, in "Emotions", *PAS LVII,* 1956/7, pp. 281-304 says that one must be responsible for what one is ashamed about and that it must be reprehensible.

[8] *The Chrysanthemum and the Sword,* London, 1947, p. 223. David A. J. Richards in *A Theory of Reasons for Action,* Oxford, 1971, gives abundant evidence of the popularity of this view.

[9] Nietzsche, in *Wir Philologen,* (*Werke* IV, 1, p. 178), says that Socrates, who in his view destroyed Homeric values, is the revenge of history for the death of Thersites.

[10] *Being and Nothingness* (translated by Hazel Barnes), London, 1969, p. 222. My comment is not intended as a criticism of Sartre, who often speaks (for example in his essay on Baudelaire) of the attempt to see oneself as though one were another person.

[11] *Op. cit,* p. 253.

[12] Helen Lynd in *On Shame and the Search for Identity,* New York, 1956, pp. 23-4: Rawls in *A Theory of Justice,* Oxford 1973, pp. 446 and 482.

[13] *Op. cit,* p. 263.

[14] Cf. *op. cit,* p. 255.

[15] Cf. *Nicomachean Ethics,* 1128b 10-35, 1179b 4-30.

[16] E. R. Dodds, *The Greeks and the Irrational*, Berkeley, 1951, especially Ch. 1 and Ch. 2.

[17] J. K. Campbell, *Honour, Family and Patronage*, Oxford, 1964. Juliet du Boulay, *Portrait of a Greek Mountain Village*, Oxford, 1974.

[18] *Op. cit*, p. 108.

[19] Cf. the paper by Abou A. M. Zeid, in *Honour and Shame, The Values of Mediterranean Society*, (edited by J. Peristiany), London, 1965.

[20] *Op. cit*, p. 256.

[21] I assume that, whatever other rôle it might play, Rawls' original contract cannot do that.

[22] In "Conscience" in *A Modern Introduction to Ethics*, (ed. M. K. Munitz) New York, 1958, p. 429.

[23] In "Guilt and Guilt Feelings" in *Guilt and Shame* (ed. Herbert Morris), Belmont, California, 1971, pp. 58-81.

[24] *Fellow Teachers*, London, 1975, p. 156.

[25] *Op. cit*, p. 160.

[26] "The Sense of Justice", p. 295. Cf. also *A Theory of Justice*, pp. 481-2.

I am grateful to Messrs. David Walker, Paul Gilbert and David E. Cooper for their help with this paper.

VII*—SELF-KNOWLEDGE AND INTENTION

by Roger Scruton

People are rational agents, they speak and they are self-conscious. I shall argue that these three features are essentially connected, and constitutive of our concept of a person. My argument will be schematic, however, since my main purpose in this paper is to show how a physicalist theory of mind (in particular a theory like behaviourism, which sees the mind as publicly observable) can account for the peculiar features of self-knowledge. A theory of personhood emerges as a corollary to the central argument.

I

I shall begin with an assumption, which is that I do not make mistakes about certain of my mental states. This, if true, is a conceptual truth. However, it may be a conceptual truth of the kind studied by the later Wittgenstein, the kind which admits of exceptions. In other words, it may be a truth about the normal case. So that, given a central example of pain, say, it would then be true that I not only do not, but cannot, make a mistake about its presence. It has seemed to many philosophers that some such thing is true. I agree with them, and I shall try to show *how* it could be true.

The assumption is not a simple one. There are at least two components:

(1) Our knowledge of certain of our mental states is incorrigible; I cannot believe that I am in pain without being in pain.
(2) Our knowledge of those mental states is 'self-intimating' in Ryle's phrase.[1] I cannot be in pain without knowing that I am.

These two components are, strictly speaking, independent of each other. But it is clear that they both attribute the same kind of authority to a man's beliefs about his own mental

---

* Meeting of the Aristotelian Society at 5/7, Tavistock Place, London, W.C.1, on Monday, 24th January 1977, at 7.30 p.m.

processes, and it would be odd if a theory were to explain the first of them without also assuming the existence of the second.

There is a further property of mental items that is consequent upon their incorrigibility. This is the property of being 'immediate' or 'immediately known'. That is, my knowledge of my own mental states has no basis. There could be no natural explanation of incorrigibility that did not bring immediacy in its wake. For suppose that I find out that I am in pain by evidence, or on the basis of some other knowledge that I have. Then it seems natural to suppose that I could make a mistake about the evidence, or about this basis, or about the inference from basis to conclusion. But then my resulting knowledge could no longer be said to be incorrigible. So, given that it is incorrigible, it must also be 'immediate'. That is part of what we mean by consciousness.

I shall not argue for the above assumptions. However, it is clear that the thesis of incorrigibility would be merely trivial if all mental states could exist equally in a conscious or an unconscious form. For statements like (1) and (2) above are merely tautologous unless we have some way of classifying the mental states referred to without describing them as 'conscious'. The existence of unconscious mental processes is clearly incompatible with the view that all mental phenomena are 'self-intimating'. And if it is possible to fear my father unconsciously then the assertion that I do not fear him is certainly corrigible. Hence my knowledge that I really do not fear him is founded on the certainty that there is no source of unconscious fear.

One might wish to argue that unconscious mental states are secondary examples, their attribution being possible only because of the prior understanding and attribution of their conscious counterparts. But I shall not take that line. It is enough for my purpose if we can identify mental states which simply cannot exist in an 'unconscious' form. I shall consider sensations. I do not think that there can be unconscious sensations, even though the processes that usually cause sensations may sometimes go on without our feeling them. Leibniz did indeed argue for the presence of *'petites perceptions'*.[2] But the important point is that the concept of the 'unconscious' gets application here, if at all, only because the perceptions in question are, as he says, *petites*. The unconscious is a limiting point, a fading into nothingness. That hardly leads us to suppose that sensations might quite literally endure, but in an unconscious state. The only kind of corrigibility that is permissible here is that which proceeds from a borderline. The case is nothing like unconscious fear, which may be stronger and more disastrous than any of its conscious counterparts. I shall concentrate on sensations, therefore, since the example will enable us to understand how the peculiarities of self-knowledge are to be accounted for. We are to study what seems to be a conceptual truth, that if a man is in pain, then he immediately and incorrigibly knows that he is.

Now it seems to me that no account of the features of self-knowledge to which I have referred follows from the Cartesian theory of mind. The idea of a special 'private' access to our own mental states can provide no explanation of the immediacy and incorrigibility of certain kinds of self-ascription. At best it provides us with a *picture* of the subject's epistemological privilege, but it is a misleading picture. The metaphor of an inner state leads us to think of self-knowledge as a kind of permanent self-revelation of each mental item to its owner. The sensations, beliefs, desires and emotions lie as it were glowing in the mind like jewels in a case, each one visible to the surveying consciousness by virtue of its own peculiar radiance. Such a picture may seem to fit sensations: it certainly does not fit beliefs, which, even though objects of incorrigible knowledge, are not permanently present to the mind. Moreover, it is a picture that seems to make the 'consciousness' of a sensation, for example, into an intrinsic feature of it. So that it now becomes impossible to suggest, what is true, that there might be creatures with sensations but without incorrigible knowledge; not because they have unconscious sensations, but because they lack self-consciousness altogether.

It seems then that if some rival theory (in particular, some form of physicalism) could explain the phenomena of self-knowledge, rather than dismiss them as an illusion, this will be a powerful argument in its favour. But of course, looked at from the point of view of the first person, it seems very odd to attempt to reconcile immediate knowledge with physicalism, and particularly odd to reconcile it with some form of behaviorism. For it is precisely the fact of immediate knowledge that gives rise to the picture of mental states as unchanging inner processes, existing above and beyond their fluctuating physical symptoms. Even when there are no symptoms the victim of pain knows that he is in pain—it still 'feels the same'—and he is in a position to follow the exact progress of the pain, knowing immediately and with certainty when it starts and how long it goes on for. For him, there is something unchanging: he does not have to study his symptoms (which is why we say that pain is not a physical complaint but a mental one)—he knows immediately the progress of his state and its precise degree of unpleasantness.

It seems natural to surmise that the peculiar phenomena of self-consciousness are a consequence of the use of language. Animals seem not to have the capacity for self-knowledge or a use for the concept of self. That suggestion can be supported in two ways, negatively and positively. The negative way would be to show that the concept of self, and the activity of self-knowledge, lie outside the reach of animal mentality, for the reason that animal behaviour is not capable of manifesting the possession of either. To describe an animal's behaviour in terms of its self-image is, strictly speaking, redundant. It performs no descriptive or explanatory function that could not be effected by the use of simpler concepts, and the supposition of simpler behavioural laws. I sympathize with that approach, and with the broadly behaviouristic outlook that it exemplifies. But it will not be my approach in this paper. I wish to suggest a more positive argument, based on a specific theory of self-knowledge, which analyses self-knowledge as a property of speech.

Let us turn away from the first person case, and consider the third person. What is it that *manifests* immediate and incorrigible awareness? It seems natural to suggest the following account: 'If I say I am in pain, then I cannot be wrong'. (I shall concentrate on the feature of incorrigibility since the other features present no added difficulties.) That will hardly do, since a man may speak insincerely about his own mental states, and if he does so then what he says about himself will be false. Moreover, even when speaking sincerely, a man may *say* something false, for example, because he does not understand the words he uses, or because he makes a slip of the tongue.[3]

Let us then phrase the thesis of incorrigibility as follows:

(A) If I say 'I am in pain' (i) sincerely,

                                    (ii) making no slip of the tongue, and

                                    (iii) understanding the words I use,

then I am in pain.

The 'if . . . then . . .' here is given whatever strength is thought to be indicative of a conceptual rather than a scientific truth. It might be thought that such a description contains no comfort for the physicalist, since the first condition—that of sincerity—begs the question which he is supposed to answer. In admitting 'I am sincere' as part of the analysis, it might be said, we have simply stated, in so many words that the subject *is* in pain. For surely the difference between the sincere and the insincere assertions of 'I am in pain' lies in the presence or absence of pain.

In so far as there is an objection enshrined in that mark, it can hardly be regarded as an objection to a physicalist analysis of incorrigibility. Besides, it is clear from the start that the case is quite unlike the normal case of insincerity. The sincere assertion that my wife has gone out for a walk does not presuppose that she has done so, only that I believe that she has. The peculiarity of self-ascription is, in Wittgenstein's words, that truth and truthfulness here coincide: the criteria of sincerity establish the truth of what is said.[4] Moreover, to say that I am sincere is not to *say* that I am in pain. (That it *follows* that I am in pain is of course precisely the thesis that I am defending.) It is to say (speaking very roughly) that my utterance is not to be explained in terms of a desire to mislead. It is to make a remark about the explanation of my utterance. The physicalist (behaviourist) will certainly wish to retort that the question is begged against *him* if it is assumed that the physical (behavioural) content of condition (i) cannot be stated separately.

Now we can rephrase (A) as follows:

(B) If I say 'I am in pain' (i) sincerely,

                                    (ii) making no slip of the tongue, and

                                    (iii) when I am not in pain,

then I have not understood the words that I utter.

Version (B) suggests at once that the burden of the problem lies not in the first person but in the third person case, precisely as it should do if physicalism is true. (B) can now be generalized:

(C) If a man says 'I am in pain' (i) sincerely,
(ii) making no slip of the tongue, and
(iii) when he is not in pain,
then he has not understood the words that he utters.

In other words, we have transformed the thesis of incorrigibility into a rule of language, applicable equally to the first- and third-person cases. A man understands self-ascription only if generally (allowing for whatever exceptions it may seem necessary to cater for) his self-ascriptions are true. A rigid rule, but nevertheless a rule. We can readily envisage its application: observing a child's behaviour we teach him to say 'I am in pain' only when he is in pain. When he gets it right every time we concede that he has understood what he says.[5] The advantages of so construing incorrigibility are twofold: first it explains how it might be a conceptual truth (in a publicly intelligible language) that a man in pain knows that he is so. The truth of the thesis is an immediate consequence of a linguistic rule. Secondly, the theory explains self-knowledge as a feature of linguistic behaviour. It therefore leads the way to a physicalistic account of it.

In a similar way we might give a derivation of self-intimation: if a man is in pain and is not prepared to assert or assent to the judgment that he is, then it follows that he has failed to understand it. That is why the remark of Mrs Gradgrind's —that there is a pain in the room somewhere but she doesn't rightly know that it is hers—is so odd. For either she doesn't mean it, or else she doesn't know what it means.

II

Now the rule I have stated is ambiguous. It does not say *which* of the words has not been understood by the man who disobeys it. Suppose, for example, that he ascribes pain accurately, and on the correct basis, to others: surely that ought to be sufficient

evidence that he understands the word 'pain', the more so
if we accept the behaviourist thesis that such words get
their *sense* from their third-person use. So is the offending
word 'I'? Surely a man understands that word just so long as
he understands a certain substitution instance of such
schemata as '*x* is thinking', or '*x* is in pain'? Why has our
subject failed to understand that, just because he sometimes
gets it wrong?

Some philosophers seem to have been prepared to argue that
'I am in pain' is not a genuine substitution instance of '*x* is
in pain'.[6] But to take such a line is surely of little consolation
to the philosopher who holds (as the physicalist must hold)
that the third person case has logical priority in determining
the sense (and the reference) of psychological terms. Besides,
it is an odd thing to say. If I am in pain, then Roger Scruton
is in pain; and *vice versa*. That seems to suggest that 'I am
Roger Scruton' is a statement of identity. In which case it will
not be a property of the term '*I*' that it cannot be substituted
in the schema '*x* is in pain': it would be a property of the
schema itself which, for some inexplicable reason, is opaque
for that particular singular term.

I want to argue that it is indeed the concept of self that is in
issue here. An imperfect grasp of rule (C) amounts to an
imperfect grasp of selfhood. So that both the word 'I' and, by
implication, the word 'he', will then be used incorrectly. It
will help to understand that suggestion if I move on to a
further objection. It might be said: how *can* there be a meaning rule like (C), a rule so absolute and seemingly so arbitrary? The answer is that the justification of such a rule is a
justification of the concepts with which it provides us, and of
the function which those concepts fulfil. There are certain
facts which distinguish people from animals, and which make
it possible to have attitudes towards people of a kind which we
could not have (except 'sentimentally') towards animals. We
need a concept in order to summarise those facts, so that we
may identify and re-identify the objects of interpersonal reaction. Now the crucial concept, the concept which is seriously
in issue here, is the concept of person, and its derivative, the
notion of self. There is no *a priori* reason why a concept
obeying the rigours of rule (C) should not take its place in our

language. Moreover, it is only if a man obeys such rules that we are able to take what he says as the primary expression of his mentality. Only for such a man does the verbal expression of pain replace pain behaviour and not just describe it.[7] I shall attempt to say what I mean by that pronouncement, why such a man might be described as a person, and why the fact of his incorrigible self-ascription is so important to us.

Wittgenstein asserts that, if a lion could speak, then we should not understand him.[8] Now consider what would have to be the case if we were to accept the speech issuing from the lion's mouth as an expression of the lion's mentality. We clearly recognize two possibilities from the outset. Either the speaker *is* the lion, or else it is not. If it is not, then it might still appear to us as possessed of a mental identity of its own. In that case it would be heard as though it spoke *out of* the skin of the lion: it inhabits the lion as a spirit might inhabit a tree. We imagine such spirits quite readily in the objects around us, and it is natural for primitive people to believe in them and pray to them. That is not to say that there is a real possibility, either *de dicto* or *de re*, that there might be a spirit in the lion or the tree. But at least it is an idea that we can entertain and plausibly describe to ourselves. Now the lion, unlike the tree, has an independent mentality of its own. Whether or not the voice is his, the lion still has his own desires, sensations and leonine satisfactions. Therefore it makes sense to ask ourselves what would have to be true if the speech which issues from him is to be an expression of the lion's mentality, rather than of some spirit which possesses him.

Consider the lion of Androcles. He roars, and a voice issues from his mouth saying, "I roar. Moreover, there is a thorn in my paw. I seem not to be able to stand on the paw in question. Indeed, my behaviour exhibits that pattern of disorganisation which is characteristic of pain. Therefore it seems that I am in pain." Suppose too that all the lion's 'self-ascriptions' are of that nature, and suppose further that many of them are simply wrong, even when emphatically asserted. In such a case the voice is clearly describing the mental state of the lion just as it would describe the mental state of any other thing, using the common public basis and neither claiming nor achieving any special immunity from doubt. The lion's voice is there-fore the voice of an 'observer' of the lion's behaviour, with the sole reservation that where the observer would use 'he' the voice uses 'I'. But then, if that is so, it seems natural to conclude that, for the voice, 'I' really *means* 'he': the distinc-tion between the two ideas has broken down. So that the voice's attributions to the lion are not the lion's own self-attributions, but rather the attributions of some other being. The lion is possessed, but not inspired.

How do we combine the lion with his vagrant spirit? Surely, the natural thing would be to grant to him just those powers of privileged self-ascription that we have been discussing. We allow to the voice a very special kind of authority in deter-mining the nature of the lion's states. The voice cannot, except occasionally and for very special reasons, make a mis-take. Moreover its knowledge is 'immediate', it does not proceed from any basis in the observable fact of pain. In other words, we require the voice to speak of the lion's pains in obedience to rule (C). This is not just a rule that the voice follows; it is also a rule that it obeys. That is how the *voice* understands its own 'self-ascriptions'. But if we make that stipulation then we can begin to understand the voice as an expression of the lion's mentality. To use a Cartesian meta-phor, soul and body have now been united. The states of the lion (of the organism) are the states of the person who speaks, and when the voice uses the word 'I' it is really referring to a self and not just to an animal organism that is perceived as external to it. In making the stipulation, and in exacting obedience to it, we have not only brought a self into being in the place of an organism; we have also given to the voice all that is necessary for an understanding of the word 'I'. Indeed, only a self could understand that word: only a self could understand, that is, the sense of 'I' in addition to its reference.

In speaking of the 'soul' and the 'body' of the lion I have been employing a Cartesian metaphor. My purpose was to show how the transition which the Cartesian would describe as a transition from creature to soul is in fact no more than a transition in behaviour, from the absence of language to the use of language in accordance with the rules of self-ascription. I have tried to provide a derivation of self-consciousness from the facts of common speech. For the Cartesian, by contrast, self-consciousness is the ultimate premiss from which all knowledge is derived. Seeing the 'privilege' involved in self-ascription as the sole guarantee against doubt, the Cartesian attempts to derive from it—and therefore from the persuasive prejudices inherent in the first-person case—a description of all that we can know. Kant deserves praise for many things, but perhaps for nothing more than his insight that the peculiarities of self-knowledge (which he referred to as the 'transcendental unity of apperception') stand in need of a philosophical explanation. Self-knowledge lies not at the beginning of philosophy but at its end.

Now of course, it is a matter of fact that the voice, when it says "I am in pain", always does so when the lion is in pain. The thesis of incorrigibility does not make the truth of sensation reports into a kind of necessary truth. It is only when that matter of fact has been observed that we can say of the lion's voice that it really *does* seem to understand the concept of self, and to recognize its own self-identity with the lion. It is of course a philosophical question to determine just what kind of 'fact' that is. A proper philosophy of mind must be prepared to give some detailed account of how things must be if there is to be incorrigible and immediate knowledge. That account has been attempted, from the standpoint of functionalism by Dennett,[9] and from the standpoint of a more generalized explanatory behaviourism by Grice.[10] But such matters are not our present concern. We wish rather to study the conceptual truth that is supposed to rest on that matter of fact, the truth that a man understands self-ascription only if he gets it right. How can we make such a strong stricture on 'understanding'?

How is it, then, that we can simply disallow the possibility of mistakes? Surely there must come a point when we have established that a child means what *we* mean by the expression 'I am in pain'. How can we then insist that henceforth he will never make a mistake in the use of that sentence? Here it is useful to refer to one of Wittgenstein's most celebrated observations.[11] There is no point in a man's linguistic practice at which it can be said that past linguistic behaviour logically determines what he will go on to do. A man may 'follow a rule' as we do, and yet, at some future time, diverge from us, insisting all the while that what he is doing is the *same* as what he has always done. That a man understands words as we do cannot be conclusively established, once and for all, in such a way as to render any future divergence of meaning impossible. So it is with self-ascription. If a man begins to make what looks to be mistakes then, after a while, we might come to the conclusion—at any time—that he has understood this use of language differently.

Moreover, nothing in rule (C) requires that every time a man declares that he is in pain, understanding what he says, then it must be *true* that he is in pain. It would certainly create a problem were we to insist on a notion of incorrigibility as strong as *that*. (C) implies only that, when a man speaks falsely of his sensations, then he is not mistaken, but insincere. Lack of space forbids my saying much about the concept of sincerity. Clearly, however, that concept will have to bear much more weight for the physicalist whom I envisage than it does for the Cartesian. We must at least beware of an analysis of sincerity that recreates all over again the absolute dichotomy between inner and outer, subject and object, reality and pretence, that is so characteristic of Cartesianism.[12]

One consequence of this emphasis on sincerity is that, if someone falsely says 'I am in pain' then we might seek to reproach him. He cannot now withdraw what he said by pleading ignorance; he can rely only on the excuse that he did not mean it. Our exacting such behaviour from a man is part of, and a necessary precondition to, our considering him as a person, and therefore a part of his own sense of himself. It is only when the practice of self-ascription is mastered that we can say, in Wittgenstein's words, that the linguistic expression of pain has *replaced* the natural expression. It has replaced it by becoming the central, most immediate, and most reliable manifestation of the subject's mental state. Only then can the subject be, for us, a person, since only then does his rational nature command the expression of his mentality.

III

In order to illustrate that suggestion I shall consider not the concept of sensation but that of intention. I shall assume that intentions are conscious, just as sensations are. Of course, that assumption will be questioned by Freudians, and in answer to their anxieties it might prove necessary to cater for exceptions, to argue that once again we are speaking of the 'central' case, and therefore that what seems to be a conceptual truth may nevertheless be bereft of universal application. The issue is a complex one, and I shall not get entangled in it. In passing, however, I cannot help wondering how a Freudian would distinguish unconscious intentions from unconscious desires. *One* way of making the distinction—that which relies on the practice of psycho-analysis—seems to result only in extending self-ascription. The unconscious intention is the one which the subject can be *brought* to self-ascribe under the analytical process.[13] Only an adherence to a Cartesian theory of consciousness will lead one to speak of such intentions as unconscious. But I shall content myself with an assumption: let it be made as weak as is required, provided only that it does not fall outside the pale of conceptual truths. In the course of the argument the reader will, I hope, see why I find that assumption persuasive. Not to make it is, I think, to lose sight once again of the distinction between animals and people.

Now it is the task of a theory of intention to say something not only about intentional action, but also about decision—about the forming of intentions for the future. If the distinction between intention and desire is ever clear it is certainly here at its clearest. And it is in such a distinction that the essence of rational agency is to be found. To borrow one of Hegel's expressions, we might say that it is in the transition from desire to intention that the characteristically human or personal 'moment of consciousness' is reached.

Expressions of intention for the future may have the same form as predictions. The normal way to express one's intention is to say 'I will do X'. (By an accident of English grammar we can of course make the distinction between predicting and deciding through distinguishing 'shall' and 'will'.) The rule for incorrigibility must take account of that. Here is one suggestion:

(D) If a man utters the words 'I will do X', and if
  (i) he makes no slip of the tongue,
 (ii) he understands the words,
(iii) he means them as an expression of intention, and

(iv) he is sincere,
then he intends to do X.

For the apodosis we may substitute another proposition that is
entailed by it, namely: that he will try to do X when the
occasion arises, unless he has changed his mind meanwhile.
Indeed, so phrased, the rule (D) reflects many of the recent
attempts to give a definition of intention.[14] It is not here important that it should be capable of serving as a definition, and
therefore accusations of circularity are not in place. All the
same, it should not be thought that 'X tries to do Y' itself involves a reference to some further intention. The concept
of 'trying' belongs to the pattern of explanation characteristic
of desire: there is no need to invoke a concept of intention in
order to give an account of it.[15]

(D) amounts to the proposition that, if a man says he will do
X and does not, at the appropriate moment, set about it, then
there are, apart from slips of the tongue, four possible explanations of failure: (a) he does not understand what he has
said; (b) he was not sincere; (c) he did not mean his utterance
as an expression of intention but as a prediction; (d) he has
changed his mind. This last escape route from the rigours of
incorrigibility is a novel one, and is clearly a necessary addition if we are not to presuppose (as we cannot) an absolute
immunity from Humean doubts about the future. To change
one's mind is to abandon one's intention in the course of time.
Now it is just possible that weakness of will is not a species of
change of mind. If that is so then we must introduce a fifth
and rather complex escape route into our rule. And it may be,
further, that the existence of such an escape route has been
in the minds of those philosophers who have spoken of the
'problem' of weakness of will. But again, that need not
concern us.

I shall concentrate on the third 'escape route', the distinction between predicting and deciding.[16] I hope to show,
through a consideration of that distinction, just why a concept
answering to conditions (D) might be useful to us, and why a
man's conformity to its strictures might be an important fact
about him, a fact sufficiently important to merit the introduction of a basic distinction between animal and person.

Now clearly, in order to form an intention it is necessary

to consider the future, and it is necessary to see oneself as playing an active and determining rôle in that future, as being able in the future to realize the objects of former resolves. One might call the attitude here involved an attitude of identifying with one's future self, and one might contrast it with another attitude—that of being 'alienated' from one's future self—in which one sees oneself not as active and determining, but rather as the passive victim of external reality, and of one's past (conceived as part of that external reality), being driven along under the impulse of forces outside one's control.

The problem is to give a philosophical account of the distinction between those attitudes. As a first step in explaining what it is to see oneself as an agent in one's future acts, one might point to the special kind of belief that is involved in intention. To form an intention for the future is to acquire a belief about one's future conduct, the distinguishing feature of the belief being its unshakeable certainty, together with its peculiar lack of evidential basis. (The features are connected: recourse to evidence can only destroy certainty of this kind.)[17] Now some might wish to deny that intention involves belief. However, it is certainly true—and no-one I think will deny this—that the man who intends something will be prone to make and accept certain pronouncements about the future. The first question, therefore, is whether those pronouncements are to be construed as expressions of belief. I do not think that it could be argued with any plausibility that his assertions lack a truth value, or that *he* regards them as incapable of being true or false. For if he did so regard them then it would be hard to understand in what way he would consider himself bound by them to produce the state of affairs that they describe. Another argument might be that assertions about one's future activity cannot be expressions of belief *because* they are not based on evidence (because they are derived in the manner which is essential to the concept of intention). Following a suggestion of Wiggins's, it might be argued that they simply do not have the right *causality* to be considered as beliefs.[18] But I doubt the force of that argument. It is surely reasonable to suggest that, while the concept of evidence is a genuine part of the concept of belief, this means that beliefs, however they are arrived at, should be *answerable* to evidence. And surely expressions of intention *are* answerable to evidence in that way. Intentions, like desires, can enter into conflict with beliefs. But, unlike desires, they cannot survive that conflict. If I say I will do X and someone shows me that to do X is impossible, then, if I believe him, I must change my mind. And I can equally be made to withdraw an intention by evidence that it will not be realized: 'I will sail to-morrow', I declare. 'But your ship is unseaworthy.' If I accept that reply, then I decide not to sail. In other words, the forming and withdrawing of intentions can be effected not merely by 'practical reasons', but by reasons for the truth of a prediction. Furthermore it is appropriate for others, if not for myself, to support my statement about the future (when that statement is an expression of intention) with evidence for its truth. 'He said he will go, and he will, because he is a man of his word.'

It might still be argued that, while an intention in this way commits one to a belief, the intention and the belief are not identical. The belief is *founded* on the intention; it comes about because, recognizing an intention in myself, I realize what I will do. Some such view has recently been suggested by Grice.[19] In what follows it should be apparent why I would wish to reject it.

Even if we accept the theory that intention involves belief, it is clear that a sincere expression of intention cannot be the outcome merely of a process of inductive reasoning, As Miss Anscombe has put it, intention and prediction differ in their 'direction of fit' with reality. In saying 'I will do X, I am taking it upon myself to ensure that X will be done; in predicting that I shall do X I am, characteristically, saying how the world will be, whatever my own responsibility in the matter. So that, in the first case, I must try to do X, and in so far as I support my assertion, it is with reasons for doing X. So I have a peculiar certainty that I *will* try to do X: not to be certain is to be insincere. By virtue of this special certainty intentions, despite the fact that they reach into the future, can obey their own version of the law of incorrigibility. It follows that the ways in which they can fail to be realized are restricted.

Now this peculiar certainty that characterizes the unalienated prospect of my own future leads quite naturally to the view that, once I have intentions for the future, then I must also have practical reason. For suppose a man expresses the intention to do X and suppose that someone points out that the only way to do X is by doing Y. Yet he denies that he intends to do Y, even though he accepts the other's opinion. That is, he is prepared to accept the following:

(a) I will do X
(b) I cannot do X unless I do Y, and
(c) I will not do Y.

Now (a) and (c) are expressions of intention. But they are also expressions of beliefs about the future, and those beliefs are certain. So the speaker must regard himself as committed to the following:

(d) It will be the case that I do X
(e) I do X only if I do Y, and
(f) It will not be the case that I do Y.

That involves a direct contradiction between beliefs. So that if a man understands ordinary inference, and has intentions, he must also understand and be affected by at least some kinds of practical inference. He must at least understand and be affected by reasoning about means.[20] Now since the ability to engage in ordinary inference is essential to understanding language. we can see one way in which the connexion between speech and rational agency might be established. At this point one can envisage a line of argument which leads to establishing, first, that intention requires self-conscious judgments about the future, secondly that such judgments require language, thirdly that language and intention can co-exist only when there is incorrigible self-ascription. If that argument could be established (and my discussion contains hints that it might) then we shall have displayed an essential connection between language, rational agency, and self-consciousness, each being both necessary and sufficient for the other. Here then, is where the transition from animal to person must lie.

Now once again we should recognize that the concept of

intention (so far only schematically characterised) can gain application only because of certain enduring matters of fact. For example, it is a matter of fact that those utterances about the future which we recognize as expressions of intention are in general followed by the attempt to realize their content. But on this matter of fact rests a whole practice of personal interaction that requires quite special concepts—and notably the concept of intention—if it is to be described. Given the general truth that a man will at some time attempt to realize his (sincere) declarations of intention, those declarations will provide us with a peculiar means of access to his future behaviour. We can now, in effect, *argue* against what he plans to do. As Miss Anscombe has pointed out, it is precisely the effectiveness of 'argument against' that is the distinguishing mark, not only of intentions for the future, but also of intentional action.[21] We know that we can attempt to change a man's behaviour by persuading him to change his declarations of intention, and he will change those just so long as he is rational and our reasons are good. Hence we have a direct means of access through reasoning to all his intentional acts. When this means of access fails—either because the agent is unable to accept reasons for or against the assertions about the future which constitute his would-be declarations of intention (the case of irrationality), or because the matter of fact connexion between present declaration and future performance breaks down (the case of insanity)—then we have no way of changing the agent's future conduct except through the manipulations of predictive science.

IV

I have referred to certain matters of fact, matters of fact which make the adherence to strict rules of incorrigibility a real possibility. Among those rules I singled out (D) for particular discussion, because it served to characterize a mental concept which is vital to the notion of personhood. We can see more clearly why that should be so. In granting intentions to a man we are declaring our trust in the fact that what he says is a reliable index of his behaviour, both now and at future times. It follows that reasons given to change what he *says* will now change what he *does*. Language becomes the principal means of access both to his present mental state and to his future activity.

Now some of our attitudes to people require us to see them as persons; other of our attitudes are consistent with our seeing them only as organisms. The first set of attitudes—those the intentional object of which is to be characterised as a person—include resentment, admiration, pride, contempt and anger. The second include desire (in the sense of *erōs*), rage, disgust. The first class of attitudes mark out a way of understanding which is more important to us than the methods of science and more real to us than its discoveries. One's attitude to a man may single him out as the focal point in a network of intentions, as a man capable of committing himself to his own future, and of taking responsibility for his own past, as a creature who has not merely identity but self-identity, and the necessary self-consciousness involved in that. One's interest in his future conduct will lead to an attempt to give and receive reasons for acting. If, however, one's interest in a man is not merely personal—if one is simply anxious to know and affect what he will do, whatever his intentions—then one will give no special consideration to practical reason. One's attitude, being 'predictive', could be satisfied by any appropriate influence on its object's conduct: for example, by the application of conditioning or drugs. In such a case one attaches no overriding weight to the man's ambitions or interests, to his expressions of hope, pride or remorse, except in so far as these are a necessary object of the scientific knowledge one requires. When we retreat, in this way, from the sphere of inter-personal reaction, we begin to treat people, in Kant's terms, not as ends but as means only. For their ends, their reasons, and the moral attitudes that arise from these, are no longer of any special interest to us; their rationality, and their claims as rational agents, cease to be the determining factor in our treatment of them. Our attitude to them becomes one of 'alienation'.

It is an essential tenet of Hegelian and Marxist thought that there can be no alienation from others which is not also alienation from self. I am inclined to believe that that is true, although I have no argument to establish it (no argument, that is, which would survive translation from its Hegelian dialect). But we surely agree that, if Hegel's view is correct, then we have every reason to treat others as ends and not as means. For self-alienation is certainly a possibility, and a disastrous one. Just as we can take an attitude to another man which does not involve our giving special priority to his self-ascriptions, so can we take such an attitude to our future self. I may cease to regard my own assertions about the future as having any special authority in determining the way things will be. In such a case I cannot really be said to have intentions: all my statements about the future become predictions rather than decisions. They are founded on, and refutable by, the available evidence for their truth-value. And that is how *I* regard them. But if I have no intentions for the future, then it seems that my attitude to my own past must be similarly depersonalized. For how can I take responsibility for anything if I can have no intention to make amends for it, and no sense that it proceeded from any planned activity which has its source in me? Attitudes like remorse, self-complaisance and pride become not just irrational but impossible. It can hardly be desirable to be like that, for, deprived of the status of rational agent by this steady erosion of self-determination, one is deprived of the very ability to see one's state as desirable. And how can one rationally desire to be in a state which one cannot see as desirable when one has it? It seems, then, that we cannot, consistently with our rational nature, reject the habits of self-ascription that are enshrined in rule (D). If that requires us to impose such a rule upon all our dealings with others—as indeed the Hegelian position implies—then we have every reason to do just that. But to suggest that we then cease to treat others as physical things, or that we then allow to them some aspect or reality that is not (and cannot be) publicly observable is (as I have tried to show) misguided.

NOTES

[1] G. Ryle: *The Concept of Mind*, Ch. VI.
[2] Leibniz: *Nouveaux Essaies*, Bk II, ch. 1, ss.ix-xv.
[3] On these points, see the admirable discussion in D. Gasking: "Avowals", in R. J. Butler (ed.): *Analytical Philosophy, Series I*.
[4] Wittgenstein: *Philosophical Investigations*, pt. II, xi, p. 222.

[5] Suggestions of this argument occur in Gasking, *loc. cit.*

[6] See for example, N. Malcom's review of the *Philosophical Investigations*.

[7] Wittgenstein: *Philosophical Investigations*, part I, section 244.

[8] *Ibid.*, II xi, p. 223.

[9] See *Content and Consciousness*, London 1969, esp. pp. 100 ff.

[10] See "Method in Philosophical Psychology", Presidential address to the American Philosophical Association, 1974-75.

[11] Wittgenstein, *op. cit.*, part I, esp. sections 172 ff.

[12] The interesting work on the concept of sincerity stems from the Idealist tradition in philosophy; not surprisingly, the results of that essentially humane tradition have found few adherents among contemporary analytical philosophers. But the results survive, and have been given fresh expression by literary critics. See, for example, F. R. Leavis: "Reality and Sincerity", in *Scrutiny*.

[13] On this point, see the highly suggestive remarks contained in Wittgenstein's *Lectures on Aesthetics, Freud, Etc.*

[14] See, for example, the seminal paper by S. Hampshire and H. L. A. Hart: "Decision, Intention, and Certainty", *Mind*, 1958. Also Hampshire's *Thought and Action*, ch. 2.

[15] This remark is directed against Jack W. Meiland: *The Nature of Intention*, chapter 5.

[16] The *locus classicus* for the distinction between predicting and deciding is *Thought and Action*. A great many philosophers have discussed the question (see, for example, Pears in Strawson (ed.): *Studies in the Philosophy of Thought and Action*). But the distinction seems to me to be far simpler and far more easily intelligible than they have usually made out.

[17] On these points see G. E. M. Anscombe: *Intention*, and H. P. Grice: "Intention and Uncertainty", *Proc. Brit. Acad.* 1974.

[18] D. Wiggins: "Knowledge, Belief, Freedom and Causality", in *Royal Institute of Philosophy, Lectures*, 1974.

[19] "Intention and Uncertainty", *loc. cit.*

[20] Of course further argument is required if we are to establish the really important conclusion, that a creature who is to this extent rational, must also be prepared to reason about his *ends* of conduct, and be prepared to accept some common principles in deriving them.

[12] *Intention, passim.*

ACKNOWLEDGEMENT

I am very grateful to Mr Mark Platts, Mr Ian McFetridge, Professor David Hamlyn, and Dr John Casey, for comments on an earlier draft of this paper.

VIII*—THE IMMUTABLE LAWS OF NATURE[1]

by Ardon Lyon

I. INTRODUCTION

There are two views about laws of nature which seem at first impossible to reconcile. On the one hand law-statements seem possessed of a truth stronger than the most utterly contingent —a truth necessary, eternal and immutable, although not logical. On the other hand just about any statement we consider which has a *prima facie* claim to express a law turns out to be not even true at all, but false, because falsified. One task of this paper will be to bring out what is true about these two views, and to show how they can be reconciled without committing dialectical hara-kiri.

What sorts of statement have a *prima facie* claim to be considered expressions of laws? At least since the time of Norman Campbell, philosophers of science have generally taken as laws of nature any and all empirical universal generalizations about what one might call 'natural facts'—as opposed to 'utter contingencies' such as that all the chairs in my room are (as it happens) made of wood. They have claimed that 'really' there are no important differences between, for example, 'Water is a liquid at room temperature' and 'The planets move in ellipses'. One result of this has been a proliferation of discussions about black ravens, whereas most scientists would presumably not consider it a law of nature that birds have a particular coloured plumage. The philosophers' argument has been that there are countless generalizations which men have accepted on the basis of superficial and obvious observation, which were used as the foundation stones of science, and which haven't generally been thought of as laws only because they weren't discovered by a more or less difficult process of experimentation. There is however no *essential* difference

---

* Meeting of the Aristotelian Society at 5/7, Tavistock Place, London, W.C.1, on Monday, 10th January, 1977 at 7.30 p.m.

between the verification procedures for statements which scientists think of as laws and those which they think of as descriptions of 'natural facts', and thus they are really both in the same (epistemological and scientific) boat. It seems to me, on the contrary, that there is a difference between these two sorts of statement, and between laws and theories, which I shall later indicate, and which have been either overlooked or misdescribed by the philosophers. So in attempting to pick out the characteristic features of laws of nature we should surely begin by considering examples that just about everyone would agree to be laws. Thus in what follows I shall consider mainly paradigmatic laws such as Boyle's Law, Kepler's Laws, or Hooke's Law.

The majority of well-known philosophers of science in the Anglo-Saxon world are still empiricists of one kind or another, despite a fashionable resurgence of Kuhno-Feyerabendian pop-anarchism and Hegelian Marxism. The most doctrinaire of these empiricists even claim that there are no *essential* differences between statements such as 'All the chairs in this room are wooden' and 'All planets move in ellipses'—the differences are only ones of degrees of universality through space and time. So I shall also try to distinguish 'utterly contingent' generalizations from other generalizations in a manner some empiricists might find satisfactory.

II. Verification Procedures

The idea that there are laws of nature probably first arose among the ancient Babylonians. They would hardly have thought of the regular occurrence of phenomena in nature as falling under the rule of law unless they believed that an element of compulsion was involved: for laws implied a lawgiver—a god or gods whose divine decrees had to be obeyed by all phenomena under their sway. Such ideas were alien to the ancient Chinese. Their conception that people should behave in accordance with *li*, custom, rather than *fa*, law, was paralleled by their belief that regularities in nature are merely customary rather than lawlike, and Needham suggests this may have inhibited their scientific discoveries.[2] The empiricists, somewhat like the ancient Chinese, think of natural regularities as just—regularities. So let us see if we can overcome empiricist objections to the distinction between laws and mere regularities, and give an account of natural necessity, without thereby implying that there must be a creator of natural laws. It does not matter whether the use of the term 'law' of nature is then for an atheist or agnostic merely a metaphor so long as we can explain the distinction between the so-called 'laws' and mere regularities.

Let us first remind ourselves of the general manoeuvres in the empiricists' attack on the conception of nomic necessity, hopefully without lapsing into mere parody. For brevity let us call the alleged two universal classes 'laws' and 'generalizations'. The empiricist thesis is a typical philosophical claim of the form 'there are really no differences between X's and Y's' despite our managing pretty well in the ordinary course of events to distinguish between X's and Y's, although sometimes, of course, we came across dubious or (a different matter) borderline cases.[3] The claim is sometimes put in the form that 'really' there is no difference in *meaning* between 'X' and 'Y', perhaps because there are no clear, objective, distinguishable and agreed criteria on the basis of which we can differentiate (or differentiate with certainty) between X's and Y's.

Now the verification and falsification procedures for statements of the form 'All A are B' are exactly the same—so the empiricist says—whether such statements are generalizations or the allegedly different 'laws'; and since the meaning of a statement is the method of its verification, we haven't two sorts here but one. Let us call this the Verification Argument. Secondly, some philosophers have tried to distinguish between laws and mere generalizations on the grounds that the former, unlike the latter, allow counter-factual inference of the form 'If this non-A were an A, it would be a B'. But counter-factual statements, in the subjunctive mood, themselves stand 'in need of analysis'; so this alleged differentiation gets us no further forward. Let us call this the Analysis Argument.

To see whether this is only a parody let us look at the work of one empiricist, R. B. Braithwaite. Braithwaite's views are interesting because in a way he *does* distinguish between laws and generalizations: he says that really or basically there is no difference between them, but that we give certain generalizations the honorific title of 'law' when we have put them in the context of an 'overall deductive system': or, as he puts it,

the distinction does not correspond to an "objective dichotomy . . . [but] is relative to the body of knowledge and reasonable belief (the rational corpus) of a particular person at a
particular time".[4] That is, once we have deduced a generalization from other generalizations which we have for the time
being accepted on scientific grounds, we call them 'laws'.[5]
Braithwaite accepts that this leads to the paradoxical conclusion that the highest level generalizations are not, according
to him, laws: and this *is* highly paradoxical, because surely
the most wide-ranging generalizations, at the top of the
scientific tree, so to speak, are precisely the ones which we
would ordinarily feel *most* inclined to classify as laws.

One of the reasons why Braithwaite comes to this conclusion is because, as he puts it, on any theory of the nature of
scientific laws other than the constant conjunction view "a
scientific law, while including a generalization, states something more than a generalization" (p. 11), or again that on his
view "scientific laws will be taken as asserting no more (and no
less) than the *de facto* generalizations which they include"
(p. 10). It may sound pedantic to insist that people, not laws,
make statements or assertions: for it might be thought that
Braithwaite has here simply used a harmless metaphor. But
once we do insist on this it becomes rather obvious that someone who asserts 'All *A* are *B*' does indeed assert just that
—no more and no less. Thus someone who says 'The planets
move in ellipses' doesn't *say* whether it's a law or a generalization, and so any attempt at an analysis of statements of the
form 'All *A* are *B*' which hopes to distinguish laws from
generalizations is doomed to failure (unless by oversight).
What is required is an analysis not of 'All *A* are *B*' but of 'It's
a law that all *A* are *B*'.

Oddly enough, the two most eminent post-war British
philosophers of science who reject the constant conjunction
view, also perpetrate this error. Thus Kneale wrote that he
wished to attack Hume's view that "to assert a law of nature
is, then, only to assert a constant conjunction without restriction in the field of our actual experience".[6] And Popper, in
agreeing with Kneale about the 'objectivity of nomic necessity' wrote: "A most penetrating criticism of the view that
theories, or laws of nature, can be adequately expressed by a

universal statement, such as 'All planets move in ellipses', has been advanced by William Kneale . . . [a law-statement is of the form] . . . 'All planets move necessarily in ellipses'."[7]

But all this is wrong, even though Kneale makes the correct point that 'all dodos have (timeless) a white feather in their tail' while (perhaps) true, is not a law, since there is no necessity in it: all white feathers might easily have been removed or bred out by mutation without destruction of the dodo in question. And Popper makes the same point about 'All moas die before reaching the age of fifty': this might be true because they were killed off before the age of fifty by a virus, but would have lived longer had the virus been absent, or if they had obtained a different diet, *etc.*

So now what we need to do in order to counter the empiricists' Verification Argument is to show the difference in verification and falsification procedures between:

(1) All A are B.
(2) It is a law of nature that all A are B.
(3) It is an accidental generalization that all A are B.

Notice that (2) entails (1) and so does (3): but in my view (2) and (3) are mutually incompatible, as I shall later try to show. Since (2) entails (1) and so does (3), it follows that whatever is evidence for (2) is evidence for (1), and whatever is evidence for (3) is evidence for (1): while whatever falsifies (1) immediately falsifies (2) and also (3). This similarity in verification and falsification procedures is perhaps one reason why an unwary empiricist might think there is no difference between (2) and (3), and why an anti-empiricist might think of laws as being of the form 'All A are necessarily B', thus conflating (1) and (2). For since finding A's that are non-B falsifies (2) and (3) equally, it may not be at first obvious what verifies (2) rather than (3) or *vice versa*.

Finding A's that are B provides evidence for (1) but not for (2) or (3) since it is equally compatible with either of these mutually incompatible propositions. Of course finding more and more A's that are B, when taken *in conjunction with* an 'overall deductive context' of what Braithwaite would call a "rational corpus of knowledge and reasonable belief" and Popper would call "a body of scientific conjectures", can then give us grounds for accepting (2) rather than (3)—but even then only if the deductive context is law-like and not purely factual or accidental, and so unless we can explain the grounds for believing whether the deductive framework is law-like we will have made no advance.

Finding an A that is not B falsifies (1) but equally falsifies (2) and (3). Here we should note that we never get *certain* falsification any more than certain verification: finding what appears to be an A which is not B leaves it open to us to suggest it might not be an A or it might be B, thus leaving room for Kuhnian, Feyerabendian or Lakatosian theses. But we should remember that we can reject things more or less *reasonably*: protective belts can be used either to hold up sensible trousers or just as a quasi-magical decoration, or for all stages in between. Another sensible move, and one that is normally used in the course of scientific practice, is to say that we have some anomalies, we know that something must be wrong, but that it would be irrational at this stage to reject any particular thing as *shown to be false*: further research may show us what was (presumably) wrong, or of course if we are unlucky it may not. Finally we should remember that there can be *indirect* evidence for or against (1), such as ancient paintings of dodos with or without white tail feathers, and for which we might have, say, anthropological evidence regarding the likelihood of their being accurate, just as we have documentary and other historical evidence regarding the likelihood of planetary sightings being accurate, depending on the availability of instruments, the likelihood of there being deliberate or unconscious cooking of the books, *etc.*[8]

Let us call any evidence for A's being B, other than direct observation of A's, 'indirect' evidence for A's being B. Then the evidence for choosing between (2) and (3) *must* be indirect, since if either is true then (1) is true and *a fortiori* all so far observed A's are B. Now why do we think it's not a *law* that all dodos have (or had) white tail feathers, even if it's *true* that they all had white tail feathers? As Kneale pointed out, this is simply because we know from observations of other birds that tail feathers can be removed, or cut off, without destroying the birds. And we know furthermore that by genetic tinkering plus evolution, or perhaps by suitable breeding or even diet we might be able to change plumage colour. Similarly, it is surely not a law that all ravens are black, and philosophers of science who use this as a paradigm to contrast with accidental generalizations inevitably misdescribe the central features of laws.[9] While it is not a law, there are still causal, and in fact genetic reasons why all ravens are black: and causal connexions are in some sense necessary[10]—there is some mechanism in the genes that *makes* them all black. Presumably ravens have the genetic make-up which produces their black colour either because that colour has survival value, or because by chance no viable mutations have altered their genetically induced colour. Many philosophers of science equate 'causal' with 'law-like'. But there are causal reasons why all the chairs in my room are wooden even though this truth is utterly contingent.

In due course I shall try to distinguish between laws and 'natural facts' by reference to two kinds of counterfactual inference. Meanwhile we note that generalizations about natural facts are statements which even if true for all time might have been false in our universe had something turned out a little differently, and in particular had we human beings attempted to make them false. To draw the contrast between these and laws, let us suggest as a first shot that laws are universal truths[11] which would still have been true under different initial conditions, and in particular which we human beings could not make false whatever steps we took to try to falsify them—not, I mean, because of mere technical difficulties, but because, had we all the technical power available in the universe, this universe is so constructed that it would be *in fact* impossible to falsify them come what may. These nomic necessities differ from logical necessities by being false in some conceivable worlds, *i.e.*, in their contraries not being self-contradictory.[12] Our evidence that it's a law and not a generalization that all A's are B is provided by (a) our having tried strenuously and failed to falsify the universal statement, by (b) our having tried strenuously and failed to falsify those universal statements from which it is deducible, and by (c) our having tried strenuously and failed to falsify various suitable hypotheses about a's which are similar to A's. Actually, (c) sometimes comes to nearly the same thing as (b), because the statements about *a*'s will be deducible from some higher level presumably law-like statements from which we can deduce that all *A* are *B* (a consilience of law-like inductions). We may have some *apparent* falsifications, or anomalies, for which we haven't even searched—they turn up only too easily!—but then to believe despite this that the statement is a law is to believe that such 'falsifications' *are* only apparent, and that there could be some explanation for such anomalies which will retain the universal statement as a truth while (a)–(c) remain true.

Similarly, our evidence that a statement of the form 'All *A* are *B*' is not a law is provided by the grounds we have for believing that it could be falsified either by natural occurrences, or by us if we tried hard enough—the appropriate contraries of (a), (b) and (c).

III. COUNTER-FACTUALS

This concludes our remarks about the different and contrary verification procedures for '*S* is a law' and '*S* is a universal generalization'. In the course of this we have used or referred to counter-factuals, so now we should say something about these and the Analysis Argument. It has often been suggested that if, contrary to the doctrinaire empiricist' claim, it is possible to make an objective distinction between mere generalizations and nomic necessities, then this distinction is reflected in the fact that laws, unlike generalizations, 'license counter-factual inferences'. Many empiricists object that the meaning of counter-factual conditionals is as unclear as the alleged distinction they are supposed to reflect, and this is partly because the procedures for verifying the truth or falsity of counter-factuals is so obscure. I have tried so far to deal to some extent with the latter, verification-procedure part of the objection by indicating the different evidence (indirect) in favour of '*S* is a law' and '*S* is (not a law but) a generalization'.

In view of the extensive literature on counter-factuals it would be impossible here to evaluate the various theories which have been put forward concerning their nature. As for any alleged general obscurity of counter-factuals, they do have a use in standard English, and anyone who attempts an 'analysis' of them must presumably know what they mean in order to ascertain whether his analysis is correct when offering it to those others who are allegedly still in the dark. Thus the generalised complaint that all counter-factuals are obscure in meaning seems a rather peculiar thesis. So I merely want to suggest here, by consideration of three little scenarios, that the truth of a counter-factual does not depend crucially, as has often been suggested, either on the falsity of its corresponding antecedent, or on there being a nomic connexion between the corresponding indicative antecedent and consequent.[13]

Scenario 1

This takes place in an art gallery.

A. "That's a very fine Sisley."
B. "It's not a Sisley. I suspect it's a Pissarro."
A. "It looks like a Sisley to me."
B. "I agree. It does. But if it were a Sisley it would be in Room 14. That's where (all) the Sisley's are hung."

There is nothing necessary about hanging Sisleys in Room 14. It is an alterable decision by the hanging committee.

Scenario 2

Here, a body has been found with a suicide note, which the police take to be genuine, but *A* thinks it was murder and therefore wants the police to search for clues, which they are reluctant to do.

A says: "Look here; you agree that if he *had* been murdered, you would probably but not necessarily be able to find finger prints. So do please at least look into this possibility." Again, we certainly shouldn't say that *A* was wrong just because we later find that the man *was* murdered (which is what *A* thinks), *or* just because we find that he wasn't. So neither the truth nor the falsity of 'He was murdered' is a truth condition of the truth of the counter-factual.

Scenario 3

A. "I think I've been bitten by mosquitoes."
B. "If you had been, you'd know about it all right."
C. "Yes, probably. But sometimes the lumps don't show up for quite some time."

We certainly shouldn't think that B was wrong just because the corresponding indicative antecedent 'A has been bitten by mosquitoes' turned out to be true. There was some *doubt* in the air, but B, who was in the garden with A when there were mosquitoes about, thinks that if A has big lumps, then he has almost certainly been bitten by mosquitoes, but if he hasn't, then he almost certainly hasn't been. Note that C says "*Yes*, probably. But . . .", and *not* "*No*: sometimes they don't show up . . .".

I think these scenarios indicate that the truth, or perhaps the appropriateness or correctness of a so-called counter-factual depends on there being a certain sort of connexion between the states of affairs described in the corresponding indicative antecedents and consequents, but not on their individual truth or falsity.[14] But the counter-factual wouldn't be *uttered* unless either:

(i) the speaker believed the corresponding indicative antecedent was false—perhaps the standard case, (as in Scenario 1), or

(ii) the speaker believed his audience unshakeably *thought* the corresponding indicative antecedent was false, and was 'going along with them' for the sake of the argument for the present time, while believing, perhaps rightly, that it was true (as in Scenario 2), or

(iii) there was simply a great deal of doubt in the air as to the truth or falsity of the corresponding antecedent and consequent, and the speaker was making some suggestions towards ascertaining this (as in Scenario 3).

I expect there are other appropriate situations, but for now I want only to throw doubt on the falsity-of-the-antecedent doctrine, and hence on all the alleged paradoxes that arise from this thesis, and also to indicate, partly by our use of such phrases as "on the whole", "perhaps", "*yes*—but not necessarily", that there doesn't even have to be a nomic connexion between the corresponding indicative antecedent and consequent for the counter-factual to be true. I think that if the connexion is either causal, or universal, or even highly probabilistic (but not necessarily causal) then the use of the counter-factual is correct when any of the conditions (i) to (iii) obtain.

It remains the case that where there *is* a nomic connexion, the corresponding counter-factual is true. This does not however universally distinguish between nomic and non-nomic connexions, as I have indicated above. But this is no cause for despair, for there are, I think, two sorts of counter-factual inference that can be drawn from the law-like statements, and philosophers of science have wrongly concentrated on the first kind rather than the second. If it's a law that all planets move in ellipses then:

(α) Anything (not self-propelled, *etc.* and) not a planet would move in an ellipse if put into planetary motion, and

(β) All planets would move in ellipses whatever else were to happen in the universe.

Philosophers of science seem to have considered only the first type of counter-factual, with their discussions of 'If this (presumably non-planet) were a planet it would move in an ellipse'. I have already indicated one reason why we think this true, namely, in terms of our evidence that we couldn't render false either the generalization 'All A's are B' or the laws from which the generalization can be deduced, no matter what technical power we had: but this sort of evidence also provides evidence for (β). Now we should point out situations where we might be inclined to assert statements of type (α) while rejecting statements of type (β). This would happen if we believed that, because of the sun's gravitational attraction, *etc.* (α) was true (and of course the corresponding generalization), but that we might have been able to make it false had we been able to carry out enough large-scale movement of gross bodies, which we cannot. I think this shows that it's statements of type (β) which really reflect the nomic character of generalizations, rather than those of type (α), on which philosophers of science have concentrated. This is brought out by the facts that (a) we are perfectly prepared to assert conditionals of the form 'If this were A then it would be B' where we believe there is no sort of necessity connecting A

and B, and (b) it's the aspect of being in-this-world-unfalsifi-able-come-what-may, as expressed in (β), which is the basic idea behind the difference between laws and mere generalizations. Thus if we think that (α) is true but not (β), then we think it a 'natural fact' that planets move in ellipses, just as that ravens are black, but *not* a law that this is so: its truth depends on the fact that no other large stars come near to the sun.

It may be objected: 'So according to your criterion (β) it's not a law that planets move in ellipses but a generalization. So either it's not a law, or your criterion is incorrect. If you use such a 'strong' criterion hardly anything which is usually considered a law will be a law. The philosophers have argued—wrongly according to you—that more things are laws than those normally considered by scientists. But according to your criterion (β) the class would be drastically reduced in size from the scientists' class.'

My first reaction to this is that the reduction in size is reasonable. For Kepler's so-called laws are at best 'local' laws, not universal ones. If we understand by a 'planet' a smallish body that revolves around a larger one, then it does follow from Newtonian mechanics, and indeed is presumably true of many planets in the universe, that they move in paths very different from ellipses because of the variable proximity of other large bodies. When Kepler first enunciated his 'laws' the planets in the solar system were the only ones being considered, and so it was reasonable to think of his three hypotheses as laws. But now we can see this is a mistake, and so criterion (β) is perfectly acceptable.

Having said this, we must immediately move on to the point that not even the solar planets move strictly in ellipses, and so both the generalization and (α) and (β) are false of the solar planets. Why then do scientists continue to call Kepler's hypotheses laws?

IV. IDEALIZATIONS

Strictly speaking, not even the solar planets move in ellipses, and so of course both (α) and (β) are anyway false. But still we speak of Kepler's Laws, and of Newton's Laws, those (strictly speaking) false statements from which we can deduce that, roughly speaking, a planet would move in an ellipse round the sun if there weren't other planets and general clutter around to pull it out of its planetary motion, which Newton's Laws themselves tell us they do—I mean assuming, contrary to what we know, that Newton's Laws are true. Thus Kepler's Laws tell us not what does happen, but what would happen in certain idealized conditions. I suppose one reason why we speak of ideal gases obeying Boyle's Law but not of ideal planets obeying Kepler's Laws is that actual gases were found so very early to obey Boyle's Law only extremely roughly, and in fact van der Waal's equation explicitly allows for those factors idealized away in the primitive derivation of Boyle's Law from Kinetic Theory as expounded in textbooks of elementary physics.[15] A more important reason is that Boyle's Law is untrue not because of external clutter, but because of the internal constitution of actual as opposed to 'ideal' gases. It's not surprising that connexions between idealized entities in idealized conditions are necessary—although, as we shall see, they are not logically necessary.

We cannot hope to give a coherent account of what all scientists or others have always meant by a 'law' as opposed to a universal generalization, or indeed as opposed to a theory or an hypothesis, because no doubt they have meant different things. But we can indicate at least the central features which bring out what they mainly have had in mind. Theories and hypotheses have been thought of as more tentative, and this has often but not always been because they refer to the behaviour of unobservable or theoretical entities. Thus Avogadro's hypothesis isn't usually called Avogadro's Law even now, although sometimes it is; and Newton's Laws are sometimes referred to as theories because, despite his famous disclaimer, they make reference to hypothetical forces. Again, through historical accident we tend to speak of Relativity *Theory* but Newton's *Laws*, whereas the latter have been more obviously falsified than the former. Thus Relativity Theory seems a more likely candidate for universal nomic necessity than Newtonian mechanics, but we still speak of Newton's Laws even though they are now pretty much universally agreed to be false. The picture behind all this, however, is that of a universal, indestructible-come-what-may system of gravitational forces with all physical bodies 'obeying' the relevant laws, and so behaving *because* of these forces.[16] Now the higher up the explanatory tree we go, the more likely we are to find genuine, factually-unfalsifiable-come-what-may statements which do truly describe the actual behaviour of real bodies—the 'ultimate' laws of nature—as opposed to those statements we can deduce from them which then describe only the behaviour that bodies would ideally have if there were not so much 'contingent clutter' messing up their behaviour— contingent clutter which itself acts in accordance with— 'obeys'—these ultimate laws. So the idealizations that we affect with the lower level law-statements seem to encompass two thoughts: although it's strictly speaking false that actual planets move in ellipses, (1) ideal planets would move in ellipses (*i.e.*, ones which weren't in some sort of minor reverberation owing to their not being (ideally) spherical, and owing to the way they were ejected from the sun, and (2) ideally, a (perfectly ordinary) planet would move in an ellipse (*i.e.*, if it weren't for the contingent clutter of the other planets, meteors, the effect of the planet on the motion of the sun, *etc.*). In the case of ideal gases, we are talking of the first sort of idealization rather than the second, because we have, as it were, internal rather than external clutter.

It is surely a commonplace—or should be—that when scientists try to describe and explain the behaviour of bodies, they idealize from their actual observations either to averages, or to behaviour when allowances are made for experimental errors (which may not average out) or to allow for undesirable and perhaps unknown extraneous influences, *etc.* In this they 'reject' the accurate measurements of anomalies, and if this weren't done, we would discover no putative laws to be connected with other laws and later perhaps rejected. It would be amusing to try to find how much science has been helped by the *lack* of accurate measuring instruments were it not for the fact that any such discovered anomalies would only have bothered scientists who were naïve falsificationists, and these are presumably mythical creatures anyway. Now it might be thought—particularly by empiricists—that once generalizations stop functioning as true or false reports of the behaviour of actual bodies, they 'flip over' into logically necessary truths because scientists render them analytically true, in the case under consideration by making the property of moving in an ellipse part of the meaning of 'planet'. I am certain this doesn't happen in practice, at least in this case, although of course in other cases it sometimes might: but what can we do to *show* that 'All planets move in ellipses', when used as an idealization, is still not analytically true, but has a function which puts it in a category between the logically necessary and the 'utterly contingent'? I think several arguments can be mustered, of which I shall mention only the two that seem to be most cogent.

First, when the move was made from 'Planets move in circles (of extreme complexity)' to 'Planets move in ellipses', the meaning of the word 'planet' simply did not change. It still meant 'wandering star' or 'body with an apparent motion from the earth out of phase with that of the "fixed stars" ', or some such phrase. The specific, detailed path of the planets simply was not and is not part of what is meant by the term 'planet': and certainly the term did not stop *denoting* the same bodies, Mars, Saturn, *etc*. It is true that we are still talking here of actual, not ideal planets: but suppose we now found it convenient to talk of the ideal planets as moving in a rather different path, since this remains close to the path of actual planets but gives us a simpler physics—and it could be argued that in speaking of geodesics we already do this— there is still no temptation to say that the meaning of 'planet' has changed, and that we are talking of a different *sort* of entity.

Secondly—a consideration that is connected with the first— scientists normally don't and certainly shouldn't use the idealized form of the statement in such a way that it is logic- ally unfalsifiable. They still do and should leave open the possibility, even now, of using a new curve as descriptive of the path of an ideal planet, a path whose convenience would be attested by an admixture of its closeness of fit to the be- haviour of actual planets (which might be worse than that of the ellipse) together with the rest of the physico-mathematical apparatus. And certainly this would happen if the behaviour of actual planets (in our solar system) were in the future to change radically—an unlikely but not impossible state of affairs. Then our idealization would use a different curve, but we would still be using it to refer, indirectly, to the behaviour of the same old bodies.

I have tried to give an account of what scientists (ideally?) do, which explains naturalistically those facts previously indicated in misleading ontological form by Pythagoreans and other rationalists, by conventionalists and by prescriptivists alike. All of those provided useful if misleading antidotes to ideas of the pure empiricists. If the empiricists' prescriptions had been strictly followed, science would have been unable to advance a jot, even though their pleas to rely on observation themselves provided useful correctives to an over-enthusiastic rationalism. Fortunately Kepler to a greater, and Galileo to a lesser, extent were both Platonists, and one can even sympathise with modern writers who claim that Aristotle's science was not, as sometimes claimed, too *a priori*, but too empirical. When however we remember Aristotle's vision of an axiomatization of scientific necessary truths, the axioms of which we would be able to apprehend by intellectual intuition only *after* we have reached them inductively from our many and varied considerations of the phenomena, I find this gives a model of scientific progress nearer to the picture I have been painting than any other of my acquaintance.

I should like finally to draw some tentative practical conclusions. If so-called laws of nature are idealizations from experience except at the very highest level, then in the human sciences we need not fear that a 'science of man' might discover immutable laws which would inform us how men behave in accordance with an iron law of necessity. So to discover laws we should not pay much attention to statistics: these are useful for the discovery of *facts*. Max Weber had already wisely seen that such laws are about 'ideal types', but he didn't realise that this is also the case with most laws in the non-human sciences: indeed he thought this showed they must use differing methodologies.[17] Such idealizations would inform us *roughly* what to expect, and for the most part—although of course they might not describe average behaviour, any more than Boyle's Law describes the average behaviour of gases. Where not describing idealizations we might be able to discover not laws but mere facts, whether universal or statistical but anyway changeable. What most natural scientists spend most of their time trying to do is just that: whether there is life on Mars, what are the multiple causes of babies' sudden 'cot deaths', whether income policies reduce inflation, how to build fabricated genes, to mention only a few currently in the news. I wouldn't deny that these are in some sense theory-laden, but what gets discovered are good old empirical facts (or non-facts) for all that. Whether there even *are* any high level immutable laws which all real as opposed to ideal bodies "must obey", of the sort the ancients thought were laid down by God, can of course never be known for certain. But not only has this model provided a most fruitful drive for the advancement of science, it also seems very reasonable indeed to think it correct.

V. SUMMARY

I have been claiming that we can usefully distinguish three sorts of generalization:

1. Purely accidental generalizations, *e.g.*, 'All the chairs in my room are wooden'.
2. Generalizations about facts of nature, *e.g.*, 'All ravens are black'.
3. Laws of nature, *e.g.*, (a) 'All planets move in ellipses'.
   (b) 'The velocity of light *in vacuo* is independent of the velocity of the emitting source'.

Each of these types is contingent, *i.e.*, false in some conceivable world, and hence what we might call *logically-falsifiable-in-principle*.

Type (1) are (rather easily) falsifiable in practice. Type (2) may or may not in fact be falsifiable in practice, but they are *factually falsifiable-in-principle*, in that if we had the technical know-how we would be able to render them false. Thus they are much more like type (1) than type (3), and indeed it seems to me that the difference between these two types is one of degree, rather than kind: thus it may be very difficult for me to put a non-wooden chair in my room, if I am very weak or very broke, while it may become very easy for scientists to breed white or pink ravens. In saying this I seem to differ from most contemporary philosophers of science, who are inclined to bracket type (2) with type (3)—apart from those of a doctrinaire empiricist kind, who anyway say that there are only logical truths and empirical truths of lesser or greater generality, and hence there are no essential differences betwen (1), (2) and (3). I have tried to indicate the verification procedures for ascertaining whether a generalization is of type 2 (or of course 1), or type 3.

Type (3) can be sub-divided into two kinds. Those such as (a) are normally false if construed as descriptions of empirical reality, but true if construed as idealizations, where they are still in fact falsifiable on what we might loosely call pragmatic grounds. Only as so construed do they express laws of nature, and this answers the puzzle I set myself at the opening of this paper. Finally, there may be those such as (b) which are true of empirical reality and *factually-unfalsifiable-in-principle-come-what-may*. These are the 'ultimate' laws of nature, and although we can never be absolutely certain that there are any, since any proposed candidate may become falsified, it is still perfectly reasonable to believe that there are. We aim to use laws of type (b) both to explain why those of type (a) would be true of empirical reality if that reality were simpler (*i.e.*, why they are true as idealizations), and also to explain the behaviour of the contingent clutter which makes those of type (a) false when construed as descriptions of the relatively complex reality in which we live.

NOTES

1 I am grateful to Stina Lyon, Stuart Anstis, Jean Henry and members of the philosophy department of York University, Toronto, for criticisms of an earlier version of this paper.

2 Joseph Needham, *Science and Civilisation in China*, Vol. II, Ch. 18, "Human Law and the Laws of Nature in China and the West", Cambridge at the University Press, 1956. Needham's magnificent work contains all we require here for an appreciation of the rise of the conception of 'laws of nature' in the Western world, as well as a comparison with the situation in China.

3 We can be doubtful or ignorant whether something is an X or a Y because we are doubtful about the features required to be an X or a Y, or because we are doubtful whether the example under consideration has these factors, or whether it has them to a sufficient degree. Quite differently, we may be aware of the criteria and know that it instantiates these criteria by an amount which puts it on the borderline between being an X and a non-X; then only conceptual confusion could make *us doubtful* about the situation: the conclusion we should draw is that the example is (clearly) a borderline X.

4 R. B. Braithwaite, *Scientific Explanation*, C.U.P., 1955, p. 304.

5 Compare Hume's view that *we* make a distinction between what we call necessary connexions and other contingent connexions, but this does not correspond to any real difference in the nature of things.

6 W. C. Kneale, *Probability and Induction*, Oxford at the Clarendon Press, 1949, p. 74.

7 K. R. Popper, *The Logic of Scientific Discovery*, Hutchinson, 2nd Impression, 1960, p. 426.

8 A beautiful example is Mendel's results with the peas, which on probability theory have an almost impossibly close fit with his theory. This may have been caused by his assistants' stopping the experiment once the hoped-for results were obtained. This is an example where trying to falsify one's hypothesis would have had unfortunate consequences—it would certainly have succeeded—even though it happened that Mendel's theory was lost for so long that at first it played no part in the evolution of evolutionary theory. If Kepler's Laws had been rejected because incompatible with (accurate) observation—which they are—this would have had a most unhappy effect on the progress of Newtonian science. Inaccuracy can sometimes be a help—but only for dogmatic naïve falsificationists.

9 For example, Carl Hempel, in *Aspects of Scientific Explanation*, Collier-Macmillan Ltd., London, 1965, pp. 175, 231, 265-267, 339, 377. Ernest Nagel, in *The Structure of Science*, Routledge & Kegan Paul, London 1961, writes (p. 61): "There is a strong *disinclination* to call a universal conditional L a 'law of nature' . . . if the *only* available evidence *for* L is direct evidence" and "our attitude to [the statement 'All ravens are black'] is *less firmly settled* than it is towards statements called laws for which . . . indirect evidence is available" (my italics throughout).

My claim is that our attitude should be unequivocal: the variety of plumage .colour of birds similar to ravens, which Nagel mentions but describes merely as "an *absence* of a comprehensive variety of *indirect evidence for* the statements that all ravens are black" (my italics), in fact provides the best conceivable evidence that it's *not* a law. Perhaps one reason why Nagel has this difficulty is that he, like the writers already discussed, asks (p. 51) whether a law of nature "asserts no more than accidental universality".

10 I have attempted an 'analysis' of causal statements in terms of counterfactuals rather than universal generalizations in "Causality" *British Journal for the Philosophy of Science*, 18.1, May 1967, pp. 1-20. A similar account has recently been given by David Lewis, reprinted in Ernest Sosa (ed.) *Causation and Conditionals*, O.U.P. 1975.

11 But see below on whether laws are even true.

12 Logically necessary truths have, not several contraries, but one contradictory. Some very basic laws, such as inverse square laws, have contraries which either would lead to such difficulties that one cannot easily see how they could possibly be true, or perhaps are such that *if* there is a force *then* necessarily there must be an inverse square law. But there need not be such forces—thus according to relativity theory there are not 'really' any gravitational forces, but this world is so constituted that things behave as though (if we are very clever but not clever enough it looks as though) there are such forces. Philosophers sometimes wonder how it is that putative laws can be false and yet appear so true over such wide areas. To understand this, compare the scientist with the detective: after we have discovered that John is the murderer it *then* becomes clear why all the previous evidence pointed, and pointed wrongly, towards Jane.

126 ARDON LYON

¹³ For a selection of articles on counter-factuals see Sosa, *op. cit.* Stalnaker, in "A Theory of Conditionals" there suggests that the corresponding antecedent need not be false and that (footnote 3) "the mood tends to indicate something about the attitude of the speaker, *but in no way effects the propositional content of the statement*" (my italics). This doesn't seem correct to me, but it is not very far removed from what I argue below. Stalnaker also believes, however, that *every* pair of true statements is conditionally related, which is hardly more reasonable than the suggestion that "if *p* then *q*" means the same as $p \supset q$.

¹⁴ Some philosophers have suggested that we should really be talking about subjunctive conditionals, rather than counter-factual conditionals, and our little conversation pieces indicate that this is right, since there may be nothing contrary-to-fact about the corresponding antecedents or consequents. But for two reasons I haven't used this terminology. First, in 'analysing nomic connexions', some philosophers have only used the term 'counter-factual conditionals', although some have also spoken of 'subjunctive conditionals'. Secondly, a search through several grammars (*e.g.*, Fowler, Jesperson, Kennedy, Schisbye and Knud) fails to indicate very clearly when it is appropriate to use the subjunctive (although talk of possibles as well as contraries-to-fact does seem to mesh in with what I have been arguing), while they do unhappily imply that use of the subjunctive is rapidly dying out in English. Kruisida and Erades, *An English Grammar*, Noordhoff, 1967, 8th edition, p. 637 even write: "The use of the stem in the above cases would not justify us to speak [*sic*] of the existence of a subjunctive in English . . . Needless to say, English does not possess such a *system*" (my italics). Some sentences discussed by philosophers of science do not seem to be in any standard English form, but for example to mix subjunctive and indicative moods—in which cases it is of course unsurprising that the writers are puzzled about what they mean.

¹⁵ Lakatos somewhere conjectured that *every* proposed law has been refuted before it has even been propounded. 'Refuted' should here mean, not 'shown to be false', but 'in logical conflict with some proposition(s) reasonably believed to be true'. I suspect that any formalized rejection rules would be bound to be counter-productive if only because so much depends on the almost accidental order in which various hypotheses and observations come to be encountered.

¹⁶ It's very misleading to say that the planets move (roughly) in ellipses *because* of those Newtonian Laws which we use in explaining to ourselves why they move in ellipses: they move as they do (in the world) because of various causal influences in the world (forces, states of affairs described in initial-condition-statements, *etc.*). This is perhaps more difficult to grasp than the fact that logical truths are not true *because* of the truth of those axioms from which *we* choose to deduce them; but even here, metaphors such as foundations, ultimate truths, support *etc.* tend to make us think of the axioms as being 'the reasons why' the theorems are true, when in fact they would be true whatever were the case: so, as one might put it, there is no *reason* for their being true.

¹⁷ J. W. N. Watkins, in "Ideal Types and Historical Explanation", *British Journal for the Philosophy of Science*, 3, 1952, has already given a very full account of Weber's methodology in this respect, and pointed out that ideal types are used in all sciences. See also Carl Hempel, "Typological Methods in the Natural and Social Sciences", in *Aspects of Scientific Explanation*, where it is argued, correctly in my view, that Weber hasn't shown that in this respect the social sciences require a different methodology from the physical sciences.

IX*—SENTIMENTALITY

by Michael Tanner

The only occasion on which Oscar Wilde approached pro-
fundity was when he was accusing Lord Alfred Douglas, at
prodigious recriminatory length, of shallowness. In the course
of his bombardment, he wrote: "The fact is that you were,
and are I suppose still, a typical sentimentalist. For a sentimentalist is simply one who desires to have the luxury of an
emotion without paying for it. You think that one can have
one's emotions for nothing. One cannot. Even the finest and
most self-sacrificing emotions have to be paid for. Strangely
enough, that is what makes them fine. The intellectual and
emotional life of ordinary people is a very contemptible
affair. Just as they borrow their ideas from a sort of circulat-
ing library of thought—the *Zeitgeist* of an age that has no
soul—and send them back soiled at the end of each week, so
they always try to get their emotions on credit, and refuse to
pay the bill when it comes in. You should pass out of that
conception of life. As soon as you have to pay for an emotion
you will know its quality, and be the better for such knowledge. And remember that the sentimentalist is always a cynic
at heart. Indeed sentimentality is merely the bank holiday of
cynicism."[1] These remarks, together with some of the things
that I. A. Richards says in his chapter "Sentimentality and
Inhibition" in *Practical Criticism*, seem to me the most perceptive brief general comments made on a subject that is of
the first importance, but discussion of which is avoided for a
variety of reasons, most of them bad. But I may as well say
at the outset that I have found it too perplexing and difficult
a subject to be able to offer more than a series of rather loosely
related thoughts; and that my attempts to impose a greater
degree of order on it had resulted in falsehoods of an especially
damaging kind—the results of trying to schematize indocile
realities, which in this case at least are reflected in the un-
wieldiness of the concepts that we use to cope with them.

---

* Meeting of the Aristotelian Society at 5/7, Tavistock Place, London,
W.C.1, on Monday, 7th February 1977, at 7.30 p.m.

However, among the issues that I shall be dealing with, though not separately, since they are not separate issues, are these: (1) What are the usual conditions under which sentimentality is predicated of people, feelings (or emotions—for my purposes there is no need to distinguish between them), and do they form a coherent and useful set, or have they (the conditions) proliferated in a confusing and unhelpful way? (2) If some more or less coherent account of sentimentality can be given, is it to be considered, at least in its more extreme forms, as a very harmful or corrupting quality? (3) Is the often-asserted link between sentimentality and cynicism, or even cruelty, more than a contingent one, if it indeed exists? (4) Is there any evidence for a claim that sentimentality is an historical phenomenon, bearing in mind that charges of it are made very much more frequently nowadays than they were, say, three centuries ago?

It might well be felt that a satisfactory analysis of sentimentality could only proceed, or be derived from, an account in quite general terms of the emotions and their relationships to their causes and objects. Of course I hope that what I have to say can be fitted into some such account, but I am not persuaded that an analysis of sentimentality needs to wait upon one; if I were, I shouldn't be attempting it, since it seems to me that the general subject of the emotions is still in a grievously confused state. I hope, rather, that by dealing with a set of phenomena, and the concepts which we use to cope with them, where the relationship between emotions, their causes, and their objects, is pathological, we might be able to advance in our understanding of more normal cases, remembering always that normality is not a statistical matter, and that it could be the case that most of our feelings were properly categorized as sentimental.

Everyone who uses "sentimental" and its cognates fairly often and fairly responsibly agrees with Wilde that a dominant element in sentimentality is that the feelings which constitute it are in some important way unearned, being had on the cheap, come by too easily, and that they are directed at unworthy objects. All these charges are part and parcel of the allegation that to be sentimental is to be shallow in a specially noteworthy way. But after that, analysis tends to peter out

while accusations continue. I. A. Richards, in the most sustained attempt to bring order into this area, distinguished,
as it was fashionable to do at that time and place, three 'senses'
of 'sentimental'. The first is a quantitative one; "a response
is sentimental if it is too great for the occasion. We cannot,
obviously, judge that any response is sentimental in this sense
unless we take careful account of the situation."[2] He immediately continues: "Another sense, of which this is not true,
is that in which 'sentimental' is equivalent to 'crude.' "[3] And
finally: "A response is sentimental when, either through the
over-persistence of tendencies or through the interaction of
sentiments, it is inappropriate to the situation that calls it
forth. It becomes inappropriate, as a rule, either by confining
itself to one aspect only of the many that the situation can
present, or by substituting for it a factitious, illusory situation
that may, in extreme cases, have hardly anything in common
with it."[4] Richards gives an excellent example in the way that
people who spent unspeakable years of misery in the war
emerge remembering the wonders of comradeship, and
nothing else.

Richards' remarks, suggestive as they are, are clearly not as
final as their being listed as the three senses of 'sentimental'
would lead one to hope. In the first place, there is a reference
in both the first and the third to 'the situation'; but there are
many cases of sentimentality where there *is* no situation in the
relevant sense, the ones that come most readily to mind being
responses to instrumental music. Or to be more precise, it is
the music itself which is the prime bearer of the charge, and
for most instrumental music it seems simply mistaken to say
that it is concerned with a situation or has an object, in the
required sense. And in those works of programme-music
where there is an evoked or implied situation—Liszt's or
Richard Strauss' symphonic poems—it is not on account of
their dealing with some set of external circumstances that we
make our judgments of sentimentality, if and when we do.
Tchaikovsky is incessantly berated for the sentimentality of
his symphonies, without a clear suggestion that they are
exaggerated responses to some programmatic situation or to
'Fate', the ostensible subject of the Fourth Symphony, to
which over-reaction would be difficult. The idea is rather

that the way he is expressing himself is in itself thoroughly
regrettable—that no kind of object, or lack of one, would
justify this kind of response or demonstration. If that is right,
it has important consequences for the usual view (I think it
fair to call it that) of sentimentality as being an essentially
relational affair. The only way that Richards could cope with
sentimentality where there is no given or implied situation is
by use of his second 'sense', in which 'sentimental' is equivalent to 'crude', and that will be found to be itself too crude an
instrument. Continuing with the shortcomings of Richards'
account: neither the first nor the third sense seems to pin-
point the reason why we want to call the death of many a
fictional Victorian child sentimental. It is surely clear that the
death of a child, at least one of Little Nell's mettle, is something towards which strong feelings are appropriate, yet that
doesn't deter us from saying truly, if normally too easily, that
Dickens' portrayal of her death, as of many another terrible
kind of incident, is grossly sentimental. Whilst it is obvious
that the first of Richards' senses doesn't apply, the third
sounds much more promising, but we shall see that it too
won't do. A third criticism is that it is only certain kinds of
exaggerated, had-on-the-cheap, hand-on-heart responses that
we characterise in this way. We don't, *e.g.*, call Othello's jealousy at Desdemona's supposed unfaithfulness sentimental,
though it is inappropriate to its object, both in quantity and
quality. On the other hand, we may well, as *Othello*'s best
critics have done, characterise his attitude to himself in his
final speech ". . . Then you must speak of one who loved not
wisely but too well . . ." as grossly sentimental. But though
that might lead to the suggestion that it's the warm, sympathetic (including to oneself) love-to-sorrow spectrum of feelings that are the only ones that, on suitable occasions, can be
called sentimental, I don't think that that will work either.
People who get into frightful states of anger or indignation
over occurrences that they encounter or hear about may often,
on that account, be properly called sentimental. The relevant
difference between unjustified, rampant jealousy and vehe-
ment anger might then be pointed up by stressing that the
anger and indignation of what one might call the profession-
ally furious don't lead anywhere, whereas Othello's jealousy

certainly does; and even if it hadn't, it would have been a dreadful cancer in his soul, while anger about a political extradition in a distant land, say, doesn't go beyond being simply anger—doesn't when it's sentimental, that is to say. And that would bring us back to something like the 'easiness', lack of cost, and so forth, which Wilde accused Lord Alfred of. But though I feel that that is much more hopeful, it still won't work as it stands, because Othello's sentimental last speech— that is not meant to be a total characterisation of it, but an element of sentimentality is evidently present—does lead him straight into suicide. And indeed sentimentality is predicable of emotions that lead people to quite drastic actions, so that it is often the case that though they may not have earned their emotions, whatever that comes to, they pay for them, *pace* Wilde. So payment for one's emotions doesn't exempt them from being sentimental. The tendency which we un-doubtedly have to align sentimentality and supineness won't work, because people are often motivated by thoroughly senti-mental responses into spectacularly violent courses of be-haviour.

So far, then, Richards' account of sentimentality hasn't been as incisively firm as it at first seemed. Wilde's apparently looser mode may in fact turn out to be more precise. However, it must be remembered that I have quoted very selectively from Richards, and that he has a good deal more to say on the subject. And Wilde, who was engaged less in analysis than in attack, may have been treated with surprised latitude. Nonetheless the connexion between having a sentimental emotion and acting on it, for example, which would seem to be severed in his account, if 'payment' and 'action' are inter-changed, might still work if we specified more precisely what occurred in someone's being sentimental and yet acting on their feeling. For the route from motive to action, when it contains or goes *via* a sentimental feeling or attitude, might be said to be inappropriate in relation to the action. One might put it exaggeratedly by saying that Kant's view of the relation of motive to action gives the impression that all emo-tions, or passions, are sentimental on this modified and ex-tended account. Every action whose motive is not the per-forming of a duty is inspired by feeling, and therefore at best compromised. Whereas we would more sanely want to say, despite the aggreeable element of fanaticism in Kant's outlook, that there are some emotions which do not play their part in being good reasons for action, a notable class being sentimental emotions.

That still leaves open the question of what sentimental feelings actually are. One element, related to criteria I have already mentioned, but separable from them, is the having of emotion(s) for its, or their own sake. This again turns out on scrutiny to be a promising lead which doesn't do as much as one might hope. That shouldn't lead to its rejection, of course, since it seems most unlikely that any single formula will get us very far. "Having an emotion for its own sake" is not a perspicuous phrase, certainly not if there is taken to be the suggestion of pleasure in the having. For I don't see that it can be denied that some sentimental feelings aren't at all pleasurable and yet people go on indulging them. The feelings typically associated with unrequited love are hideously painful, yet it is part of the syndrome that one goes on turning them over, inflicting ever greater degrees of torture on oneself, in no way enjoying it all, unless in the sense that, as people say, they at least know that they're alive—but alive in such a way that they might well rather be dead. In such extreme cases it might well be disputed whether the feelings *were* sentimental, since so few of the normal conditions for that obtain. Perhaps it would be conceptually neatest, and also accord most accurately with our intuitions at this point, if we agreed that only emotions in which there was a pleasurable element, of however overlaid or involuted a sort, were properly to be called sentimental, and that one might indulge feelings that were atrociously painful; and nothing more.

Yet another way, related to previous ones, in which we might try to focus on the central concept, is that such feelings tend, after a certain point, to dislocate themselves from their objects, if they have them. This is clearly related to Richards' third sense, but not identical with it. For where he stresses the dislocation alone, I would want to amplify and claim that once the dislocation has taken place, there is a tendency to auto-generation, so that it isn't so much inappropriate

strength or object that is in question, but a disturbing autonomy which retains the *cachet*, if any, of the emotion when it
was in more or less proper relationship to its object, which
may have been a perfectly worthy one. The element of
dishonesty, probably of self-deceit, that is agreed to be
characteristic of attitudes, people or whatever when they are
sentimental is connected with the sense of the developed
feelings having lost touch with their origins, in insidious and
dangerous ways. And there is a general implication, though
not an universal one, that the self-development is illicitly
pleasurable. And this would help to explain our readiness to
call unrequited love, sometimes, sentimental, whilst jealousy,
the most violently unpleasant of feelings, is never considered
sentimental, however ridiculous, arbitrary and unjustified it
may be. It is always ghastly. Again on the other side, at least
some states of grief, which have a general but not overpowering melancholy tone, can be in a certain degree pleasant, and
on that account sentimental, and tending towards that not
wholly disagreeable lassitude which made Dr. Johnson stigmatise grief as "a species of idleness". So even an emotion
that might seem predominantly painful may have compensa-
tions enough to lead us not to curtail it. In this slightly
nebulous respect Spinoza seems to have been exactly wrong
about pleasure and pain. His view, famously, is that pleasure
is the passage, or the accompaniment of the passage, from
lesser to greater activity, and pain the passage, or its accompaniment, from greater to less.[5] But just as in Book II of the
Ethics he unwittingly shows the dangers of confusing epistem
ology and the philosophy of mind, so here he shows the
dangers of confusing philosophy of mind and ethics. Whether
he is talking of *titillatio* or *laetitia*, he is concerned that they
should be by-products of something which he regards as
always good: increased activity. But apart from having the
strange consequence that God cannot be happy since he is
unable to become more active, it fails, as his account does at
every stage, to take account of the pleasures of indolence,
routine or "wallowing".[6] Nevertheless, like all fascinated and
exasperated readers of Spinoza, I feel that he has got hold
of something of great importance, while doing nothing to
make clear, by examples or any other means, what it is. But

his stress on human bondage to the passions, though he suggests an over-intellectualised way out of it, which is inevitable given his general cast of mind, may help us to see why we regard sentimentality as at least regrettable, and at worst thoroughly vicious. For Wilde's brief against the sentimentalist, and Richards' three senses of 'sentimental' all have in common, contained implicitly in them, the passivity of the mind in relation to feelings. The only activity which the sentimentalist manifests naturally is, one might say, the activity of rendering himself more passive. It is characteristic for the sentimentalist to inhibit those checking devices which are available, though hard to handle, for interrogating one's experiences, for asking whether one's feelings are primarily controlled by their object, if they have one, and what *kind* of communication they are maintaining with it. And though Spinoza gives us no help on the subject, there clearly is a distinction to be made between feelings which we allow to happen to us, and those which we activate, though it is not a clear distinction.[7] But that, even so, won't demarcate sentimental from unsentimental feelings for us, because it is of course perfectly possible to lead a thoroughly sentimental yet highly active life, one characterised by that kind of abandoned enthusiasm for which the German *Schwärmerei* is so incomparably expressive a term. The *Stürmer und Dränger*, and the heroes and heroines of sensibility in the eighteenth century, energetically courted emotions that then took over, got out of control, and were therefore attributable to the workings of destiny. Bearing such specimens and their latter-day descendants in mind, it would be tempting to suggest that there are two broad categories of sentimentalist: those who let life do what it will with them, and languish in more or less exquisite torment; and those who seize every opportunity for 'drinking life to the dregs' *etc.*, and therefore require a quite different account of their emotional lives. But striking as the differences are, it is the underlying identity of their feelings which is crucial. For in the end both court the same emotions, and it is simply a question of whether they think they can indulge them most satisfactorily by adopting a preliminary active or passive rôle, the aim of both being that variety of passivity sometimes called 'being carried away'.

At this point, when many suggestions have been toyed with, and none developed, it may seem likely that the drift of my selection is towards a set of stringent recommendations for emotional hygiene, in which I may finally produce an account of sentimentality which will suggest that the vigilance with which we monitor our emotional lives may well leave little chance or *any* emotions to survive; and indeed there are anti-sentimentalists whose aim would seem to approximate that, and who do not, in Wilde's term, take any bank holidays, who can't be said to be sentimentalists in matadors' clothing. It will not, in fact, be the upshot of my argument that a censorship of the feelings should be established, but rather—and the suggestion is no doubt as banal as its execution is uncommon—that what should be established is an education and discipline of the feelings, the ideal condition of man being one in which he has no fear of his feelings, however voluminous and powerful they may be, because of his confidence in their vitality and their vitalising effect on others. An ideal *so* 'ideal' may well seem to most people not worth enlarging upon.

Returning now to consider further the possibilities of analysis that I have sketched, the first question to cope with is whether there is anything intrinsic to sentimental feelings by virtue of which they are so categorised. I think that the answer is that sometimes there is, and sometimes not; in the latter set of cases, there is always the possibility that they will slither towards the first class. My first and chief reason for thinking that there are some feelings that are intrinsically sentimental is derived from the phenomenon of instrumental music, with which I have already dealt briefly. Whatever we may think of the usual list of musical sentimentalists, unquestionably some music is sentimental. There is often no prospect for analysing sentimentality here in terms of a misplaced or displaced relationship to an object, since there is no object. A weaker suggestion of a familiar kind would be that though there are no objects in these cases, it is *as if* there were. The emotions embodied in César Franck's Piano Quintet, to take an obviously noxious example, are very like the emotions expressed in some of the oleaginous religiose passages of French operatic composers from Gounod to Massenet. That granted, one may have been spared exposure to *Thaïs* and its ilk, and indeed to any pseudo-religious dramatic and vocal music, and still find the Piano Quintet shocking, as even Liszt did. Nor need one express one's objections to it in an 'as if' form, in order to stigmatise it as sentimental. That isn't to say that one won't characterise it by the use of 'life' terms—'masturbatory' seems to be an obvious candidate. But that still doesn't mean that it has even an implicit object; the feelings it expresses, and in suitably responsive listeners evokes, are comparable no doubt to the feelings one has when there are objects around—objects of one's feelings, I mean—but objects being regarded sentimentally. That is, there is the strongest sense of emotions which have been best described by Wilfrid Mellars as "eroticism curbed, or rebellious passion that struggles to break free."[8] One can tell from the music itself (I leave aside the verification-procedures in this type of enterprise) that it is *curbed eroticism* that is being expressed, and curbed eroticism of a particularly enjoyable kind; part of the enjoyment comes precisely from the curbing, which means that it can continue more or less indefinitely, as Franck's music often threatens to do. There is thus a very sharp contrast with the Prelude to Act I of *Tristan*, where the eroticism which is curbed for the first half is very evidently straining to be unleashed, and indeed is unleashed with notoriously overpowering effect. But that doesn't, naturally, clinch any point, for there have been innumerable would-be *Tristan* Preludes since the original, in which passion is unleashed but the whole thing is rotten, rancidly sentimental. The varied assessments that I'm handing out are no doubt based on reactions that I wouldn't have if I hadn't had some relevantly similar emotions in contexts where there were objects. But though one way of arguing from that would be that the relationship between the emotion and the object in *those* situations was what led me to call the emotion a sentimental one, and that it was the similarity in emotional tone which led to the same attribution in objectless situations, there is a quite different line which we might more wisely take; that even though the emotions found in a piece of music were similar to the emotions found in situations where there were objects, it is not on *that* account that they are sentimental: rather, perhaps, one can see from the instrumental-music cases that sentimentality is an intrinsic quality of some emotions, though it may be tempting when one thinks of situations where there are objects to claim that the sentimentality resides in the relationship between the feelings and what they are feelings about, or towards.

Neither of the positions strikes me as true *überhaupt*, but I think, though I should have great difficulty in marshalling adequate arguments to persuade the unconvinced, that each of them is true for some cases. An opponent of my second suggested line might, for instance, press on with his claim that the feelings expressed and aroused by a piece of instrumental music may be sufficiently like those expressed or aroused by some situation where there is an object calling forth undue quantities, or the wrong quality, of emotion for it to be said that there is an implied object. And it could be argued, I think incorrectly, that when we call a piece of music sentimental it is always because it suggests implied objects; though that clearly wouldn't be a sufficient condition for sentimentality in music, since some evidently unsentimental pieces also have implied objects. The Eroica Symphony, which is not in the least sentimental, is in an interminably debatable sense 'about' heroism, which could thus be said to be its object. The Adagietto for strings and harp from Mahler's Fifth Symphony, on the other hand, is sentimental without being about anything at all, not even death in Venice; it was sentimental from the day that Mahler composed it, which was why it came in so handy for Visconti's piece of prolix kitsch.

The opposing views about whether sentimentality can be an intrinsic property, or is necessarily relational, can probably only be satisfactorily dealt with by introducing further and wider considerations about the inner life. My view is that it would be preposterous at the present ill-formed stage of the philosophy of the emotions to take up a strong line. But I do think that recent Anglo-American philosophers have underestimated severely the incidence of objectless emotions, partly because they have been in general behaviouristically inclined, partly because they have preferred to discuss feelings for which there are frequently employed names. They have neglected to observe that the connexions between the emotional lives of almost everyone and the objects that those emotions have, when they have them, are loose to an extreme degree. What might have been felt to be Wilde's insufferable élitism in writing "The intellectual and emotional life of ordinary people is a very contemptible affair" seems to me to be perfectly just, and he erred only in thinking that the emotional lives of most extraordinary people—he was thinking particularly of himself—are in a better position. In spite of constant appeals from some literary critics, educationalists and novelists—I think here of Lawrence's remark that "a man who is *emotionally* educated is as rare as a phoenix"[9]—most people are content to remain, to a great extent, in bondage to the passions, perhaps because no-one has ever suggested to them that the emotions might be educated, or been truthful about how arduous a business it is. Considering how much almost everyone is in hapless thrall to their feelings, it is truly astounding how little interest they take in precisely what they are; and philosophical interest in them is a very stop-go affair too. There was a brief period in the late nineteen-fifties when English philosophers debated whether there was a huge number of indefinitely discriminable emotions, or very few, the criterion being chiefly a matter of variations in overt response. After a couple of interesting books, the subject seems to have been virtually abandoned again. Yet it does seem obvious that if the education or cultivation of the feelings is feasible, it is of the utmost importance, since most people spend their lives in the limbo between boredom and misery, and the misery, granted a solution of what Lawrence refers to as "the bread-and-butter problems of alimentation" has largely to do with the disorderliness of their emotional lives, a very large ingredient in which is sentimentality—aimless or pointless feelings, existing prior to any object fitting or unfitting, and therefore always ready to latch onto the first even faintly plausible candidate for their expression, or betrayal, to use Collingwood's apt word.

There is a clear danger that in attempting to locate the central aspects of sentimentality one will oscillate between dealing with specific feelings and with the people who have them, trying to get to grips with the concept by dealing with a given emotional state, and moving outwards from there into the pattern of life of a person whom we would call sentimental, and hoping that this oscillation will give the impression that it is, indeed will be, a dialectical progress towards understanding. It won't. The difficulty is exacerbated by the extreme proximity of at least some sentimental feelings to a phenomenon that "flourishes in the same hedgerow" and yet is in all crucial respects quite different: the phenomenon of emotional generosity, something that I take to be, together with vitality, to which it is closely linked, the most desirable of all human qualities. Now one way in which we distinguish, if we recognise the quality of emotional generosity at all, between it and sentimentality, is in the freedom with which the generous (the adverb 'emotionally' is to be understood from now on) act on their feelings without anxiety about the point and value of doing so—and the lack of anxiety is well-grounded. So once more feeling and action become fairly closely linked in making the distinction between sentimental and other feelings. And from the outsider's point of view, there may rarely be anything more to go on in making the essential discriminations. But there *is* a further difference. I have, in order to support that claim, to report on my findings about myself, an activity that angels left to fools about a quarter of a century ago. However: in the complexity of the relations between my feeling and my actions, I feel confident in assessing some of my emotions as being of a kind that naturally leads to action, unless there are other inhibiting factors, as of course there naturally often are. It might be that it is the recalcitrance of the world in refusing to suffer one's emotional expressions that leads to so many of them remaining wholly within, and either dying of inanition or burgeoning without point, and thus leading one willy-nilly to sentimentality. But it also seems to me that some of my feelings are of a kind that inhibit action, because they themselves are enjoyable to have, but if acted upon, one would cease to have them, and one doesn't want to. Such a feeling does seem to me intrinsically sentimental, even though there may be equivalent feelings which prompt one to action. The kind of feelings I am thinking of are righteous indignation on the basis of which no action can be taken, and in general that range of feelings which help to increase one's sense of one's own superiority so long as no activity is required. An enormous amount of meditation on the sufferings of the Jews in the Third Reich is of this kind, though it is almost impossible to persuade indulgers that it is. It is in this region that Wilde wrote more wisely than he knew when he spoke of having emotions without being prepared to pay for them. But the emphasis should fall on the being prepared; payment may not be required, or it may not be expected but have to be made. Many sentimentalists pay horribly in the end for their sentimentality. It is the attitude they adopt towards the payment that marks them as sentimenal or not.

So far we can say that sentimental people have been shown to (1) respond with extreme readiness to stimuli; (2) appear to be pained, but actually enjoy their pangs; (3) respond with equal violence to disparate stimuli at an amazing pace, the amazement being engendered by the speed with which one piece of intensity is as it were casually replaced by another; (4) avoid following up their responses with *appropriate* actions; or if they do follow them up appropriately, it is adventitious.

But this needs modification. We would call a person sentimental precisely on account of certain things he did, which were entirely appropriate to his feelings. A man who goes to inordinate lengths to avoid treading on snails is in a difficult position; we are very likely to call him sentimental for making such a fuss over snails, and perhaps more likely if he puts his feelings into practice than if he doesn't. It is in such cases, where sentimentality is predicated of someone irrespective of whether or not he puts his beliefs into practice, that it finally becomes clear that all such predications are made on the basis of a set of standards regarding the relationships between feelings, attitudes, beliefs and actions which will necessitate, if we are to defend them (as I, of course, cannot, here), a full account of our deepest moral commitments.

So: it is sentimental to feel in a certain way towards some objects, on account of what those objects are; or to feel in certain ways irrespective of the objects concerned; or to feel in certain ways and not to act accordingly. Sentimentality, then, is the name of several kinds of disease of the feelings.

in which the elements of feeling "in the void", of unfocused emotion, and of being prepared for huge bouts of emotional response to virtually random, or alternatively direly predictable stimuli, are all closely connected. The point can be made clearer by returning to music. The greatness of some interpretative artists, of whom the obvious and overwhelming example for our time is Maria Callas, consists precisely in their focusing our attention on what, in other hands, or from other larynges, becomes simply an excuse for indulgence. Only after one has listened to Callas sing "Un bel dì", for example, is one at all likely to know what it is about in any but the vaguest way, and what progression of feeling it so movingly notates.

Opera and song provide some particularly helpful material for dealing with some of the issues I've been discussing. It is notoriously characteristic of opera that many of the most popular works in the genre have ludicrous or indecipherable plots, absurd words, and that the dramatic situations merely provide an occasion for display of various kinds, ranging from the bloodless Melba-type coloratura to the flamboyantly expressive. Verdi's works are largely in the second category, except that the emotions in the majority of them are so blatantly primitive, or as the apologists put it, "painted in primary colours", that it is *de rigueur* to regard him as honest, forthright and wholesome, while Puccini, whose operas are distinguished by vastly superior texts, is brusquely dismissed because of his indulgences, languors and stridency. We tend to have a strange prejudice that female slaves captive to Babylonians and singing brash tunes are somehow superior to seamstresses dying of consumption in Parisian garrets. But if one is to defend emotional purity—though not at the cost of wholehearted emotional commitment—it is all the more important to be firm about one's lack of snobbery about the life of feeling.

The poems of Wilhelm Müller which comprise the cycle which, reordered by Schubert, constitute *Die Winterreise* are in no way superior to some of the most despised opera libretti, except that there are no plot difficulties to cope with. The reason why the poems, mostly, are embarrassingly sentimental, achieving only an odd moment of distinctive and

striking imagery, while the cycle as a whole—Schubert's cycle
—is one of the supreme things in art, possibly the greatest
of all modern tragedies, is that Schubert not only by a variety
of means turns the commonplace into the uncanny and the
searching, but that Müller's indistinguishable dollops of goo
achieve, thanks to Schubert's inspiration, a sharp separation
when they are made parts of a genuine and agonisingly honest
exploration, a pilgrimage into an insanity of self-knowledge.
The youngster who begins the cycle as an unremarkable
sufferer from unrequited love stumbles on, driven by the pain
of what lies behind and the desperate search for what may
still await him; and even when what lies before him is a hazy
Romantic equation of rest and death, he is still a figure of
truly heroic stature by virtue of his cruel refusal of comfort
from the direction of a mawkish churchyard, by his
Nietzscheanly explosive high spirits in the deranged "*Mut*":
"*Wenn kein Gott auf Erde sein, sind wir selber Götter*",[10] and
by his final acceptance of the unrelievable misery of his condition; any amelioration would be a failure to face the truth—
a condition that has, by the end of the cycle, become universalised to a degree where the fact that he was driven onto
his pilgrimage by rejected love has become irrelevant.
Schubert, art's most terrible loss, provides here, as so often,
the test-case; the enormous pull towards the ideals of oblivion,
"lapsing-out," unspecified and unspecifiable forms of merging,
and the knowledge that it is impossible, a dream that can only
be lingeringly entertained if it is firmly placed in a context
of realism. He knew so much about some forms of sentimentality that he could incorporate them, seemingly without
critique, only to leave us with a final impression that nothing
has been shirked, no unrealities finally allowed.

To revert to Wilde, and his claim that sentimentality is
merely the bank holiday of cynicism. The ease with which the
sentimentalist has his emotions, gets rid of them, and moves
on to another set, is not casually related to cynicism. For it is
definitive of cynicism to regard human beings as shallow,
manipulable and crudely categorisable. To be a cynic is to
reject any analysis of human motivation which appeals to
depths and complexities of the selfish and the noble, the
spontaneous and warm intertwining with the calculated and

therefore in some sense 'cold'. It is a view of men which, by predicating necessary shallowness of them, is itself condemned to shallowness. It is thus especially appropriate to the vulnerable adolescent seeking protection from a world seen as threatening, to the manipulator of people who would hate, nonetheless, to feel that the human material he was manipulating was susceptible to more than a very limited amount of damage or pain, and to the disillusioned middle-aged whose feelings have been sufficiently often disregarded for him to want to deny their existence, if they have survived. But each of these classes of people, even the second, is liable to experience the impact of the, to them, painful fact that there *are* feelings which others value and organize their lives upon. But the feelings which are worth having are those which it costs an effort to have—which doesn't mean that the effort is what makes them worth having, but is a consequence of the complexity of the data with which we have to deal. To have them it is necessary to understand what they are. To understand what they are it is necessary to run the risks involved in the depth-probing which results in their emergence and growth. The process is long, slow, time-consuming, painful and demanding of a degree of commitment that it is fearsomely difficult for most people to make. In this sense most people are cynics and sentimentalists. For a further feature of sentimental feelings is that analysis of them—placing them in relation to their objects, positioning them in relation to other items in one's emotional economy—shows that they are 'easy', easy to come and easy to go, parts of "undisciplined squads of emotions". Unsentimental emotions are typically deepened and made more secure by pondering and analysis; which is one reason why the alleged dichotomy of thought and feeling is so harmful.

While the alleged connexion between cynicism and sentimentality seems clear, it is less evident that a strong connexion exists between sentimentality and cruelty. It is admittedly likely that someone whose feelings come and go so swiftly and easily that they are more aptly described in the reductive Rylean terminology for the whole of the inner life of twinges and pangs, will not think hard before wounding someone else, but what has been more noteworthy is the sentimentality shown by the cruel than the cruelty shown by the sentimental.

Hoess weeping at a performance of the Verdi Requiem given by Jews who were to be incinerated the next day is certainly a bizarre episode, but I am not at all sure that making an Adorno-type meal of it, taking it as darkly indicative of the moral ambiguity of art, and so forth, is necessary or desirable. It does show how far sentimentality can go, and how staggeringly superficial people can be in the presence of great art, but that is no news. The episode is merely to Hoess' discredit, and not at all to Verdi's, or anything else. Or if it is, that remains to be shown. Any discussion of the subject that I have read suggests more a thrilled sense of inscrutable connexions than a desire to understand anything.

I return, finally, to the notion of paying for an emotion; when Wilde invoked it he was appealing to something very deeply rooted in our view of the world, namely that an inner life which is self-generating and insufficiently related to the world of action is corrupting and dangerous. It is a fascinating aspect of the work-ethic, all the more surprising coming from Wilde. But important as we feel it is that feeling shouldn't terminate in utterance and gesture, we don't usually enquire to what degree the correlation should be maintained, and it's worth mentioning music for the last time to make things clearer. William James' famous claim that whenever one is moved by a piece of music one should go out and *do* something, as a specific against irresponsible cultivation of the inner life, strikes most people as touchingly wrong-headed; if only because it isn't clear, after listening to most pieces of music, what kind of thing one should do which would in any serious sense be relevant to them. And on the rare occasions when music does convey particular injunctions, they tend to be of the "Embrace the world!" variety, which may be hard to manage. Yet unless we are going to take an incredibly drastic view, and regard music as an illicit stimulant, those of us for whom it is among the two or three most important things in life need to be able to cope with the allegation that we are merely being sentimental in a rather grand and unusually impenetrable disguise. That threat doesn't seem to me to be difficult to ward off, though it deserves lengthier treatment than I can give it. But the object to which we respond— the music itself—is something that, when it does offer emotional stimulus, may be judged as sentimental or not by a sense which we acquire and develop of the degree of organisation that is possible in the emotional life. The greatest instrumental music is that which offers us symbols or patterns of something like an ideal of intensity and balance of feeling; the most corrupting music is of the kind that urges an illusion of order, or offers the exciting and appalling temptations of disorder. And the most recent example of elephantiasis in music, leaving aside the anti-musical endeavours of Stockhausen in his bitterly regrettable latest phase, was of course that which followed in the wake of Richard Wagner: huge bombastic tone-poems, of which Schoenberg's *Pelleas und Melisande* is one especially blatant case. It isn't surprising with an artist of such supreme quality that the sense of something desperately wrong, a spiritual sickness expressed as an artistic tumour, led to the production of a 'system' which, if not used with the intelligent plasticity of its originator and his most gifted disciples, resulted in boring rigour or the illusion that because the music could be analysed in a particular way, the feelings expressed in it were to be apprehended as fully formed and controlled, though in fact they were nothing of the kind. All sentimentality, one might say, aspires to the condition of music. But much music is the surest safeguard we have against the temptations of sentimentality.

But I am inclined to think that nothing can secure us against sentimentality to anything like the degree that we need. Most of our basic attitudes and feelings are sentimental, on the analyses I have adumbrated of the concept. For my answer to the question whether sentimentality is an historical phenomenon is that it is, to this extent: enormous numbers of our feelings and attitudes towards the most basic issues are based on some more-or-less traditional Christian outlook. But we are no longer living in a Christian society, in any serious sense, and most of us are not Christians. Our general view of the world is not at all like Christ's. And yet we depend for much of our emotional and spiritual succour on art and teaching that not only presupposes the truth of Christianity, but actively propogates it. Many an atheist thinks that the *B minor Mass* is one of the greatest works of art; that is what I feel. But I am not at all clear that I should. The brevity with which I have mentioned this matter means not that it is an after-thought, or tangential to the subject-matter of the paper, but that I am too disconcerted by it to know what to say.

At various points I have contrasted sentimentality with the fulness of emotional vitality which I take as the ideal of life, even if it involves, since these things cannot be calculated very finely, risks of overdrawing our emotional reserves. Against the pointless inner proliferation of feeling which is sentimentality we may place, as something at least as frightful, the state depicted by the *Wasteland*, as it is summarised by Collingwood, our greatest English aesthetician: "The poem depicts a world where the wholesome flowing water of emotion, which alone fertilizes all human activity, has dried up. Passions that once ran so strongly as to threaten the defeat of prudence, the destruction of human individuality, the wreck of men's little ships, are shrunk to nothing. No one gives; no one will risk himself by sympathizing; no one has anything to control. We are imprisoned in ourselves, becalmed in a windless selfishness. The only emotion left us is fear: fear of emotion itself, fear of death by drowning in it, fear in a handful of dust."[11] Reckless indulgence of emotion, or terror of it, may equally be the consequence of living on the emotional inheritance of the Christian era. Of the two alternatives, abandonment to unearned feelings may well be the lesser evil; certainly Collingwood's chilling prose makes the other seem even worse. But sentimentality deserves to be taken more seriously than it takes itself.

NOTES

[1] *The Letters of Oscar Wilde*, edited by Rubert Hart-Davis, p. 501.
[2] *Practical Criticism*, p. 258.
[3] *Ibid.*
[4] *Loc. cit.*, p. 261.
[5] *Ethics*, Book III, Definitions II and III of the Passions.
[6] I am aware that Spinoza means something fairly different from what we ordinarily mean in his use of such terms as 'activity.' I should be grateful if, in showing my naïveté on this subject, some Spinozist would also show precisely how Spinoza uses ordinary terms, and that he does not lapse into attaching the force to them which they normally have, *if* he doesn't.
[7] For a helpful but difficult discussion of related issues to this, see Richard Wollheim, "The Mind and the Mind's Image of Itself" in *On Art and the Mind*.

8 *Man and his Music*, 1-volume edition, p. 915.
9 *Phoenix I*, p. 539. Lawrence's italics.
10 "If there are no gods on earth, then we ourselves are gods."
11 *The Principles of Art*, p. 335.

X*—ON THE LOGIC OF RELATIONS

by Stephan Körner

The purpose of this essay is to argue for the revision of a widely accepted account of relations by combining some of the technical achievements of mathematical logic, as embodied in the lower predicate calculus, with some philosophical insights of Brentano's analysis of relations. The result is meant to be a logical theory which would be compatible with ontological positions as divergent as the theses of Aristotle that relations are less real than quality or quantity, of Leibniz that they are *entia rationis* or of Russell that they are not. Brentano took no serious notice of mathematical logic. Had he done so, many papers by his successors on intentional relations, opaque contexts, identity and related topics need not have been written.[1]

The main step which has to be taken in order to arrive at the revised theory of relations is quite simple. It starts from Brentano's account of *relativa* as connecting a *fundamentum relationis*, which occurs in *modo recto*, with a *terminus relationis*, which occurs in *modo obliquo*. And it consists in interpreting this account by adding so-called "relational expressions" to the predicates of the lower predicate calculus. The interpretation will be elaborated in part I which after a preliminary comparison of directly and obliquely occurring expressions (§1) proceeds to a discussion of relational expressions, including compound predicates with names, predicates and sentences as their internal components, as well as relations in the narrow sense of the term(§2). The purpose of part II is to show the relevance of the preceding general discussion to some questions about extensionality, intentionality and modality (§3); about various constraints on the substitution of equivalent expressions for each other (§4); and about different ways of "rectifying" obliquely occurring expressions (§5).

---

* Meeting of the Aristotelian Society at 5/7, Tavistock Place, London, W.C.1, on Monday, 21st February, 1977 at 7.30 p.m.

I

1. On the direct and oblique occurrence of names, predicates and sentences.

The difference between the direct and indirect mode of a linguistic expression may manifest itself in its form or in the form of wider expressions in which it occurs as a part. It may also manifest itself in the manner in which the users of the expression behave. In sketching a logical theory one must naturally put the main emphasis on exhibiting, or indeed on instituting, formal differences between the direct and the oblique *occurrence* of linguistic expressions in contexts which themselves are texts, rather than on exhibiting non-formal differences between the direct and indirect *use* of expressions in non-linguistic contexts.

A name occurs directly or referentially if, and only if, it occurs as naming, or referring to, a real particular, *i.e.,* a particular in the actual world. Thus in the statements that Mr. Healey is parsimonious and that Mr. Micawber is parsimonious only the first name occurs directly. The nature of real particulars is here not in question. They could be—and have been assumed to be—material objects, persons and material objects, Whiteheadean events, platonic Forms *etc.* The real particulars acknowledged by a person may, moreover, fall into two classes, namely particulars which exist independently (*e.g.,* horses or men in Aristotle's ontology) and particulars which exist only as aspects or features of independent particulars (*e.g.,* numbers in the ontology of Aristotle). Our characterization of the direct or referential occurrence of names thus presupposes a differentiation of experience into particulars and attributes, but does not presuppose that there is or can be only one such differentiation.[2]

A name occurs obliquely if, and only if, it occurs as an internal component of a predicate *e.g.,* '*x* is less-parsimonious-than-Mr. Healey' or '*x* is more-parsimonious-than-Mr. Micawber'. Whenever it is convenient to indicate explicitly that an expression occurs as an internal component of a predicate, the expression will be preceded by a dash or connected by dashes with the other parts of the predicate. Some names, like that of Mr. Healey, occur both directly and obliquely.

Names which, like that of Mr. Micawber occur only obliquely, are fictitious names. That a name occurs only indirectly is in ordinary discourse often tacitly understood, that is to say, without the explicit application of some such predicate as 'x imagines-in-accordance-with-Dickens'-novel-that-Mr. Micawber ...'. This compound predicate in which the name of Mr. Micawber occurs obliquely, *i.e.*, as an internal component, is, of course, applicable to real particulars, especially readers of Dickens' novel. If a name occurs non-referentially one normally has a more or less clear idea of what it would be like if the name had also a referential occurrence. The idea may, however, be so confused that it cannot even be consistently expressed. This familiar fact does not preclude the adoption of normative standards requiring that the idea *should* be capable of a formulation which is consistent and, perhaps, in addition possesses other features. (See section 5, where this "rectification" of obliquely occurring expressions is discussed.)

A monadic predicate—for the moment we need consider no others—occurs directly or applicatively if, and only if, it occurs as applying to one or more real particulars. Thus the predicate 'x is human' occurs applicatively in 'Mr. Healey is human', but not in any sentence in which the fictitious Mr. Micawber is characterized as human. A monadic predicate occurs obliquely if, and only if, it occurs as an internal component of a predicate, as does the predicate 'x is a woman' in 'x-is-lover-of-all (some)-women'. Some predicates occur both directly and obliquely. Predicates which occur only obliquely, are fictitious predicates. That a predicate occurs indirectly is in ordinary discourse often tacitly understood. For example, in the statement that Mr. Micawber is human not only the name 'Mr. Micawber' but also the predicate 'x is human' is used indirectly, since in this sentence it does not apply to a real particular, but is understood to be an internal component of some such predicate as 'x imagines-in-accordance-with-Dickens'-novel-that-Mr. Micawber-is-human-and- ...'. If a predicate occurs obliquely one normally has a more or less clear idea of what it would be like if the predicate had also an applicative occurrence. The idea may be so confused that it cannot be consistently expressed.

A sentence occurs directly or implicatively if, and only if, it occurs as expressing a true proposition and, hence, as

STEPHAN KORNER

materially implying any other sentence expressing a true proposition. Thus, looking back at the preceding examples, whenever a predicate occurs applicatively the corresponding sentence occurs implicatively. A sentence occurs obliquely if, and only if, it occurs as an internal component of a predicate e.g., '*x* believes-that-Mr. Micawber-is-human'. Some sentences, such as '-Mr. Micawber-is-human' occur only obliquely. In ordinary discourse the direct and the indirect occurrence of sentences are often only tacitly distinguished. Again, if a sentence occurs obliquely, one usually has a more or less clear idea of what it would be like if the sentence also occurred implicatively. That the idea may not admit of being consistently expressed does not—as has been pointed out already— preclude the adoption of normative standards requiring that it be capable of a formulation which satisfies various conditions of acceptability.

2. *Relational expressions and their species.*

As our examples show, the difference between directly and indirectly occurring expressions corresponds to a structural difference between predicates which do and predicates which do not contain a name, predicate or sentence as an internal (synsemantic, syncategorematic) component. For the purpose of a more systematic treatment of these and cognate distinctions it is useful to introduce the notion of relational expressions of which relations in the narrow sense of the term are merely one species. In doing so it will be sufficient to consider expressions of form $x \ [Ry]$ in which x and y will respectively be called the "external" and the "internal" variable. What will be said about expressions containing one internal variable can be easily generalized to expressions containing two or more internal variables.

An expression $x \ [Ry]$ is a (dyadic) relational expression if, and only if, the external variable x can be replaced by some directly occurring expression and the internal variable y can be replaced by some *directly or indirectly* occurring expression in such a manner that the result is a true sentence. Relational expressions may be subdivided into three classes, namely: (1) relations (in the narrow sense), *i.e.*, relational expressions which yield true sentences, only if y is replaced by a directly occurring expression. (2) compound monadic predicates, *i.e.*, relational expressions which yield true sentences, only if y is replaced by an indirectly occurring expression (3) impure relational expressions which are neither relations nor compound monadic predicates but yield true sentences, both if y is replaced by some directly occurring expression or if it is replaced by some indirectly occurring expression. In order to indicate these distinctions in a formal language one might, for example, represent relations by xRy, compound monadic predicates by $xR - y$ and impure relational expressions by $xR ? y$. Each of these classes of relational expressions can be subdivided according to whether the external and internal variables range over names, predicates or sentences.

In order to indicate explicitly the type of expression by which the internal and the external variable must be replaced if a true sentence is to result from the replacement, $a, b, c,$ will be used for variables ranging over names of particulars; F, G, H for variables ranging over predicates; and f, g, h for variables ranging over sentences. For constant names, predicates and sentences the same letters will be used and provided with a subscript. Examples of relations are 'a collides with b' (where a and b range over names of material objects); 'f logically implies g' (where f and g range over sentences); 'a knows f' (where a ranges over names of persons and f over sentences). Examples of compound, monadic predicates are 'a desires $- b$' (where a ranges over names of persons and b over names of particulars; and a believes $- f$ (where a ranges over names of persons and f over sentences).

An example of an impure relational expression is 'a is taller than $?b$' where a and b range over the names of entities which have or are imagined to have a certain size. The substitution instances of this and other impure relational expressions resemble either the substitution instances of relations as with 'The Empire State Building is taller than the Eiffel Tower' or they resemble the substitution instances of compound, monadic predicates as with 'Mr. Healey-is-taller-than-the-first-inhabitant - of - Lilliput - seen - by - Gulliver - in - accordance - with-Swift's-tale'. In a formal language, which our sketch is meant to suggest, the difference between directly and obliquely occurring expressions can be read off from a difference in their form. (Although the analysis of impure relational expressions into combinations of pure ones seems feasible, it is by no means straightforward.)

The need for relational expressions other than relations in the narrow sense manifests itself especially in the analysis of intentional phenomena *i.e.*, of the connexion between a *res cogitans* and its *cogitata*. Compound monadic predicates containing indirectly occurring names, predicates or sentences as components are clearly intentional since the oblique occurrence of an expression involves a thinker's idea of what it would be like if the expression also occurred directly. On the other hand, not all intentional predicates are compound monadic predicates since, as Brentano well knew, some intentional predicates are relations (in the narrow sense). Yet, all intentional predicates logically imply compound monadic predicates. More precisely, the applicability of any intentional predicate logically implies the applicability of a compound, monadic predicate of form $aR - b$, $aR - F$ or $aR - f$. A few examples must here suffice.

A clear example of a predicate which is both, intentional and a relation (in the narrow sense) is the relation of imagining each other. Whereas 'John imagines − Venus' does not express a relation because it does not imply that each of the names occurring in it occurs referentially, 'John and Venus imagine each other' does express a relation—be it because it has to be understood in the light of an ontology which acknowledges goddesses as real particulars, be it because the woman whom John imagines and who imagines John was christened 'Venus'. It is furthermore clear that the applicability of 'a and b imagine each other' to John and Venus logically implies the applicability of the compound monadic predicate 'a imagines − Venus' to John and of the compound monadic predicate 'b imagines − John' to Venus.

Another clear example of a predicate which is both intentional and a relation is the relation of correct belief. Whereas 'John believes-that-Columbus-discovered-America' or, more briefly 'John believes-f_1,' does not express a relation because it does not imply that the name and the sentence occurring in it occur directly (the name referentially, the sentence implicatively), 'John correctly believes f_1' does express a relation between John and the sentence f_1. It is furthermore clear that the applicability of the relation 'a correctly believes f_1' to John and f_1 logically implies the applicability to John of the compound monadic predicate 'a believes $- f_1$'. As against this the applicability of a non-intentional relation, *e.g.*, 'a is to the left of b' does not logically imply the applicability of a compound monadic predicate.

II

3. On compound monadic predicates, extensionality and modality.

By admitting relational expressions, in particular compound monadic predicates of form $aR - b$, $aR - f$ and $aR - F$, into the lower predicate calculus one increases, of course, its expressive power. But in doing so one does not in any way affect the referential occurrence of names, the applicative occurrence of predicates or the implicative occurrence of sentences. The enlarged theory is in particular no less "extensional" than the original: Monadic predicates—whether compound or not —are applicable only to real particulars; any sentence resulting from such an application to a real particular is *with respect to this particular* existentially quantifiable (*e.g.*, $a_0R - b_0$ implies $(\exists x)(xR - b_0)$); any sentence formed by the application of a predicate to a real particular or by existential or universal application has a truth-value and contributes in the usual manner to the truth-value of any truthfunctional compound of which it is a truthfunctional component.

The intentional or non-intentional character of a sentence must be distinguished from its modal character. More precisely, whether a sentence is logically necessary, ontologically necessary, contingent, logically possible *etc.*, does not depend on whether or not it contains a compound monadic—or more complex—intentional predicate. While we are only concerned with alethic or, as I shall say, implicative modalities which can be expressed in the language or metalanguage of the lower predicate calculus, it is important not to underestimate its power to express even subtle modal differences.

The fundamental implicative necessity is logical necessity

whose syntactical and semantical definition is here taken for granted. Because classical quantification theory is sound and complete we shall indicate the logical necessity of a sentence f by $\vdash f$ (and not distinguish between $\vdash f$ and $\vDash f$). In terms of logical necessity we can define various kinds of relative necessity with respect to various conjunctions of non-logical principles N, which may be ontological principles, physical principles *etc.* If, for example, N is a conjunction of ontological principles to which, as Kant put it, every judgment must conform "if it is not to lose all its content", then the definition of ontological necessity takes the form:

(1a) f is ontologically necessary $\underset{\mathrm{D}}{=} f \wedge (N \vdash f)$

or (1b) $\underset{\mathrm{D}}{=} f \wedge \vdash (N \rightarrow f)$

or, briefly (1c) $\underset{\mathrm{D}}{=} \vdash N^f$

If one were to introduce the stronger notion of physical necessity one would have to replace the conjunction N by, say, $M \wedge N$ where M is a conjunction of physical principles. In a similar manner one defines

(2) f is logically possible $\underset{\mathrm{D}}{=} \neg(\vdash \neg f)$

and (3) f is ontologically possible $\underset{\mathrm{D}}{=} f \vee \neg(N \vdash \neg f)$[3]

The implicative necessity—or other modality—of a sentence can also be formulated as the applicative necessity of a predicate. In the Kantian ontology, for example, the ontological necessity of the second analogy can be expressed either by characterizing the sentence 'Every event is caused' as ontologically necessary or by characterizing the predicate 'being caused' as applicable with ontological necessity to any real particular to which the predicate 'being an event' is applicable. Yet either formulation conforms to our formal definitions and can be expressed in terms of the logical validity of sentences and of logical implications between sentences within the framework of the lower predicate calculus.

The defined modalities thus are, or are included in, the so-called modalities *de dicto*. They must be distinguished from the so-called modalities *de re* which cannot be expressed in the lower predicate calculus. It is sufficient to consider *de re* necessity, which expresses a necessary connexion—not between one sentence and another or between the applicability of one predicate and the applicability of another—but between a predicate and an individual *qua* individual. For example, to assert the *de re* necessity of 'Socrates is mortal' would be to assert that Socrates *qua* Socrates—and not, *e.g.*, *qua* human being or *qua* animal—is necessarily mortal.

It is by no means obvious how the distinction between an individual's necessary predicates (those which it necessarily possesses *qua* individual) and its other predicates can be implemented by a formal theory. One way of achieving this implies the assumption that individuals can be given names of which they remain the recognizable bearers "in all possible worlds". Theories of this kind have been adumbrated by Isaiah (LVI,5) who ascribes to God the power of conferring "an everlasting name which cannot be cut off". One such theory is a corner-stone of Leibniz's *Theodicée*. Others have been elaborated by contemporary modal logicians.[4] It may well be that the impression of a need for such theories arises from underestimating the power of the lower predicate calculus—and its metatheory—to cover a much wider spectrum of modalities than the protagonists of *de re* modalities would have us believe.

4. *Equivalence and substitutivity.*

The equivalence of two expressions in virtue of which one may be substituted for the other—*e.g.*, as leaving the rhythm of a poem or the force of an insult intact—depends on their function. In logic one is concerned with the co-reference of names, the co-implication of sentences, the co-application of predicates and lastly the co-designation of names on the one hand and predicates on the other. If one rejects the *de re* necessity of a thing's possessing a certain name, then a statement asserting the reference of a name to a thing or the co-reference of two names to it, say

(4) *a* coref *b*

is contingent. In the case of the co-implication of sentences one can distinguish between different modes of co-implication, namely logically necessary, ontologically necessary and contingent (where we again ignore the possibility of interpolating, say physical necessity between ontological necessity and contingency). Of the following statements of co-implication:

(5) $\vdash f \leftrightarrow g$, $\vdash_N f \leftrightarrow g$, $f \leftrightarrow g$

each unilaterially implies its successor.

To the different modes of co-implication between two sentences f and g there correspond analogous modes of co-application, which may be represented by, say

(6) $\vdash (\forall x) (F(x) \leftrightarrow G(x))$, $\vdash_N (\forall x) (F(x) \leftrightarrow G(x))$,
$(\forall x) ((F(x) \leftrightarrow G(x))$

In the case of co-designation a name, say, a and a predicate, say, $F(x)$ designate the same particular, the name by naming it, the predicate by applying to it and only it. Co-designation, which may be represented by, say,

(7) a codes $F(x)$

is always contingent because the statement that a name names a particular is contingent.

Since there can be no co-reference between two names unless both occur referentially it would be a mistake to deduce from the premises (a) John believes-that-Cicero-denounced-Catilina and (b) 'Tully' coref 'Cicero' the conclusion (c) John believes-that-Tully-denounced-Catilina. The mistake arises, as Brentano pointed out long ago, from confusing the direct or referential occurrence of a name with its oblique occurrence.

Just as there can be no co-reference of two names unless either occurs referentially—and hence no referential equivalence or intersubstitutivity of a referentially and a non-referentially occurring name—so there can be no co-implication of an implicatively and a non-implicatively occurring sentence; no co-application of an applicatively and a non-applicatively occurring predicate; and no co-designation between a predicate and a name if the predicate is used applicatively and the name non-referentially or the name referentially and the predicate non-applicatively. The rule might be briefly summarized by the slogan "No direct co-signification without direct signification" and justly be called Brentano's rule.

Because co-implication and co-application may be of different strength, the application of Brentano's rule must be combined with that of another rule which might be called the rule of Theophrastus. According to it the conclusion of a deductive inference has the modal strength of the weakest premiss—assuming, of course, that the premiss is essential, *i.e.*, cannot be dropped without affecting the validity of the inference. As has been noted, logical necessity is stronger than ontological necessity, which is stronger than contingency which in turn is stronger than logical possibility. The interpolation in this sequence of other modalities, such as physical necessity or ontological possibility presents no difficulty.[5]

Having exemplified the application of Brentano's rule in resolving a typical paradox which arises from a conflation of the direct and oblique mode of an expression's occurrence, we seem to be obliged to exemplify the application of Theophrastus' rule in resolving some characteristic paradoxes which arise from conflating modalities of different strength. Our first example is due to Kneale (*op. cit.* p. 611) who uses it in an attempt at discrediting the rule of Theophrastus: From (a) 'It is logically possible that the number of apostles is not smaller than 13' and (b) 'The number of apostles = 12', there seems to follow (c) 'It is logically possible that 12 is not smaller than 13' which is indeed 'ridiculous'. But the paradox disappears if in (b) the identity sign is properly interpreted and (b) replaced by (b') 'The class of apostles is contingently co-designative with the numeral "12" (*i.e.*, happens as a matter of contingent fact to have 12 members)'. The conclusion then has to be reformulated by (c') 'It is logically possible that a class which is contingently co-designative with the numeral "12" should not be smaller than 13' (that a class which as a matter of contingent fact has 12 members should have a number of members which is not smaller than 13).

Similar remarks apply to the apparent paradox that from the premisses (a) 'It is logically necessary that if there is life on the evening star, then there is life on the evening star' and (b) 'The evening star = the morning star' there follows (c) 'It is logically necessary that if there is life on the evening star, then there is life on the morning star'. However, since (b) must be interpreted as expressing the merely contingent co-application of 'evening star' and 'morning star' (c) must be replaced by (c') 'It is contingently true that if there is life on the evening star then there is life on the morning star'. The paradox arose once again from ignoring the different modal strengths of the premisses and, hence, the correct modal strength of the conclusion.

From co-reference, co-implication, co-application and co-designation, which are equivalences between linguistic expressions, one must distinguish the equivalences between temporally or otherwise distinct aspects of things, in virtue of which two different aspects of a kind of thing—such as a table or a person—are judged to be aspects of the same particular thing and as representing this thing and each other in certain contexts and for certain purposes, defined by law, social practices *etc.* Equivalences of this kind play an important rôle in the constitution and individuation of things, rather than in the designation of already constituted and individuated things, in the application of predicates to them and in making statements about them.[6]

Just as modal statements *de dicto* allow for the substitution of equivalent expressions if the rules of Brentano and Theophrastus are satisfied, so under the same conditions do they allow for existential quantification. Thus the logically necessary statement of the arithmetical theorem that $9 < 10$ implies that there exists an x such that the predicate $x < 10$ is with logical necessity applicable to it; and the contingent statement that the number of planets < 10 implies that there exists an x such that the predicate $x < 10$ is contingently applicable to it. In all such cases the applicability of the predicate has the same modality as the assertion of the sentence which has been subjected to existential quantification.

5. On the normative rectification of obliquely occurring expressions.

The oblique occurrence in a compound monadic predicate of of a name, a predicate or a sentence makes some distinctive, though indefinite, contribution to the meaning of the compound predicate. For although the oblique occurrence of an expression is associated with *some* idea of what it would be like if the expression had a direct occurrence, this idea—as has been noted earlier—may not even be internally consistent. (To deny this would be to deny, for example, that a scientist or mathematician who believed a certain theory to be true could not have believed the theory to be true, if it later turned out to be internally inconsistent.)

There are various ways of making the correspondence between obliquely and directly occurring expressions more definite by imposing standards of acceptability on the obliquely occurring expressions or, briefly, by rectifying them. Among the rectifications, which have been proposed, one can distinguish two main types, namely, logical rectifications, which impose purely logical requirements (expressible in terms of logical consequence and other metalogical notions of the lower predicate calculus); and ontological rectifications, which require conformity to certain supreme principles which, though non-logical, are regarded as necessary conditions of all acceptable ("meaningful", "coherent" etc.) thinking. Here it will be sufficient to exemplify both types of rectification very briefly by considering indirectly occurring sentences expressing beliefs.

One method of logically rectifying them consists in a stipulative definition of the correctness of a sentence expressing a belief. Consider the following:

(i) Columbus correctly believed $-f_1$ (that he discovered America).

(ii) Columbus incorrectly believed $-f_2$ (that he discovered India).

(iii) Cagliostro incorrectly believed $-f_3$ (that he discovered the elixir of eternal youth.)

If Columbus correctly believed $-f_1$, it must be the case that f_1 is true and that he believed at least some of the logical consequences of f_1. A strong, but rather unrealistic, definition of correct belief would require him to believe *all* logical consequences of f_1, so that—with obvious abbreviations—(i) can be formalized as

(ia) Columbus bel $-f_1. \wedge .$ Columbus bel-Cn $(f_1). \wedge .f_1.$

The analogous formalization of (ii) is

(iia) Columbus bel $-f_2. \wedge . \neg$ (Columbus bel-Cn $(f_2). \wedge .f_2).$

If we assume that to the obliquely occurring sentence $-f_3$ there corresponds no directly occurring sentence and if we indicate this assumption by adding the superscript zero to it, then (iii) can be formalized as

(iiia) Cagliostro bel $-f_3^0$.

One could, without going beyond the extended lower predicate calculus, also formalize various weaker notions of a sentence expressing a correct belief, *e.g.*, by requiring that Columbus did not believe the negation of any logical consequence of f_1.

All these stipulative definitions presuppose that whereas simple and compound predicates are syntacticaly distinct, semantically they are both alike interpreted as monadic predicates which are applicable to real particulars. (Thus the set determined by, *e.g.*, 'x believes $-f_3$' is a proper subset of the set determined by 'x is human'.) It is, moreover, worth emphasizing that the obliquely occurring $-f_1$, $-f_2$, $-f_3$ and any other obliquely occurring sentence is *not* a meaningless expression, a true or a false sentence, a sentence without a truth-value or a sentence with a truth-value other than truth or falsehood. It is none of these, but a syncategorematic part of a compound monadic predicate. Similar remarks apply to logical rectifications which are global in that they concern the whole system of the sentences expressing a person's beliefs, *e.g.*, the requirement that this system be internally consistent. Further examples of actually adopted, merely proposed or as yet only conceivable, logical rectifications could be easily produced.

It is even more obvious that there is a great variety of ontological rectifications since every metaphysical doctrine proposes some overriding constraints on the system of a person's beliefs. A recently revived example of such a metaphysical doctrine implies the assumption of *de re* modalities, expressing necessary connexions between individuals *qua* individuals and some of their predicates and the assumption of "rigid names", which allow the identification of individuals in different possible worlds. It is sometimes argued[7] that the possibility and, indeed, the ontological necessity of such transmundane identification follows from the fact that, say, 'I did not miss this morning's lecture, but I might have' and 'I did not miss this morning's lecture, but there is a possible world in which I did' are full paraphrases of each other. Yet, once a person is identified in the actual world and the fact established that he did not miss this morning's lecture, one can—without assuming *de re* necessities about him and without assuming his transmundane identifiability—assert that the false statement to the effect that he missed the lecture is logically possible, ontologically possible or possible with respect to still more specific assumptions (compare the definitions 1-3 in §3).

It is not a task of this essay to argue either for the rectification of indirectly occurring expressions or for leaving the correspondence between indirectly and directly occurring expressions in its naturally indefinite state. Nor is it among its tasks to argue for or against any particular kind of rectification. However, the analysis of the correspondence between directly and obliquely occurring expressions would be incomplete if it did not exhibit the difference between unrectified and rectified correspondence, between logical and ontological rectification and if it did not indicate different—including mutually exclusive—versions of either.

NOTES

[1] Among them is this essay, which grew out of work with R. M. Chisholm on an edition of some of Brentano's posthumous papers. *See* F. Brentano, *Philosophische Untersuchungen zu Raum, Zeit und Kontinuum* (Hamburg, 1976).

[2] For details see *Categorial Frameworks* (Oxford 1970 and 1974), the ontological pluralism of which is however not shared by Brentano.

[3] For details see my "Material Necessity" in *Kant-Studien* (vol. 64, No. 4, 1973).

[4] See esp. S. Kripke "Naming and Necessity" in *Semantics of Natural Languages* ed. by G. Harman and D. Davidson (Dordrecht, 1971).

[5] See W. and M. Kneale, *The Development of Logic* (Oxford 1962) p. 102, where a Latin version of the rule is given as *Sectetur partem conclusio deteriorem*.

[6] See *e.g.*, my "On the Identification of Agents" in *Philosophia* vol. 5 (No. 1-2) 1975.

[7] *E.g.* by Linsky, *Reference, Essentialism and Modality* (ed. L. Linsky, Oxford 1971) p. 100.

XI*—FEELING, THINKING, KNOWING

by Louis Arnaud Reid

I

In an article on Jung,[1] James Hillman writes that at the end of
the century "there were no clear distinctions among the various components of the mind which had been grouped, or discarded, in that bag called 'the affective faculty'. From the time
of the Enlightenment in Germany, the soul was divided into
three parts: thinking, willing and feeling. Fundamentally,
this third region of the psyche, like Plato's third class of men,
was inferior." Furthermore, this bag of feelings was always in
opposition to thinking, or, as Moses Mendelssohn said: "We
no longer feel as soon as we think". Hillman adds that the
opposition between thinking and feeling is still found in the
scientistic psychology of head without heart, and the romantic
psychology of heart without head.

'We no longer feel as soon as we think'. This might be sup-
plemented by other over-simple generalisations: 'As soon as
we think we make statements': 'To claim to know anything
entails (*inter alia*) being able to state it clearly': 'Knowledge
is expressed in the form "that-*p*"; what cannot be so expressed
is not knowledge'.

These are, doubtless, oversimplified—though the paradigm
'that-*p*' is normally taken for granted in epistemological discussions: moreover, this is an assumption which has domi-
nated western thought. On the other hand philosophers and
plain men constantly give cognitive *nuances* to feeling-words
and ideas, suggesting 'feelings' and 'intuitions' which have
something of a cognitive-claiming character. We all at times
speak of cognitive 'feelings' about moral and humanitarian
matters, about people, works of art, political decisions. Ryle
listed different uses of the word 'feeling', some of which are
cognitive-claiming.[1a] Jung uses 'feeling' in various cognitive

---

ways, but very pragmatically and often inconsistently. 'Feeling' is used cognitively by philosophers—existentialists, pheno-menologists . . . by James, Bradley, Alexander, Whitehead, MacMurray, Langer . . . by Gestalt psychologists—in a large variety of ways. In the 'twenties (and more recently)[2] I argued for feeling as cognitive. Very much the same line was taken in the 'fifties about 'emotion'—often too easily run together with feeling, as if the two were identical. There was a sort of redis-covery of the cognitive element intrinsic to emotion—by Bedford, J. R. Jones, Kenny, Peters, Mace . . . 'Emotions', it was argued, cannot be understood merely in terms of internal ongoings, but are integral with cognition and behaviour rele-vant to the situations in which they arise. Peters' term 'ap-praisal' (cognitive appraisal) of the situation, sums up the best of it. (It is substantially the same as what I was trying to say, but of feeling, in the 'twenties.)

Although 'feeling' has been so variously used, and there is a large literature of emotion, the dominance of the 'that-p' concept of knowledge has been so powerful and sustained that it has tended to force the reduction of other sorts of knowing to its own pattern. This is particularly questionable in claims to know *values*—moral, personal, aesthetic—where, though knowledge-that may have its important place, it is not every-thing. Feeling there at least seems to have an essential cogni-tive part to play. I can do no more than suggest now that neglect of that is not only detrimental in philosophy itself, but has serious moral, social and educational consequences as well. I believe the time is more than ripe for a fresh look at the rela-tions between feeling and knowing.

II

The treatment of feeling by many 'straight' psychologists earlier in the century was thin. (And in some later textbooks, it is perhaps not surprising that writers self-blinded by wholly behaviouristic approaches, have not even mentioned 'feeling' in their indexes!) Earlier, feeling was mainly regarded as hedonic tone—sometimes as the tone of emotion—with a range from the (positively) pleasurable to the (negatively) unplea-surable. Whether there could be 'neutral' feeling in between, was a matter of controversy. Feeling was sharply distinguished from the character of the concrete mental states of which it was the character or quality. And it was said to be intransitive, and definitely non-cognitive. Feeling (some held) does not even 'know' facts of inner occurrences: feeling is 'the way you feel'.[3]

I remarked on the habit of running the words 'feeling' and 'emotion' together, as though distinctions don't matter here. They do. But since this paper is on feeling, not emotion, I cannot say anything adequate now about emotion and its relation to and distinction from feeling. I can only affirm, without supporting argument, (1) that actual emotions are largely episodic, whilst feeling, I shall suggest, is underlyingly present through conscious life: most of the time when we feel we are not having emotional feelings at all. (2) Emotional feelings occur when there is an 'appraisal' by the psychophysical organism *as a whole* (not 'cognitively' only, but cognitively-conatively-affectively-organically), of any situation which we are in, and in which, because of this total appraisal, we are stirred up, excited, *etc.*, in countlessly different ways, in a marked degree —a degree not precisely definable. And there, for now, I must leave 'emotion'. It is just possible that the rest of the paper may, indirectly, show my statement to be less bald than, standing by itself, it must appear to be.

III

Because there is no generally accepted usage of the word 'feeling' (except for the earlier, inadequate uses), I shall start with a clean slate and stipulate my own—bearing in mind that stipulative uses can be justified if they can clarify and illuminate. I have hinted at the seriously detrimental effects of the division between feeling and other aspects of active mind. If we can reconceive feeling in its setting in the whole economy of the psychophysical organism in living transaction with a world which is independent of it, and recognise feeling as in organic relation with everything else, I believe that such reconception will throw light in various ways on knowledge and understanding.

'Feeling' is indefinable, except by so-called 'ostensive'

definition: it can be *displayed* in examples of its different manifestations. According to Susanne Langer, feeling, the mark of mentality, emerges at a certain stage of evolution, when a "neurophysiological process can be said to 'break through to feeling' ".[4] Like—but it is of course only an analogy —the incandescence of a piece of iron at a high temperature, feeling is living process becoming aware of itself.[5]

At this primitive stage, feeling just seems to happen, and this consciousness, the emergence of the primitively psychological from the irritable physiological, is a mystery no one yet has begun to understand. But two things have to be kept in mind: (1) the *inseparability* of organic processes from the organism's feeling of it, the fact that, as Langer puts it, the "being felt is a phase of the process itself".[6] On the other hand (2) there is the *conceptual distinction* between the feeling, which is (if primitively) mental, and the organic processes which are felt.

Even at this stage, the notion of feeling as living process becoming aware of itself has a dimly cognitive flavour, even if the cognition is, so far, of a rudimentary kind. Feeling, on one side of it, is feeling-of, and on the other side, it has a content—at this low level, sensation-content. There is never just feeling: feeling awareness could not be without being feeling of something. At the human level, the denial by earlier psychologists (*e.g.*, Woodworth) that feeling is cognitively transitive, was wrong. We can't experience the feeling of sensations of toothache or tiredness without, indivisibly, feeling toothache or tiredness (though we need not be naming them). Yet granting this, it is important to keep the conceptual distinction between feel*ing*, or immediate experien*cing*, and the *content* of that feeling. Feeling is the most immediate, inward and private thing we know, and it is the inner side of conscious experience in the widest and most usually accepted sense of that term, conscious experience which in human beings includes action of various kinds, thinking, imagining, having moral and aesthetic experiences, maybe religious ones, coming to know and coming to terms with the external world, ourselves and other people . . . Feeling is the immediate experience of indwelling in that conscious life in its most inclusive sense. To symbolise the conceptual distinction between feeling and its content—without which discussion can be muddled—I shall sometimes use 'IE' for the participles denoting the process or event of feeling or immediate experiencing, and 'C' to stand for content of feeling. Feeling as it actually occurs is always IE(C).

I suggested above that feeling is 'underlyingly' present throughout conscious life. Usually it is tacit (Polanyi's word) not focal. We are, of course, often consciously aware of feeling, and under a very wide range of conditions, usually when hedonic tone (positive or negative) is marked, and when we say there is 'affect'. By affect I mean here not just hedonic tone, but the markedly toned feeling of the whole complex which is felt (IE)C. This toned feeling of the whole complex has what may be called 'quality', strictly speaking unnameable because each complex felt is a particular, different from every other; and the quality of feeling or affect shares in this particularity.

But apart from very definite affect of which we are consciously aware, there can be underlying affect which is less strong or definite, as in a general mood; and this can colour the rest of conscious experience. We are depressed, or sad, or elated, or happy . . . The 'spectacles' are dark or rose coloured . . . Then there are many occasions when there is no noticeable affect at all, and we are not consciously aware of feeling as such. But even then, there can be said to be underlying feeling. Lacing one's shoes, putting out the milk bottles or the cat, as routine activities, normally have no affect worth mentioning. But if we retrospect, we can recognise the feeling of being on the inside of the experience, and recognise that if it were not for the underlying intuitive feeling-awareness, we could not have had the focal experience of carrying out these activities.

IV

It is clear (and no one disputes) that feeling is on one side very private and subjective, and that this has often been identified with hedonic tone. But here we are interested in the relation of feeling to the cognitive functions of mind. When, however, the words 'cognition' and 'cognitive' are used, it will be necessary for the purposes of this particular discussion to remember several things. (1) The term 'cognition' must be taken in a very open way and given a wide range of application. 'Cognition' must not be confined here to the 'that-p' form, to beliefs expressed in clear propositional statements, rationally checked for their truth in prescribed (and proscribed) ways. This is one main sort of knowledge, but one only. I want to include also direct experience-knowledge, acquaintance-knowledge (not in Russell's restricted sense), as well as knowing-that, *connaître* and *kennen* as well as *savoir* and *wissen*. (2) I am assuming that there are degrees of knowing, and error and truth mixed. *Mis*apprehension is cognitive, though erroneous, and 'truth' a regulative ideal of cognition. (3) I am talking now of *claims* to knowledge. Validation, testing, 'proof' of knowledge-claims also of course need consideration. I shall have a word to say on this at the end.

Negatively, emphasis on the private and subjective aspect of feeling has led to its isolation from the rest of active knowing mind. In the objective stress on fields of propositional knowing such as mathematics and the sciences, it is easy to overlook feeling as having any part to play in such knowledge. On the other hand everyone knows that the active truth-seeking mind has its 'passion for truth'. Again, feeling can be a pioneer for knowledge-to-come; tentative hypotheses are often 'felt' before they are explicitly formulated; there are 'feelings-after', hunches, and so on. Emotions, of course, are deeply suspect. Even the passion for truth can be distorted into bias. This is fair enough, and it is true that what T. H. Huxley called the 'clear cold logic engine of the mind' has a dominant part to play in some kinds of propositional knowledge. The main aim of the business is to get as near to impersonal and objective truth as possible. We do attach proper names to great discoveries—Newton, Darwin, Einstein, Planck . . . But it is, in the end, the truths that matter and not the fact that their discoverers had significant cognitive-feeling-experiences about them, or that they may have had to suppress their feelings and desires. This, at any rate, would be a prevailing view among many scientists. I do not say all, or always. And I am certainly not saying that the total human *value* of the life of science can be summed up by saying that it is productive of important propositional truths. But in doing science the truths can be, with justification, distinguished, even separated, from the value experiences.

It is when we come to values, and to our claims to know them, that the importance of feeling, its relation to knowing, and its function in the process of knowing, begins to stand out most clearly. On the one hand, we cannot know values at all without, at some stage (not all the time), feeling them. On the other hand we cannot justify our judgments of value without various detachedly cognitive processes of thought and action. Feeling and active thinking and doing are all in organic relation to each other in a way here which is much more clearly marked than when we are thinking, relatively impersonally, about value-free matters of fact, about what 'is the case'. There, the main function of feeling in relation to the search for factual knowledge might be called an *auxiliary* one: here, as I am suggesting, feeling is intrinsic at some stage to the knowing, or organically related to it. In both cases we require the transitiveness, the self-transcendence, of cognition apprehending what is independent of the apprehending mind. But in knowing values, I am saying, it is different: in moral, or aesthetic, knowledge the feeling of the value of what we know is inseparable from and continuous with the self-transitive knowing of it. In cognitive experience of value, feeling is part of the knowing, and colours what is known. Aesthetically, in poet's mood, the

> . . . daisies pied and violets blue
> And lady smocks all silver-white
> And cuckoo-buds of yellow hue
> *Do paint the meadows with delight* . . .

Intrinsic values can be thought of generically as what we are interested in, care about, desire, feel-for (or feel-against). Value is a bipolar concept: there is a psychophysical pole, a *pro* or *con* approach, and an objective pole. This is obviously a minimal account: value situations in the most general sense are situations in which we feel-about-something, and the 'value' is what we feel-about. We have to feel: sometimes feeling leads is to values of lasting and enlarging importance; sometimes they turn out to be spurious, false. The *rationale* of different sorts of value judgments is clearly of paramount importance.

V

Leaving all this for the moment, I want to return to the 'that-*p*' concept of knowledge, in order to consider how it affects the very possibility of a catholic or inclusive account of knowledge. I am assuming the familiar current theory of propositional knowledge-that which takes the form: 'I am sure about (or believe) *p*: it is true (or 'the case'); and I have a right (or good reasons) to be sure'.

Such a statement is on its own showing a self-restricted account in that it applies to the propositional *genre* only. But if we go further, and take it as 'the' paradigm of knowledge, the way is automatically closed to consideration of other kinds of knowledge-claims, already mentioned. Apart from knowing-how, which Ryle expounded, there is the knowledge 'with the direct object', acquaintance-knowledge of persons and things, in general, experience-knowledge of fact or value. These cannot be exhaustively explained in terms of propositional knowledge-that, knowledge-about.

Knowledge of *fact* cannot so be exhaustively explained. There is, always, the cognising of a *given* element. Take a borderline example. Sitting waiting in my stationary car, I suddenly feel a sharp impact on my back. There is an instant of felt sensational experiencing (IE) of what we can subsequently describe in words as 'impact-of-car-hitting-my-car-from-behind' (IE)C. But for the first instant, there are no words. Words start when I exclaim 'What's that!' Then comes the diagnosis. But the very question 'What's that?' (subtly transformed from an exclamation to a question) presupposes experience-'knowledge' of a *that* about which the question is asked.

Usually knowledge-about (expressible in statements) and experience-knowledge overlap, or coincide, though they are still distinguishable. If the word 'intuition' be taken here to mean apprehension of a field as a whole, and I have (say) an immediate intuition (experience-knowledge) of an area of my Study, my intuition has content, of which it can be said that, on the one hand, I know it as simply given in the experience of perception now, without words (and I know 'about' it in *that* sense). On the other hand, I know its content as a precipitate of knowledge-that, acquired, partly through language, accumulated and assimilated from the past. I know-that there are books, chairs, desks, *etc* . . . But these have their place in the field of my total intuition which in itself is not expressible in propositional language. As before, knowledge-about as expressed in words, presupposes wordless non-propositional experience-knowledge, is dependent on it.

It is true that when we are focally interested in propositional knowledge-about particular facts, experience-knowledge falls into the background: this is true in abstract thinking, perhaps outstandingly so in the focus on symbolic meaning in pure mathematics. When, on the other hand, we turn to knowledge of *values* (where feeling as cognitive plays an essential part), experience-knowledge can be of central importance. I will take an example from aesthetic value now, and return to it later.

Suppose, in the Tate, I am struck, almost stunned, by the complex magnificence of a huge Turner. Here, obviously, I could say, and go on saying, all sorts of things about it—its colours, patterns, composition, its space . . . And often, in criticism, description and analysis play an important part in helping our appreciation. But these are all subsidiary to, parasitic upon, something else, the direct wordless intuition of the picture as a whole. It would be shocking nonsense to suggest that all the most excellent statements about the picture, however many, could possibly, in themselves, and without being assimilated into something different—the intuition of the picture—add up to aesthetic knowledge. There is a positive content in experience-knowledge of art which cannot be propositionally 'said' at all. And this is central.[7] The same sort of thing can be said of knowledge of persons.

Since the 'that-*p*', 'knowledge-about' model, with its focus on the truth of statements, will not do for aesthetic and other kinds of knowing, it is worth considering whether a sort of 'Copernican' revolution in the theory of the relation of knowing to truth may not open the way to a more catholic view of knowledge.

I said earlier, of attempts to get as near as possible to

impersonal and objective truth (*e.g.*, in science) that subjective processes of coming to know—the experiences of the feeling, knowing minds who propose and in some degree possess the knowledge—tend to be forgotten and to fall into the background. A habit develops of thinking of systems of true propositions as though they existed on their own, as though knowledge could, almost, be defined in terms of the truth of independent-standing propositions. I say 'almost', because in the definition, 'belief' or 'being sure' are mentioned. Yet the living mind which searches after knowledge, falls into the shadowy background and propositional truth seems to assume dazzling, blinding importance. One kind of truth, propositional truth, is like the sun, the knowing mind a dark planet, or, if illuminated, deriving its light as knowing from the impersonal source, its only, single sun.

But suppose we get away from the notion of truth—after all never satisfactorily defined—as belonging to propositions. Suppose we think instead of the searching mind as the active centre (a very uncertain 'sun'!) from which the very possibility of all cognitive illumination emanates, and think of tentative truth-claims, perhaps of many kinds, as functions of the seeking mind working on its job, trying to do it well, and in some degree, even if small, succeeding.[8] Or more widely, of truth and other sorts of validity as a quality of the measure of the success of the whole psychophysical organism as it tries, cognitively and in other ways, to come to terms with itself and with the world it inhabits. This view cannot be developed now: but however vague it sounds, it at least does not submit knowing and knowledge to the domination of one— never defined—propositional model of truth. And positively, it will be possible then to consider openly other kinds of cognitive claims of the exploring psychophysical organism— feeling, active, creative, as well as knowing. Having removed a barrier, it will then be easier to consider these other ways mentioned—the tentative seeking to know persons, moral good, aesthetic value.[9] And it will be easier to see how feeling functions as an organic part of the cognising, as it does not so function in more detached and impersonal knowing. All this can, of course, merely be suggested. And questions of attempted justification of the claims, I shall mention only very briefly at the end, referring particularly to aesthetic knowing.

VI

In knowing persons, we have, in addition to learning many things *about* them as we go along, to feel with, and often for, them in direct encounter. What I meet when I encounter another person is not just a cluster of descriptive predicates nor just a 'case' with certain classifiable characteristics. I meet a person now, face to face, and it is for this individual (individual not instance) for whom I have to have empathy and sympathy, manifestations of cognitive feeling. If there is absence of cognitive feeling, there is a lack of something in the knowing. And here I am not thinking of what is called 'emotional involvement' with the other person, but of a self-transcending cognitive effort in which cognitive feeling plays an indispensable part.

Moral knowing has, of course, been enormously written over (as has knowing of other persons). Here I am concerned chiefly with knowledge of basic principles of good—rather than with rules of right-doing—and with knowing good directly and intuitively.

There has to be a point somewhere in the knowing of the morally good when we cognitively *feel* it as good. An example is the direct intuitive apprehension of *caritas*, care for the good of others; sometimes it is compassion. To feel *caritas* as good we have to know it directly in a bit of actual immediate experience, in some personal situation. Knowing and feeling here are inseparable.

I am saying that (at some stage) feeling plays an essential part in the knowledge of a person and in the knowledge of an intrinsic moral value like *caritas*. I am *not* saying that feeling alone—perhaps a moment of felt insight—can apprehend *caritas* clearly in its fullness; its existential meaning can be known more fully only by knowing it in its operation in the total complex of human living which *caritas* can infuse and transform. And this knowledge and understanding demands all the powers of knowing, critical thinking, active feeling mind, working together. The same is true of the knowledge of other moral values—integrity, justice . . .

To put it more generally: the feeling being discussed now obviously is not like what had to be mentioned earlier, the feeling of a bodily, sensational experience of, say, toothache, or having a hot bath. (Such feeling is recognisably cognitive, but in a weak and uninteresting sense.) It is not even just a warm immediately felt mental or spiritual appreciation of some shining manifestation of *caritas* or integrity—however apposite on the occasion that may be. What is before us now is feeling entering as an element into some of the highest and most human enterprises—personal, moral, and, as we shall see, aesthetic. It is feeling as a necessary part of apprehending important and complex human values. Feeling, I am suggesting, can feed, nourish, enlarge and enrich the content of that thinking. This in turn can, retroactively, affect the concrete realisation of the values. The concern is with feeling, thinking, acting—distinguishable of course, but thought of now not in abstracted separation from one another, but as related, as interacting in the way that only the parts of an organism (here the psychophysical organism) can interact with one another. They contribute to each other, modify each other and the whole, so that thinking, feeling, knowing, and action, working together, can become a function of the whole organism. In the space left, I can only hint at how this happens in art. (It is developed more fully in my *Meaning in the Arts.*)

The phenomenological story of the place of feeling in the arts is an endless one. Not only are there many forms of art, each with special characteristics, but each work is an individual; and feeling, as concrete, will be individual too. But that the knowing of any individual work or art involves cognitive aesthetic feeling, cannot I think reasonably be in doubt. The knowledge and understanding of a poem or a picture or a piece of music requires the use of several modes of understanding; but what unites them all into relevance is the cognitive feeling of and for the individual work as a complex whole and as it is presented. To say this is not to retreat into subjectivity, as if the feeling were merely a private ongoing within the mind-and-body: that would be the watertight faculty-view all over again. If the feeling is regarded as sharing in the self-transcending activities of the active cognitive organism, then it fulfils a function which they alone could not achieve.

Of course the embodied mind, as active and knowing, has

to divide up things in order to deal with them: we can (more or less) only do one thing at a time, and can only give focal attention to this or that abstracted aspect of a cognised situation at any one moment. But feeling, with its inner continuity and flowing changes of toned-quality as the content of feeling changes, is the tacit underlying influence. For example, a performing musician has much 'cognitive' work to do in studying his score; musical analysis and synthesis is one part of learning music. He has to attend, too, his senses alive and active, to the medium of the music, and to muscular and many other skills involved in performance. Though there is constant overlapping, it would be fair to say that for most accomplished musicians (it may be different in geniuses like Mozart) these processes take time, and have (more or less) to be done at different times, in a relatively slow learning process. But though these *seriatim* processes are necessary, they also have to be 'forgotten' as far as the focal attention of the mind is concerned, and the effects of all of them have to be gathered into the fluid, single, concentrated relevant cognitive *feeling* for the actual music as a complex unity. Musical knowledge in action is felt knowledge in action. Until this happens there can be correctness, technique, conscientiousness, but not musical vitality. It is the vitality of knowing here, the living embodiment of felt knowledge in the psychophysical organism of the musical performer, and the aesthetic embodiment of it in the performed music, which is the crux of it all.

And, perhaps, a further point can be made. Feeling, here affect, is not only a uniting cognitive awareness of the living whole. It is a reinforcement of vitality. Silvan S. Tomkins,[10] writing of emotion as motivating power, and speaking of instinctive drives, argues that drives without affect are not in themselves sufficient to fulfil their functions. Two of his examples are anoxic deprivation and sexual tumescence. In gasping, choking, drowning, it is not simply the imperious demand for oxygen which drives, but also the rapidly mounting panic. Pilots who refused to wear oxygen masks at 30,000 ft. suffered a more gradual anoxic deprivation, which resulted not in panic, but euphoria. Some met death with a smile on their lips. "It was the affect of enjoyment which the more slowly developing signal recruited." And in sex, tumescence, product of the sexual drive, is not in itself enough; it requires the excitement of the whole man, not merely his sexual organ. I suggest that these, very different, examples could be taken as reinforcing the claim that feeling, in the aesthetic situation, is an 'amplifier',

On the side of artistic creation, too, feeling has an important part to play. In artistic creation there is a stage in which something like what Piaget calls 'syncretistic thinking' takes place. Anton Ehrenzweig, concerned with art, speaks of the contrast between our highly differentiated thought and 'undifferentiated' thinking. He writes: [11] "the deeper we penetrate into low level imagery and fantasy the more the single track divides and branches into unlimited directions so that in the end its structure appears chaotic. The creative thinker is capable of alternating between differentiated and undifferentiated modes of thinking, harnessing them together to give him service for solving very definite tasks. The uncreative psychotic succumbs to the tensions between conscious (differentiated) and unconscious (undifferentiated) modes of mental functioning. As he cannot integrate their divergent functions, true chaos ensues." Without digressing on this interesting remark about the psychotic or begging any questions about the unconscious, we can apply another word, 'dedifferentiated', which Ehrenzweig also uses in discussing the creative thinker. I think the actual word, though better than 'undifferentiated', is less than perfect. For if we consider what happens within the margins of the artist's *conscious* experience, there can never be a complete escape from the differentiations which with the aid of language we have learned to make from babyhood on. In other words, in conscious life, even to its margins, there can never be complete *de*-differentiation. (I am not denying what may happen in the 'unconscious' or through its influence; here and now it is simply not being discussed.) I think a better word is 'dediscursive'.

And that this kind of thinking and feeling does occur in the process of artistic creation, there is no doubt. The processes of artistic creation vary enormously with different artists, and are not well understood; and there are no rules. But in (say) the composing of poetry, there can be a time when the poet is relaxed from the focal tensions of ordinary thinking or logical rules. He lets himself sink into what can best be called a feeling state, in which floating images, snatches or strings of words, enter his mind and are received semi-passively, without critical scrutiny, seeming to form themselves as they 'will' into patterns which he accepts without trying, at that moment, to make sense of them. In terms of everyday thinking they may be 'nonsense'. The poet at this stage is in a child-like—but not a childish—receptive mood. He accepts the images and words, in a sense attends to them and in a queer way can enjoy them. He may be able to retain them in memory for later poetic use, or he may scribble, not caring whether they are 'nonsense' or not: perhaps he enjoys it all in a kind of ecstasy which is difficult to describe to anyone who does not know it directly, and which to commonsense may seem quite mad. But later, the poem may come.

The story of this artists' madness must be as old as history. Socrates speaks of the poets in this way, poking gentle fun at them. As usual, Shakespeare puts it better than anyone:

"The poet's eye, in a fine frenzy rolling
  Doth glance from heaven to earth, from earth to heaven
  And as imagination bodies forth
  The forms of things unknown, the poet's pen
  Turns them to shapes and gives to airy nothing
  A local habitation and a name."

Painters know it too in their own ways. The ordinary laws of *Gestalt* are relaxed; spaces between solid objects become positive shapes, sky is no longer background to landscape but integral with it; composition is sometimes like automatic writing. And in the coming together into an artifact, feeling for the whole, alike in poetry and painting and other arts, dominates the forming and direction of the parts. At the receiving end of art, again, we have to allow global cognitive feeling to have its way. Through cognitive, but dediscursive, feeling we become able to grasp new structures, new values, new aesthetic meaning so completely embodied in its formed medium that it cannot be 'said' in any other way, and certainly not said in ordinary discursive language.

VII

The discussion in this paper has been mainly of cognitive claims arising out of direct value-experiences in which feeling plays an essential part. These cognitive claims inevitably issue, at some stage, in value-judgments which take the form of propositional statements claiming, at least tentatively, to be true. But claims are one thing; the validation of them, another. The validation of judgments of value—ethical, and here particularly aesthetic—is a highly complex and controversial problem, on which there has been a large amount of writing. In aesthetics, it is much tied up with the claims of works of art to be individual and unique. As it is impossible here to say anything philosophically significant on this question, I must—with art in mind—content myself with a mere statement of belief.

I believe there *can* be validation of judgments about art. There are no knock-down arguments or proofs. But 'arguments' of a sort, and the giving of 'reasons' or 'grounds', there can be. In attempted justification of aesthetic judgments about art, the form of thinking is different in some essential respects from argument and reasoning in other fields. But there is no doubt that there can be reasonable discussion between people of perceptive aesthetic experience. And though there will always be, and very properly, disagreements and disputes about aesthetic 'taste' ('no disputing about tastes' is false here), enlightened discourse among enlightened people, who combine assertion with listening and learning, can modify and correct partial views and improve aesthetic understanding, moving through more liberally grounded opinion nearer to 'knowledge'. And some things we can safely be said to *know*—for example that Shakespeare is a better poet than McGonagall. But I don't think the fact that even McGonagall 'knew' it is much evidence!

VIII

In conclusion: I have used 'knowing', 'knowledge', 'cognition' in a wide, and on some views a loose sense. As far as the propositional form goes, this is no worse than Plato's ranging about from *Eikasia* and *Pistis* to *Dianoia* and *Epistēmē* or *Noēsis*. At the bottom end, crazy beliefs, conjectures, opinions are not 'knowledge' in the sense of *Dianoia* or the (ideal) *Noēsis*. But they are all, in our wide sense, 'cognitive'. And if direct 'experience-knowledge' is postulated as being cognitive, its range is equally wide, from worm-like (cognitive) feeling, or vague, scarcely differentiated human feelings of 'something there', right up to the developed and educated direct insights into (say) moral goodness or the complex aesthetic quality of works of art—these being nourished and illuminated by reflective thinking assimilated into the insights. The contextual meanings of Plato's *Noēsis* or Spinoza's *Scientia Intuitiva* of course make these words inapplicable here. But the profound insight into a work of art has something of the supposed directness of *Noēsis*. If, on the other hand we go on just assuming what is etymologically, epistemologically, psychologically (and occasionally even clinically) in effect a schizoid division of thinking and knowing from feeling, these insights will be incomprehensible. And we shall go on suffering from the many damaging effects—not only in philosophy but in education and elsewhere—of the denial of human wholeness.

NOTES

[1] In Chapter 8 of Magda B. Arnold (ed) *Feelings and Emotions* (Academic Press, New York and London, 1970).

[1a] "Feelings", in Elton (ed) *Aesthetics and Language*, Blackwell, 1954.

[2] In *Knowledge and Truth* (Macmillan, 1923): "Instinct, Emotion and the Higher Life" (*British Journal of Psychology*, 1923): "Towards Realistic Psychology" (*Journal of Philosophy*, 1924): "Immediate Experience, Its Nature and Content" (*Mind*, 1931): "Feeling and Understanding", *in Aesthetic Concepts and Education* (Ed. R. A. Smith, Illinois, 1970).

[3] Robert S. Woodworth: *Psychology; A Study of Mental Life*, 18th ed. (London, Methuen, 1946), p. 405.

[4] Susanne K. Langer: *Mind: an Essay on Human Feeling* (Johns Hopkins Press, 1967) Vol. 1, p. 9.

[5] *Ibid.*, p. 21.

[6] *Ibid.*

[7] Professor P. H. Hirst, in "Literature and the Fine Arts as a Unique form of Knowledge" (*Cambridge Journal of Education*. Vol. 3 No. 3), argues that works of art are a special kind of propositional statement. In the same *Journal* (Vol. 4, No. 3) in an article, I have tried to refute this view.

[8] I first suggested this idea in a rudimentary way in *Knowledge and Truth* (*sup.* 1923), Chapter VII (esp. 199 *sqq.*) with a tentative concluding chapter on "Non-propositional Truth".

⁹ This last is developed more fully in my "Feeling and Aesthetic Knowing" in Ralph A. Smith (Ed.) *Journal of Aesthetic Education*: Double Bicentennial Issue: July-October 1976.

¹⁰ In Chapter 6 of Magda B. Arnold (ed.), *op. cit.*, "Affect as the Primary Motivational System", pp. 101 *sq*.

¹¹ *The Hidden Order of Art* (Paladin, 1970): pp. 14-15.

XII*—INSINCERITY AND COMMANDS

by Jane Heal

In this paper I want to consider some similarities and contrasts between assertion (the speech act typically performed when an indicative sentence is uttered) and command (the speech act typically performed when an imperative sentence is uttered). In particular I shall ask whether a command can be insincere in the same sort of way that an assertion can be. The starting point for discussion will be a variety of unusual speech acts which might be proposed as examples of insincere command; but I hope by discussing these to throw light on some broader issues. In what follows I use the word "command" to cover all varieties of imperatival speech acts: orders, requests, instructions, pleas, *etc.*

In considering varieties of sentence and the actions we do with them it would be satisfying to discern a general pattern common to all fundamental sorts of speech act and to trace the differences between the varieties to differences in the items which form the pattern. So, to take a very simple example, if we accept something like H. P. Grice's theory about language we can set up an elegantly symmetrical description of assertions and commands: an assertion is an attempt to get a hearer to acquire a certain belief *via* revelation of the speaker's intention that he should acquire that belief while a command is an attempt to get the hearer to acquire a certain intention *via* revelation of the intention that he should acquire that intention.[1] It indeed seems plausible that assertion is in some way closely linked with belief while command has a link with intention. But is it right to think that the link is of exactly the same shape in the two cases? Consideration of insincerity may help us with this question. If the structure of the two speech acts is the same we would expect to find the same kinds of deviations from the normal pattern possible in both cases. So, given the plausible assumption that insincerity is a structural feature of some

---

* Meeting of the Aristotelian Society at 5/7, Tavistock Place, London, W.C.1, on Monday 21st March 1977, at 7.30 p.m.

sort, failure to discover a convincing specimen of insincere command suggests a difference in structure between assertion and command.

The *Oxford English Dictionary* account of "insincere" runs, in part, as follows:

> Assuming a false guise in speech or conduct: dissembling; disingenuous; said of persons and their actions or behaviour.

If intentional deception were the necessary and sufficient condition for insincerity there would be no problem in finding insincere commands. There are certainly commands by the utterance of which the speaker intends to mislead the hearer in some respect. But mere intention to deceive is not a sufficient condition for insincerity. Suppose I hear a burglar and, to convince him that I am asleep and no threat to him, I emit a snore or two. Do I snore insincerely? A snore, faked or genuine, does not seem to be the kind of thing which can be sincere or insincere. Even when we consider a kind of action where the question of sincerity does arise, for example assertion, not any kind of intended deception is sufficient to render it insincere. If I give less information than I might in answer to a question, thus deliberately suggesting that I know less than I do, my *assertion* is not *ipso facto* insincere. Insincerity, then, seems to be a particular kind of deceptiveness, the possibility of which arises only in connexion with certain sorts of actions. The insincerity which interests us can be given a rough ostensive definition by pointing to the following kinds of case: exclaiming "How delightful!" when one does not feel pleasure; smiling in a friendly manner at a person one does not like and intends to harm; offering sympathy when in fact unmoved by the hearer's sorrow; and, of course, paradigmatically, lying—*i.e.*, asserting that so-and-so when one does not believe that so-and-so.

The question "Can a command be insincere?" then seems to come to this: "What, if anything, is the command analogue of a lie?"

Some philosophers think that the notion of insincerity is unproblematically applicable to commands. D. M. Armstrong writes:

[A] speaker may be insincere. He may be speaking *"contra mentem"*. Such insincerity is not confined to assertion (lying) but may be involved in almost every sort of speech act. (As an example of an insincere *command* consider the following case. I have been myself commanded to say "Get out" to you and I dare not disobey, so I issue the order. But nevertheless I hope that you will disobey. My command to you is insincere.)[2]

J. R. Searle maintains that a request is insincere if the speaker does not want what he requests.[3] R. M. Hare says that a command is insincere if the speaker does not intend that the addressee should do what is commanded.[4] None of these philosophers discusses in detail what he means by "insincere" but none suggests that insincerity when predicated of commands has a different basis or significance from insincerity predicated of assertions.

Other philosophers have been more doubtful. A. Kenny writes:

> The concept of *meaning an utterance* . . . has application to statements as well as [commands] . . . "It was only a joke" and "It was just a story" are two common ways of denying that a statement was *meant*, that is, meant to be taken seriously.
>
> Now this notion of *meaning* plays different parts in connection with statements and in connection with commands. For a statement to be either truthful or untruthful it must be meant; and a truthful statement differs from an untruthful one in being believed by the utterer. But a command . . . is sincere if it is *meant* by the utterer, and insincere if it is not.[5]

So, for Kenny, assertions can be classified in two ways, first as meant and not meant and then, within the category of the meant, as sincere or insincere. With commands, by contrast, classification as meant or not meant coincides with and exhausts all that could be involved in classification as sincere or insincere. B. A. O. Williams comes to a similar conclusion; according to him commands can be odd in a variety of ways but we lack "any general parallel to *straightforward* cases of insincere assertion."[6]

Let us test these claims by examining some examples.[7] I shall take eight features which a command might exhibit and which might be thought to constitute insincerity and will show that for the first seven there is a close and obvious assertion analogue exhibiting the same feature, an analogue which is *not* a lie. The eighth case fares better but is still unsatisfactory. Consideration of why our examples fail leads to some more general reflections on the nature of insincerity, assertions and commands.

When a person tells a lie he directs an assertion at an audience but he does not believe what he asserts. So in our search for an insincere command it is natural to look (as Searle and Hare suggest) among commands where the speaker either does not want or does not intend what he commands.

> (A) The speaker does not want what he commands, *e.g.*, I request my friend to stop singing because it is waking the baby, although I enjoy the singing and do not want it to stop.

Here "do not want *X*" is compatible with "intend *X*" and to say that the speaker does not want what he commands is just to say that he issues the command reluctantly. But one can issue an assertion reluctantly and this is something clearly different from being insincere since the classifications lying/ truthful and glad/reluctant cut across one another in the case of assertions. (It is worth noting that the same is true of many of the features we shall discuss below; in assertion, classification by these features cuts across and is thus clearly distinct from classification into truthful and lying.)

Let us turn to cases in which the speaker does not intend what he commands.

> (B) The university politician says "Don't mention the matter to Jones" intending that his countersuggestible colleague shall do just that.

The assertion parallel here must be stating that so-and-so in order to induce a belief, in a distrustful hearer, that not so-and-so. But ordinary lying operates by assuming, and abusing, trustfulness in the hearer and is thus clearly something different from exploiting countersuggestibility.

(C) A parent addresses a rebellious son, "Never darken my doors again". But he is divided in his mind; part of him, perhaps we might say "his real self" intends his son to disobey.

There seem to be here, rather confusingly, two possible assertion parallels—stating that so-and-so while not really believing it and stating that so-and-so while not really intending one's assertion to be taken seriously. (One utterance could exhibit both oddities simultaneously.) But both cases are strikingly different from lying which involves no such self deception or division of mind.

(D) A burglar breaks into my house; a neighbour notices something wrong and comes to make enquiries; the burglar forces me at gun-point to say "Everything is all right; please go away." But I hope the neighbour will not go away.

The assertion analogue to this sort of command, issued under duress, is surely the assertion, also issued under duress, which I make when I say "Everything is all right." But again this is notably different from the ordinary lie where no duress is involved.

(E) An officer, seeing his men about to flee and desiring to preserve some semblance of authority, orders them to retreat.

He does not intend what is commanded because one cannot intend what one takes to be already the case. So his command is superfluous and known to be superfluous.

One could similarly put up a show of informing someone of something he already knows. And this, once more, is quite different from lying.

(F) "Your money or your life" yells the small boy, leaping out at his mother.

The assertion parallel must be a joking or pretend remark, not a lie.

(G) A bank robber dresses up as a traffic warden and issues directives to the public.

This case does not fit the description "command where the speaker does not intend what is commanded". But, as a possible variety of deceptive command, it deserves consideration. However, as in cases (A) to (F), it fails as an example of insincere command because the assertion analogue, which must surely be getting credence for one's statement by appropriating a uniform or status one is not entitled to, is again something quite different from making a lying or untruthful assertion.

In summary, we have examined so far seven features which a command may exhibit:

(a) being issued reluctantly
(b) being counter-suggestively intended
(c) springing from a divided or self-deceived mind
(d) being issued under duress
(e) being known to be superfluous
(f) being issued in jest
(g) relying for efficacy on usurped status or authority.

Commands with features (b) to (g) are all in various ways misleading or deceptive and with commands exhibiting (b) to (f) the speaker does not intend what he commands. Assertions may exhibit all these features. And in assertion none of (a) to (g) corresponds to what we normally mean by lying. Kenny's description—"command which is not meant"—seems most at home with case (F) but is also applicable to several of the others (e.g., (C), (D) and (E)). So it looks increasingly as if his view, that insincerity in command can only amount to "not being meant", is justified. But before we adopt his position let us have one final attempt at tracking down a genuine, full-blooded, insincere command.

As an interpersonal communicative action an assertion is (often) an attempt to convey information i.e., to induce some belief in the hearer. An assertion is insincere if one asserts something, and so tries to get the hearer to believe it, when one does not believe it oneself. So, it seems, the mark of an insincere assertion is that the hearer is to acquire a belief the speaker does not share.

Let us carefully construct the exact parallel of this for commands. Let us take it that commands are aimed at producing intentions. (Some may feel that it would be better to take commands as being directed at producing *actions*. I shall return to this point.) The analogue of inducing a belief one does not share will be producing an intention one does not share. So the mark of an insincere command is that the hearer is to acquire an intention (to do what is commanded) but one which the speaker does not share.

From one point of view, that of assessment for "fit with the world", *fulfilment* is to *intention* what *truth* is to *belief*. In an insincere assertion the speaker intends the hearer to acquire a belief which the speaker does not believe to be true; in an insincere command he intends the hearer to acquire an intention which he does not intend to be fulfilled.[8]

Following this clue we see that our major mistake earlier lay in our interpretation of the formula "in an insincere command the speaker does not intend what he commands." We assumed that if the speaker did not intend the hearer to do what was commanded then he did not even intend the hearer to *try* to do it. In working with this mistaken model all we arrived at were cases parallel to cases of assertion where the speaker does not intend the hearer to believe what is asserted. Hence we arrived at no cases of commands which could provide the desired analogy with lies because it is (often) important to a lying assertion that the hearer should believe what he is told.

So here finally is candidate (H) for the title of insincere command:

> (H) An officer has a grudge against one of his subordinates and wants to make his life miserable; he therefore issues the command "Have all the equipment in first-class condition by 1800 hours" intending that the subordinate should set out on the task but should fail, thus providing a pretext for punishment.

I shall argue below that even this case (H) does not in a full-blooded way merit the name "insincere command". But first I shall comment on some features of the proposal and indicate some of its virtues.

I have been operating with the unargued assumption that

intention is a propositional attitude. The form of words "I intend that so-and-so", *e.g.*, "I intend that the money shall go to charity", is acceptable in English although the accusative and infinitive construction, "I intend the money to go to charity", is more usual. In the first person case the infinitive construction (with the accusative omitted) is almost obligatory. But I cannot see reasons for thinking this anything other than a superficial syntactic restriction.

It is a consequence of this assumption that we can speak of shared intentions just as we can of shared beliefs. If you and I both intend that the money shall go to charity we intend the same thing. (In my use of "share" we do not share an intention if each of us intends that he himself shall have the money, although in one use of "same" we do intend the same.)

The notion of sharing does however have a slightly different rôle in connexion with intention from the rôle it plays in belief. Two people could share exactly the same beliefs on some subjects, down to the very last detail. With intentions, by contrast, when we come to spell them out including all possible detail it seems that my intention must always at the end of the trail concern some action of my own. If I intend that the money shall go to charity, I must intend to do something toward achieving that state of affairs. It is this commitment to, and expectation of, needing to act oneself which makes the difference between intending something and merely expecting it with approval. So when *A* intends *B* to do *X*, and *B* himself also intends to do *X*, then *A* and *B* share an intention—that *B* do *X*. If we were considering beliefs we might here have reached the most detailed possible specification of each person's belief and found them completely coincident. But with intention there must be at least one more detail to put in—namely, that *A* intends that he himself should do something to forward *B*'s doing *X*. However, this contrast between belief and intention with respect to the idea of sharing does not affect the proposed account of insincerity in commands.

An advantage of the account of insincerity embodied in case (H) is that we can use it to dissolve some problems and unclarities which arose earlier.

We saw that, with assertion, classification by features

(a) to (g) cut across classification as sincere or insincere while we could not find how to make an analogous cross cutting classification with commands. This can now be rectified. I shall not describe examples of all the particular kinds but it is easy enough to see how (with our current understanding of "insincere") a command could be reluctant and sincere as well as reluctant and insincere, superfluous and sincere as well as superfluous and insincere, *etc.*

Another problem concerned commands involving self deception or divided mind. In considering case (C) there appeared to be two points at which division of mind might affect an assertion; the speaker might not really believe what he said or he might not really intend to be believed. The two corresponding points in command can now be identified— the speaker might not really intend what he commanded (although intending it to be attempted) or he might not really intend the indicated task to be undertaken.

Finally we have the problem of whether commands are aimed at producing intentions or at producing actions. This question can be rephrased as "Are commands aimed at producing intentions or at producing fulfilled intentions?" For assertions the analogous question would be "Are they aimed at producing beliefs or at producing true beliefs?" and the answer is clear: assertions are *qua* individual communicative actions, aimed at producing merely beliefs, but the speaker represents himself as aiming at producing true beliefs. On the current proposal we should say something similar for commands; the speaker represents himself as aiming at action, *i.e.*, fulfilled intention, but the essence of command as an individual action is that an intention is to be produced.

When we think of the nature and function of language as a whole institution it may be correct to see indicative sentences as conventional means for conveying information (*i.e.*, inducing *true* beliefs) and commands as a conventional means of influencing action (*i.e.*, inducing *fulfilled* intentions). But in both cases the possibility of abusing the institution exists. And inasmuch as "assertion" and "command" are both to be defined as "action in which the relevant institution is seriously invoked—whether deceitfully or honestly", then in both cases the necessary and sufficient conditions for performing the

speech act will mention only the intention to induce propositional attitude (belief or intention) in the hearer.

The class of actions in which the institution of assertion is
abused loom much larger in our view of the world than the
class of analogous commands. This is explained by at least
two factors. First, commands like case (H) are simply not very
numerous. Secondly, and more interestingly, the question
"Does the speaker intend me to complete successfully the
action he commands me to do?" is a less important question
from the hearer's point of view in deciding how to react to a
command than is the question "Does he believe what he says?"
in deciding how to react to an assertion. This may seem surprising, but consider case (H): from the subordinate's point
of view it may be sensible for him to try to obey the command
even when he knows that the officer does not intend him to
succeed. It may be sensible because the consequences of immediate disobedience are disastrous and there is just a chance
that he may succeed in doing what is commanded and so
thwart the officer's plan. Discovery of insincerity in a command does not automatically remove its power to influence
action. By contrast, with assertions if the speaker is accurately
informed in the matter under discussion and the hearer dis-
covers that the speaker does not believe what he says then it
would be irrational to respond to the assertion with belief.

These differences in the relative importance of deceit in
assertion and command stem not from any differences we have
so far discerned in the structure of the two actions but rather
from the nature of belief and intention. With both belief and
intention the rational thinker aims both to have his propositional attitudes rationally justified (by appeal to reasons,
evidence, etc.) and also to have them accord with the world;
he desires to have his beliefs both sensible and true and his
intentions both sensible and fulfilled. Two people may have
opposed beliefs (i.e., ones which cannot both be true) and one
or other of them must then be disappointed in that his belief
will fail to correspond with the world. They may also have
opposed intentions and again one or the other must be disappointed. Thus far belief and intention run parallel. But a
difference comes in this: Consider two people each of whom
has available all relevant information; it may be rationally

justified for them to have opposed intentions while it cannot be rationally justified for them to have opposed beliefs. If two people discover that their intentions are opposed this need not lead either to reappraise his position, for each may correctly think that his set of beliefs and intentions is the best possible for him; but discovery that another person has an opposed belief produces a situation in which one or other party must have a less than perfectly suited set of propositional attitudes. It is this asymmetry which in part underlies the comparative unimportance of commands like (H) compared to lying assertions.

Lies are a recognised sub-class of assertions. But commands like (H) have no separate name and one might even doubt whether they are commands. Perhaps they are rather pretended commands? To make this move is to suggest that it is a necessary condition for issuing a command that one should aim at action in one's hearer. But even if this is an accurate account of how we use the words "command", "request" and the like (and I do not think that it is accurate), the underlying institutions of assertion and command run parallel. A lie is a pretence at honest assertion, similarly a command like (H) is a pretence at normal command. Thus a supposed contrast between assertions—aimed at producing a propositional attitude—and command—not aimed at producing a propositional attitude—is bogus.[9] As far as our investigations at present go the two sorts of action can be regarded as very closely analogous in structure, differences springing from the nature of the propositional attitudes involved in the two cases.

Are we then justified in claiming that there can be commands which are insincere in the full-blooded sense? There may still be uneasiness with the proposed account and I shall now try another line of approach which will reveal some possible grounds for this.

Our starting point in the earlier discussion was the unassailable truism that an assertion is insincere if the speaker does not believe what he says. We then assumed that an assertion, as an interpersonal communicative action, is an attempt to influence the beliefs of another; thus we arrived easily at the idea that one assesses an assertion for sincerity by comparing the belief the speaker intends to produce in the hearer with the belief the speaker himself holds. We then applied this strategy to commands and discovered that parallels could be found.

But the trouble with the whole line of thought is that the way we have chosen to spell out the notion of insincerity in assertion is highly suspect.

Let us note first that features (a) to (g) which we identified as possible features of both assertions and commands are also possible features of almost any action directed or seemingly directed at producing an effect on another person. For example, suppose that you approach a house where I am standing in the doorway; when you are a few feet away I step forward, bar your way and attempt to push you backwards; I thereby attempt, or seem to attempt, to prevent you entering the house. All the following things are possible: (a) I am making a genuine but reluctant attempt to prevent your entering; (b) I am trying to make you interested in entering the house by seeming to prevent you; (c) I am self-deceived in that I do not really intend to prevent your entering; (d) I am acting under duress and hope that I will not be able to prevent your entering; (e) I know that my action is superfluous because you do not intend to come in but I am keeping up some sort of show; (f) my action is a joke and not intended to be taken seriously; (g) I am presenting myself as having authority to bar you, and means of doing so, which I do not in fact have.

Features (a) to (g) can thus be present in vast numbers of actions, most of which are not communicative or even quasi-communicative. Since this is so it would be strange to find that any of (a) to (g) was adequate to define insincerity since insincerity seems to be sensibly attributable only to communicative or quasi-communicative actions.

But looked at in this light the next proposal, that embodied in case (H), is no more acceptable. Case (H) suggests that we find the elusive *definiens* of insincerity by comparing the state which the speaker intends the hearer to be in with the state the speaker is in: an utterance is insincere if the speaker attempts to put the hearer into a state when the speaker is not in that state. But this feature can also be present in non-communicative actions. When I bar your way into the house I intend you to be in a certain state (being outside the house) when I myself am not in that state. It is absurd to say that my action is therefore insincere. It will not help if we add the condition that the states in question must be those of holding some propositional attitude. I can try to induce fear in another while not myself being frightened or I can attempt to induce, by non-linguistic means, a belief I do not share, without being in either case insincere.

Not only is such discrepancy between the addressee's state and the agent's state not sufficient for insincerity; it is not necessary either. Consider the following situation: I know that you know that *p* but I also know that you do not know that I know that *p*; I assert that not-*p*. My utterance is insincere. But I do not intend to produce or reinforce in you a false belief because I know that your belief that *p* is unshakable. The insincerity cannot lie in a supposed discrepancy between what I know (that *p*) and what I intend you to believe (that not-*p*) since there is no such discrepancy. The insincerity lies rather in a discrepancy between what I believe and what I represent myself as believing.

We were right to think that an insincere assertion is one in which the speaker does not believe what he says. And we may be right that the core notion of assertion is that of conveying information to others (although as the above case makes clear many assertions deviate from this paradigm). But we were wrong to combine these two ideas as we did. The key point about insincerity in assertion is not that one misleads the hearer about the world but that one misleads him about one's own state of mind. Perhaps the use of the word "lie" (which does have strong connotations of conveying false beliefs about the world) rather than the more neutral "insincere assertion" has helped to fudge this point. The account of insincerity now offered is clearly at home with the cases mentioned at the start of this paper—the insincere exclamations of delight, false smiles, *etc*. The word "expression" is one which comes easily to hand here. To be insincere is to express or purport to express a state of mind when one is not in that state of mind.

Where does this leave insincere commands?

Our question must be: Do commands express states of

mind? Is there some state of mind to which the utterance of
a command stands as assertion stands to belief, smiling to
goodwill, and so on?

In using the phrase "piece of behaviour by which a person
expresses his state of mind" we are usually gesturing towards
a class of pieces of behaviour contained in but smaller than
the class of pieces of behaviour which are evidence for a
person's state of mind. Features of this subclass will emerge
by degrees as we consider some examples.[10] A first point to
notice is this; if a person expresses his state of mind, even
when he does so spontaneously and unthinkingly, there must
be the possibility of his not expressing it, of his choosing to
keep his thoughts or feelings to himself. The piece of behaviour he produces must be something he could refrain from
producing while still remaining in the same state of mind. We
here arrive at a familiar distinction between expressing one's
state of mind and merely exhibiting symptoms of it. An
involuntary and uncontrollable manifestation is not something by which I express a state of mind, e.g., I do not express
embarrassment by blushing. I cannot blush insincerely although I may engineer a misleading blush.

There is another class of pieces of behaviour which are
evidence for states of mind but which are by these considerations ruled out as actions by which a person expresses those
states of mind, namely actions done in fulfilment of intentions. If I intend to eat this food now then the question of
whether I should eat this food now is not open to me; if it
were still open I should have yet to form an intention. By
eating the food now I do not express my intention to do so
but act in fulfilment of it.

But what about my action of, for example, picking up a
fork? The question of whether I should do this, given that I
have the intention to eat, is open to me since there are alternative methods of setting about eating. So could this action be
something by which I express my intention to eat? It seems to
me that this is not a happy description except in exceptional
circumstances. If I pick up my fork ostentatiously, cutting
across some dispute which is impeding the meal, my gesture
may be quasi-communicative; by my action I may mean (in
a Gricean way) that I, at least, intend to abandon the

argument and get on with eating, Inasmuch as my action thus amounts to a statement about my intention it is also an expression of that intention. But unless there is, as in this case, some desire to manifest to others (or oneself) one's intention, picking up a fork is not something by which one expresses one's intention to eat. To employ means to some end is not *ipso facto* to express the intention to reach that end and, as we should expect, the question of sincerity does not normally arise in these contexts. Deliberately to mislead someone into thinking that one intends to eat by picking up a fork is not (unless some very special story is told) to act insincerely.

How does this bear on commands? We are considering the possibility that by issuing a command a person expresses his intention that the addressee do what is commanded. But a command in the usual case is an attempt to get the addressee to do what is commanded. So the possibility presents itself that issuing a command is an action in fulfilment of that intention, a means of pursuing it, rather than an expression of it.

The two descriptions are not mutually exclusive. Picking up a fork in the special circumstances imagined fits both; it is an expression of intention to eat and also a move to fulfil that intention. We can find cases where the two descriptions are even more closely linked, in that it is precisely by expressing an intention that an agent moves to fulfil that intention. Consider the utterances generally agreed to be expressions of intention. We have not only "I will do X" but also 3rd and 2nd person versions, "He shall do X" and (the interesting one from our point of view) "You shall do X". This last can be directed at someone in an attempt to get him to act as when one says to a child in a firm tone of voice "You'll apologise immediately".

Could we not then regard the imperative form of words as an alternative realisation of the same linguistic rôle as is played by the commonly recognised expressions of intention? Certainly the two utterances "You'll do X" (in a firm or threatening tone of voice) and "Do X" can operate in similar ways. Both may serve to influence the actions of the hearer by revealing to him the intentions of the speaker, knowledge of which provides the hearer with reason to act.

Indeed a command must work this way; it is essential to its effectiveness as a conventional linguistic device that the hearer recognise the intention with which it is uttered, since there is no natural causal link between the utterance and the hearer's doing what is commanded. The making public of the intention that the hearer act is thus vital to the rôle of command in influencing action while making public intention to eat is not essential to the role of wielding a fork in enabling one to eat. So we cannot rule out the idea that in issuing a command one expresses an intention by the test that we used above to rule out the idea that in picking up a fork one expresses an intention.

But there are nevertheless important differences between a command and saying "You shall do X". The imperative form of words is tied by the conventions governing its use to the action of attempting to influence the behaviour of others. The other form of words has a much wider range of uses. It can occur in soliloquy as a spontaneous voicing out of thoughts, and it can also be addressed to another person not in an attempt to influence him but merely because one desires to manifest one's state of mind. For example, having suffered an insult and being at the time unable to retaliate, one may say "You shall smart for this"; the utterance is clearly not quasi-imperatival since at the moment of utterance one is in no position to influence the hearer's actions and the related imperative ("Smart for this!") is quite out of place.

I suggest then that if a type of action (smiling, asserting or the like) is one by producing a token of which a person expresses a state of mind (in that sense of "expresses" which correlates with the possibility of insincerity) then the following things are true:

(1) the action is one that a person can sensibly refrain from while remaining in the given state of mind,

and (2) the action can be produced merely to inform others of one's state of mind or for no purpose beyond the satisfaction of voicing out one's thoughts or feelings.

Commands fail to satisfy the second condition; they do not have the range of uses characteristic of types of action by which people express states of mind. A command may, in particular and unusual circumstances, be an action by which intention is expressed. But to explain the general notion of command we should not talk of expressing but merely of a conventionally established means of influencing the actions of another. To put it briefly, the imperative form of words is too much a tool for a specific purpose for it to be a vehicle of expression.

So we come finally to endorse Kenny's view of the matter.[11] Intentions are not connected with commands in quite the way that beliefs are connected with assertions. Commands may exhibit all the oddities discussed under (A) to (H) above as may non-linguistic actions. And, as with non-linguistic actions, these questions can be asked: "Does he mean that seriously? Does he really have the intention his overt behaviour suggests?" But the further question "Is he sincere?" cannot get a grip. This question arises, I contend, only when we have a piece of behaviour which is both deliberately directed at another in a communicative way and also is of a type satisfying (1) and (2) above.

We can discern broadly two views on the nature of language. One sees it as a tool for interpersonal communication, the other as a vehicle for, or expression of, thought. The moral of our discussion of insincerity is that, *prima facie*, imperative utterances fit the first model while indicative utterances fit the second.

However it does not seem to be a *deep* fact that commands fit the first model. We could manage pretty well if we had no imperative mood but only the intention expressing "You shall . . ." (Note that if we did operate this way then insincerity in our new style "commands" would be what is imagined in case (H)—namely giving someone to understand that one had an intention, and thereby influencing his intentions, when one did not have the intention in question. So the feeling that with case (H) we had approached as nearly as we could to the command analogue of a lie was not misplaced.) On the other hand, it is not clear either that it is a deep fact that assertions fit the second model. One could argue that non-informative uses of indicative sentences are in some way secondary to or parasitic on communicatively intended uses and thus that the notion of expressing one's state of mind must be elucidated *via* the notion of interpersonal communication.[12] Thus what is said in this paper does not have direct implications for the nature of any possible language or the speech acts it must make available. But it would be a bad starting point for further discussion to misrepresent the complexities of our own linguistic institutions.

NOTES

[1] See H. P. Grice, "Meaning", *Philosophical Review*, LXVI (1957), pp. 377-388.

For elaborations of these views, some of which abandon assertion/command symmetry see

H. P. Grice, "Utterer's Meaning and Intention", *Philosophical Review*, LXXVIII (1969), pp. 147-177.

D. M. Armstrong, "Meaning and Communication", *Philosophical Review*, LXXX (1970).

D. K. Lewis, *Convention*, Harvard University Press, 1969.

J. F. Bennett, *Linguistic Behaviour*, Cambridge University Press, 1976.

[2] D. M. Armstrong, *loc. cit.*

[3] J. R. Searle, *Speech Acts*, Cambridge University Press, 1969, p. 66.

[4] R. M. Hare, *The Language of Morals*, Oxford University Press, 1952, p. 13.

[5] A. Kenny, *Action, Emotion and Will*, Routledge and Kegan Paul, 1963, p. 219.

[6] B. A. O. Williams, "Consistency and Realism", *Aristotelian Society, Supplementary Volume*, 1966, pp. 1-22.

[7] Case (A) is suggested by Searle's remarks, Case (D) by Armstrong's, and cases (B) and (C) by Williams' discussion.

[8] An entirely different line of thought about insincerity in commands is raised here by the reflection that perhaps *rightness* is to *intention* what *truth* is to *belief*. It is plausible to think that a piece of advice is insincere if the speaker does not think that the action he advises is the right thing for the hearer to try to do. So perhaps a command is insincere if the speaker attempts to induce an intention he does not think right for the hearer? This suggestion merits fuller discussion than space here allows. I make only two brief points against it. First, it has plausibility only for some sorts of command. Does the master ordering his slave to bring him wine take any interest in, or represent himself as taking any interest in, what is right or best for the slave? Second, the kinds of difficulties outlined at the end of the paper which arise in treating imperative utterances as expressions of intention apply just as strongly to the idea that they should be treated as expressions of the conviction that the commanded action is right for the hearer. If the connexion I argue for, between the notion of expression and the possibility of insincerity, is correct then my final conclusion, that commands cannot be full-bloodedly insincere, still stands.

[9] *Cf.* Bennett, *op. cit.*, pp. 133-137.

[10] For some discussion of the very obscure notion of "expressing" see W. P. Alston, "Expressing" in *Philosophy in America*, ed. Max Black.

[11] The account given of Kenny's views is, in certain respects, distorted. He holds that for optatives and expressions of intention, as well as for commands, insincerity can only amount to "not being meant"; and moreover he seems to want to explain this supposed fact by some basic contrast between the nature of volitional and of cognitive propositional attitudes. But in my view it is the way in which a type of behaviour is linked to a sort of mental state which dictates whether or not insincerity gets a grip and not the nature of the state itself. Does not an *agent provocateur* in a revolutionary cell both intend his utterance to be taken seriously and speak insincerely when he says "Down with the capitalists!" or "If only the Red Dawn would hasten"?

[12] For some discussion of this topic see P. F. Strawson, *Meaning and Truth; an Inaugural Lecture*, Oxford Uniservity Press, 1970.

XIII*—THE NAMES OF
SECONDARY QUALITIES

by Peter Alexander

I

Commentators on Locke often say that his primary qualities
are 'Solidity, Extension, Figure, and Mobility' and his secondary qualities are 'Colours, Sounds, Tasts, etc.'. (These lists are
from *Essay* II.viii.9–10 but their actual composition is unim-
portant for my argument.) In an earlier article (Alexander
(1), p. 229) I proposed the hypothesis that Locke uses such
words as 'colour' and 'red' for *ideas* of secondary qualities
rather than for secondary qualities themselves. This is not a
trivial hypothesis depending merely on the view that he holds
that *all* words stand for ideas. He clearly means 'extension'
and 'figure' to be names of primary qualities, as in II.viii.18,
for example; my contention is that it is part of the distinction
between primary and secondary qualities that, in contrast,
neither 'colour' and 'odour' not 'red' and 'sour' are names of
secondary qualities.

In my earlier article I did not attempt to establish this hypothesis and I now wish to do so. Its establishment would, I
believe, be an important step because it would remove some
apparent contradictions which have troubled even Locke's
most sympathetic critics. (See Curley, p. 440 and Bennett,
pp. 107ff.) The most important of these is that he appears to
say both that *all* qualities are in objects independently of perceivers, being powers to produce effects upon us or other objects (e.g. II.viii.8–10 and II.viii.23) and that in a world lacking perceivers there would be no secondary qualities (as, allegedly, in II.viii.17).

We have, fortunately, left behind the view that says bluntly
that, for Locke, secondary qualities are 'subjective' or 'mind-
dependent' or 'in the minds of perceivers' whereas primary

---

* Meeting of the Aristotelian Society at 5/7, Tavistock Place, London,
W.C.1, on Monday 2nd May 1977, at 7.30 p.m.

qualities are not. However, the price to be paid for this has
been regarded by some to be the admission of an inconsistency in Locke since, in spite of his official doctrine that
secondary qualities are merely powers in objects to produce
ideas in us, when talking of fire and snow he says

> But *Light, Heat, Whiteness,* or *Coldness, are no more
> really in them, than Sickness or Pain is in* Manna. Take
> away the Sensation of them; let not the Eyes see Light, or
> Colours, nor the Ears hear Sounds; let the Palate not
> Taste, nor the Nose Smell, and all Colours, Tastes,
> Odors, and Sounds, as they are such particular *Ideas,*
> vanish and cease, and are reduced to their Causes, *i.e.*
> Bulk, Figure, and Motion of Parts. (II.viii.17.)

About porphyry, he says

> Hinder light but from striking on it, and its Colours
> Vanish; it no longer produces any such *Ideas* in us: Up-
> on the return of Light, it produces these appearances on
> us again. Can any one think any real alterations are made
> in the *Porphyre,* by the presence or absence of Light;
> and that those *Ideas* of whiteness and redness, are really
> in *Porphyre* in the light, when 'tis plain *it has no colour
> in the dark*? (II.viii.19.)

However, these passages are inconsistent with the official
doctrine only if 'colours', 'tastes', 'odours', 'sounds', 'whiteness' and 'redness' are taken to name secondary qualities. I
believe that this inconsistency is not Locke's. He did not
mean to say that in a world lacking perceivers there would be
no secondary qualities; he did not even say it. In these two
passages he is talking of *ideas* being removed when the conditions for perceiving are not satisfied. For him, the fact that
without perceivers objects would have no colours, tastes,
odours or sounds does not entail that they would have no
secondary qualities. The mistake can be seen by a careful
reading of the very passages upon which it is based, when it
becomes clear that Locke adhered consistently to the maxim
heading II.viii.7: 'Ideas *in the Mind, Qualities in Bodies*'.

Before embarking on detailed argument I will risk a general remark which embodies a challenge. I believe that there

is no passage in the *Essay* in which Locke clearly indicates that he is using such words as 'red' and 'colour' as the names of secondary qualities or classes of them. On the contrary, the most natural reading of the relevant passages supports my view.

II

In introducing my topic I have almost ignored an ambiguity which I must discuss. This I will do in the next section. Here, as a preliminary, I must explain a conception which appears to me to be of considerable importance in the interpretation of Locke; I mean the conception of *texture*. I believe, as I have pointed out elsewhere, that Boyle uses 'texture' as a technical term and that Locke follows him, though perhaps not unswervingly, in this. (Alexander (2), p. 54 and (1), p. 230–1)

Talking of the effects of bodies upon the sensories of animals to produce 'sensible phenomena', *i.e.* sensations such as sensations of colour, Boyle says

> . . . however we look upon them as distinct qualities, [they] are consequently but the effects of the often mentioned catholick affections of matter, and deducible from the size, shape, motion (or rest), posture, order, and the *resulting* texture of the insensible parts of bodies. (Boyle (1), p. 26, my italics.)

A little earlier he has said

> And when many corpuscles do so convene together as to compose any distinct body, as a stone or a metal, then from their other accidents (or modes) and from these two last mentioned [*sc.* posture and order], *there doth emerge a certain disposition or contrivance of parts in the whole*, which we may call the *texture* of it. (Boyle (1), p. 22, my italics.)

Boyle repeats this definition in various places.

This is an important part of the corpuscular hypothesis, which Locke clearly accepts from Boyle. Single corpuscles have only the primary qualities shape, size and mobility. (Solidity is problematic.) When corpuscles 'convene' to form objects other qualities 'emerge'. 'Posture' and 'order' refer to the orientation of each corpuscle in relation to the others in the group. The resultant pattern of corpuscles, depending ultimately on their primary qualities, is the *texture* and such patterns cause sensations in us and other effects in other objects. For example, one *superficial* texture causes the sensation of red in us and a different one causes the sensation of blue in us by reflecting and absorbing light corpuscles in different ways; the descriptions of these textures would have to be in terms of the arrangements of the primary qualities of the constituent corpuscles on the surface of objects. Thus single corpuscles do not have textures any more than they have postures and orders. Secondary qualities *are* textures, that is, patterns of primary qualities.

I believe that this is what Locke has in mind when he says, about porphyry, '. . . whiteness or redness are not in it at any time, but such a texture, that hath the power to produce such a sensation in us' (II.viii.19) and when he asks, about almonds, 'What real Alteration can the beating of the Pestle make in any Body but an Alternation of the *Texture* of it?' (II.viii.20). In III.vi.9 he talks of 'that Texture of Parts, that real *Essence*, that makes Lead, and Antimony fusible; Wood, and Stones not'. I think that for Locke, as for Boyle, secondary qualities are those textures of objects that produce sensations of colour, etc., in us. Both are trying to avoid explanations that rely on occult qualities and if causes of sensations were something over and above these textures they would be occult. If we could describe a texture in complete detail we could understand how it would act upon other possible, and fully described, textures.

If I am right, there are things in Locke which I must explain, notably the fact that in II.viii Locke has about twenty two lists which appear to be lists of primary qualities and four of them include texture. According to my view, textures cannot be primary qualities. Locke's definitions in II.viii.9 show, I believe, that he does not mean them to be. Textures are not utterly inseparable from body 'in what estate soever it be', through all changes: a single corpuscle is a body but cannot have a texture. The mind does not find textures in single corpuscles. Sense does not find textures, of the sort here discussed, in portions of matter large enough to be perceived: patterns of *corpuscles* are unobservable. In the example of the division of a grain of wheat, in the same section, Locke mentions solidity, extension, figure and mobility but not texture.

So why does Locke include 'texture' in what seem to be lists of primary qualities? It is noticeable that he discusses in some detail all the items in those lists except texture. This suggests two things. First, it suggests that he did, like Boyle, regard texture as derived from primary qualities. Second, it suggests that the word 'texture' had a familiar use in scientific and philosophical circles at the time so Locke did not need to explain it. This is supported by the *Oxford English Dictionary*. Under 'Texture' we find

> 4. In extended use: The constitution, structure or substance of any thing, with regard to its constituent or formative elements.
> a. Of organic bodies and their parts. 1665 Boyle *Occas. Med.* IV.iv *The Leaves . . . of a Tree . . . are of a more solid Texture and a more durable Nature than the Blossoms.*
> . . .
> b. Of inorganic substances as stones, soil, etc.: Physical (not chemical) constitution; the structure or minute moulding (of a surface). 1660 Boyle *New Expt^s· Phys. & Mech.* xxii, 165 *Air is . . . endowed with an Elastical power that probably proceeds from its Texture.*

The quotations from Boyle are the first in each list of examples.

So why *does* Locke include 'texture' in lists of primary qualities? I wonder if he does. The central chapter for this question is II.viii, so I concentrate on that. It is noticeable that Locke gives various lists which appear to be lists of primary qualities but that he does so in at least three different contexts and this may partly explain differences between the lists. He is sometimes talking about any actual particle of matter whatsoever, sometimes about observable bodies as such and sometimes about the features of observable bodies that cause ideas of secondary qualities in us. In II.viii.9 where he defines primary qualities, and so must be talking of any body, even an isolated corpuscle, he does not include texture.

The four lists in which he does include texture are in sections 10, 14 and 18 of Book II, Chapter viii. For example, in 10 one list is 'Bulk, Figure, Texture, and Motion of parts'. There are two points about these lists to which I wish to draw attention. The first is that each list contains also 'motion of (insensible) parts', showing that complex bodies are being discussed. The second is that each list is given in the context of a discussion of the causes of ideas of secondary qualities in us. The list in section 18 is in a sentence which does not even use the expression 'primary qualities'. If we are talking of the causes of ideas of secondary qualities, completeness requires the mention of textures and I suggest that these four lists could be read in the spirit of my first quotation from Boyle as 'bulk, figure, the *resulting* texture, and motion of parts'. (There are three other lists that might be relevant, in 23 and 24, but these are lists of qualities of bodies *affected* by other bodies or of qualities of our sense organs; two of them mention motions of parts and analogous arguments could be used.)

However, that looks odd at first sight if, as I suspect, the primary qualities are bulk, figure and mobility. If that is so, the motion or rest of a corpuscle contributes to texture just as its bulk and figure do, so why does texture not come at the end of the list as a resultant of the other three? This, too, can be explained. Motion of parts is not, of course, a primary quality since a single corpuscle has no independently movable parts; the primary quality is *mobility*, the ability to be at rest or in motion, which every corpuscle has. In a complex body the corpuscles (parts) may be in motion relative to one another or they may not. Their rest or motion contributes to the texture. The simplest case is when they are at rest and then texture depends merely on bulk, figure and their relations. If they are in motion that is an additional factor in the texture but not a necessary condition of there *being* a texture.

Few commentators have discussed what Locke means by 'texture' and if my interpretation is rejected it is necessary to ask what he can mean by it that is consistent with other things he says.

I am suggesting, then, that secondary qualities, being

qualities of objects, are textures in the sense explained. However, Locke holds that secondary qualities are *powers* in objects to produce sensations, these powers residing in patterns of the groups of corpuscles which constitute objects. Am I then identifying powers with textures? I am at least entertaining the hypothesis that Boyle and Locke did identify them.

There would appear, on the face of it, to be objections to this. Does it make sense to identify powers and textures, for powers are surely dispositional and textures are not? Moreover, Locke and Boyle say such things as that the powers of objects 'depend upon' or 'reside in' the patterns of primary qualities. Locke, in II.viii.19 talks of 'such a texture, that hath the power to produce such a sensation in us'.

Concerning the first point, there was little idea, at the time, of chemical action; what we think of as chemical action was then thought of as mechanical. I suggest that powers are to be conceived of in a mechanical and, especially, a *geometrical* way. To say, for example, that one object has the power to penetrate another is just to say that the corpuscles of the two objects are so arranged that the second has interstices of such a shape and size that projections on the first will *fit* them. To describe the texture of the first object completely is to describe something which fits other textures. The texture of gold is such that the particles will fit neatly, in some regular fashion, into the interstices in the texture of *aqua regia* and that is what dissolving is. To describe in terms of its shape and size a cone-shaped corpuscle is to describe its ability to fit a cone-shaped cavity of a certain size; *the ability to fit* is not something more in the corpuscle still to be described. The corpuscular philosophy of Boyle and Locke was kinematic rather than dynamic, as Newton's was.

As for what Locke and Boyle say about powers depending upon textures, consider this: to say that one object has the power to penetrate another is to describe from the point of view of gross observation an ability which can be explained in terms of, is obvious from, a complete description of the unobserved textures of the two objects. In II.viii.15 Locke says 'what is Sweet, Blue or Warm in *Idea*, is but the certain Bulk, Figure, and Motion of the insensible Parts in the Bodies them-

selves, which we call so.' Boyle says that the power of a key to
turn a lock is nothing distinct from its shape and size, which
fits the shape and size of the inwards of the lock and that the
attributes of being soluble in *aqua regia* and insoluble in
aqua fortis 'are not in the gold anything distinct from its
peculiar texture'. (Boyle (1), p. 18).

III

I am now able to discuss the ambiguity I referred to at the
beginning of the last section. Consider, again, my hypothesis:
Locke uses such words as 'colour' and 'red' for *ideas* of secondary qualities rather than for secondary qualities themselves.

However, since Locke holds that '*Words, in their primary
or immediate Signification, stand for nothing, but the* Ideas
in the Mind of him that uses them . . .' (III.ii.2), it would be
trivially inconsistent for him to say that 'red' stands primarily
or immediately for a secondary quality. So, can a secondary
quality, as distinct from an idea of a secondary quality, be
named at all? I think it can, as will emerge. What is clear is
that the *primary or immediate* signification of words 'standing for secondary qualities', if there can be such, must be
ideas of secondary qualities.

At this point we must recognize that the expression 'idea
of a secondary quality' is ambiguous; we must take into account the fact that Locke uses the word 'idea' for both 'sensation' and 'concept'. He usually uses it, in this context, to mean
a sensation; thus 'red', I allege, is the name of an *idea* of a
secondary quality, in this sense. More fully, it is the name of a
sensation caused in us by a secondary quality. He calls this
sensation the idea of a secondary quality because the only way
in which the secondary quality, *i.e.*, a peculiar texture, can
appear to us is as that sensation.

At present we have neither names for secondary qualities
nor descriptions of the specific textures which produce specific sensations in us. Locke appears to think that we may
eventually obtain limited knowledge of these textures but not
universal and perfect knowledge (IV.iii, *passim* & IV.xii,
passim). If we could arrive at descriptions of textures it would
be by scientific inference. The only descriptions we have of

secondary qualities are of the form 'the power to produce the idea of red in us' but these are uninformatively of the *virtus dormitiva* kind. Descriptions of textures would be informative descriptions of secondary qualities, qualities of objects. We should then have what I am calling 'concepts of secondary qualities' and not just sensations caused by secondary qualities.

My hypothesis, then, is that Locke intends such words as 'red' to be used, in philosophical contexts, as names of ideas (sensations) caused by secondary qualities but not for ideas (concepts) of the causes of those sensations, i.e., secondary qualities. This concerns primary or immediate signification.

Can we say that descriptions of textures could, for Locke, stand for secondary qualities or must we say that they could stand only for ideas (concepts) of secondary qualities? Here Locke's resemblance thesis becomes important. However we analyse this thesis, it seems clear that it is meant to catch whatever we mean by 'having an accurate idea of' something. One consequence of the thesis is that the names of ideas (sensations) of primary qualities will serve also as names of primary qualities; 'extension' names both an idea and a quality. One aim of natural science is to provide descriptions of natural phenomena and this involves arriving at accurate ideas of them. So we can say that one aim of science is to get ideas (concepts) of particular secondary qualities which are accurate. Then descriptions of these would also serve as descriptions of secondary qualities. If we then invented names for various textures, or secondary qualities, they would also serve as names for our ideas (concepts) of them. The ideal is to bring our descriptions of the world in terms of secondary qualities to the same level as our descriptions of it in terms of primary qualities.

Is this consistent with Locke's view that words stand for ideas? As has been pointed out from time to time, his statements such as '*Words in their primary or immediate Signification, stand for nothing, but the* Ideas *in the Mind of him that uses them . . .*' (III.ii.2) do not entail that words stand for *nothing but* ideas. (see, *e.g.*, Kretzmann, pp. 175 ff. and Butler, pp. 131 ff.) The reservation 'in their primary or immediate Signification' must be taken seriously. Locke thinks

that men are *right* when they suppose that words stand also
for ideas in the minds of others and for the reality of things,
because he *does* think that if words did not so stand we should
talk in vain, not be understood and not talk of things as they
really are (III.ii.4 & 5). There cannot, then, be any objection,
on grounds of inconsistency, to saying that the names of ideas,
whether sensations or concepts, of qualities can be *also* the
names of those qualities.

If I am right colours, tastes, odours and sounds are not,
for Locke, secondary qualities but sensations; secondary
qualities are colourless, tasteless, odourless and soundless textures of objects. However, I believe that my negative thesis
can be established independently of the truth of my positive
thesis.

IV

I now turn to a more detailed consideration of my thesis that
Locke uses such words as 'colour' and 'red' for ideas of secondary qualities rather than for secondary qualities themselves
In this thesis ideas of secondary qualities are to be taken as
ideas caused by secondary qualities, *i.e.* sensations.

In II.viii.2 Locke warns us that we must distinguish ideas
from their causes. He says

> These are two very different things, and carefully to be
> distinguished; it being one thing to perceive, and know
> the *Idea* of White or Black, and quite another to exam-
> ine what kind of particles they must be, and how ranged
> in the Superficies, to make any Object appear White or
> Black.

He here lists as ideas 'Heat and Cold, Light and Darkness,
White and Black, Motion and Rest'. It is to become evident
later that the arrangements of particles in the superficies are
among what he calls 'textures' and that among these textures
are secondary qualities, in objects, corresponding to ideas
such as white and heat in us.

> Section 7 of the same chapter contains a similar warning
> . . . it will be convenient to distinguish them [*sc.* our
> ideas], as they are *Ideas* or Perceptions in our Minds; and

as they are modifications of matter in the Bodies that cause such Perceptions in us . . . .

(It is worth noting that Boyle uses such expressions as 'modification of matter' for what Locke calls 'primary qualities'.)

In considering the extent to which Locke heeds his own warning let me start with the passage which might be thought to work most strongly against my view. Chapter viii of Book II must surely be the most relevant to this question since it is here that he distinguishes ideas from their causes, qualities from ideas and secondary qualities from primary qualities. Within this chapter, sections 9 and 10 are probably of the greatest importance since they contain the first and, as I think is generally agreed, the most satisfactory statement of the distinction between primary and secondary qualities. Thus, in first explaining secondary qualities, Locke says

> 2dly, Such *Qualities*, which in truth are nothing in the Objects themselves, but Powers to produce various Sensations in us by their *primary Qualities*, i.e. by the Bulk, Figure, Texture, and Motion of their insensible parts, as Colours, Sounds, Tasts, *etc*. These I call *secondary Qualities*. (II.viii.10)

The form of this passage has misled readers in two ways, most notoriously and inexcusably because they have stopped paying attention after the word 'themselves' and so failed to notice that 'nothing' goes with 'but'. However, here I want to draw attention to a less vulgar and obvious error. I believe that the word 'These' in the last sentence refers back not to 'Colours, Sounds, Tasts, etc.' but to 'Qualities' in its first appearance or to 'Powers to produce various sensations in us', or both. The phrase 'as Colours, Sounds, Tasts, etc.' lists sensations (*i.e.*, ideas). In other words, the passage should be read as if it were written

> Secondly, such qualities which, in the objects themselves, are nothing but powers to produce in us various sensations, such as colours, sound, tastes, etc., by their primary qualities, i.e. by the bulk, figure, texture, and motion of their insensible parts. These qualities (i.e. powers) I call secondary qualities.

We must bear in mind that Locke heads the two sections before this (7 and 8) 'Ideas *in the Mind, Qualities in Bodies*', sections 11 and 12 '*How primary Qualities produce their Ideas*', sections 13 and 14 '*How Secondary*' and section 23 '*Three sorts of Qualities in Bodies*' and that he several times says that secondary qualities are 'merely', 'barely' or 'only' powers. Then my reading of the above passage seems more natural than one that takes 'Colours, Sounds, Tasts, etc.' to be a list of secondary qualities. It has the more important advantage that it saves Locke from such infelicities as the view that ideas can be in objects.

It will be as well now to remove what looks like another telling and ready-to-hand objection to my interpretation. As recently as section 8, Locke has said

> Thus a Snow-ball having the power to produce in us the *Ideas* of *White*, *Cold*, and *Round*, the Powers to produce those *Ideas* in us, as they are in the Snow-ball, I call *Qualities*; and as they are Sensations, or Perceptions, in our Understandings, I call them *Ideas* . . . .

The first occurrence of 'they', referring back, as it seems, to 'Ideas', has led people to think that Locke was confused about whether qualities are ideas and whether ideas are in objects, or else that he here identifies secondary qualities with ideas of them and so contradicts other statements he makes (*e.g.*, Bennett, p. 107).

This, I believe, indicates a failure to see Chapter viii as the developing argument that it is and to note the position of the passage about the snowball in that argument. Part of what Locke is doing in these sections is leading us from thinking with the vulgar to thinking with the learned. More importantly, he is attacking a loose and misleading way of talking about ideas, probably current among philosophers since Descartes.

The detailed discussion of 'the nature of our Ideas' in II.viii begins at section 7, the snowball passage is in section 8 and the distinction between primary and secondary qualities in sections 9–10. Locke begins the chapter by mentioning simple ideas of sensation and, in section 2, listing as examples 'the Ideas of Heat and Cold, Light and Darkness, White and

Black, Motion and Rest'. Up to section 7 he has not yet introduced the term 'quality', although he has distinguished between ideas and their causes, and he uses the word 'idea' loosely to stand indifferently for qualities in things and ideas of them in us. (It may be important that in I.i.8 he says that he uses 'idea' to 'express whatever is meant by phantasm, notion, species' and to remember that 'phantasm' and 'species' were by some taken to be external to minds.) He is leading us from this vulgar way of thinking to the more accurate way of thinking which his use of 'quality' allows. When he lists examples of simple ideas in Section 2 he is still using 'ideas' in the vague and ambiguous sense. He wants to ask 'What are heat and cold?' but he cannot formulate this question or its answer accurately until he has made some distinctions. Having said that the materials of knowledge are simple ideas but not yet having distinguished qualities from ideas, he formulates his project thus

> To discover the nature of our *Ideas* the better, and to discourse of them intelligibly, it will be convenient to distinguish them, as they are *Ideas* or Perceptions in our Minds; and as they are modifications of matter in the Bodies that cause such Perceptions in us . . . . (II.viii.7.)

Ideas can be thought of as mental entities, when they must be in perceivers, or they can be thought of as contents, when they can qualify either perceivers or objects. Locke is suggesting that common sense and some of his opponents do not distinguish these carefully. Thus when we think of ourselves as feeling a hot object we think of the sensation as having the character of the heat in the object. We have ideas of heat and cold; heat and cold are in objects; so we can think of those ideas, *as contents*, as in objects. Speaking with and to the vulgar we can use *idea* as a neutral word to refer to both a sensation and what it represents and to ask whether a given idea is the same in objects as in the mind.

However, this *is* a vulgar way of thinking; it can lead only to confusion and Locke is out to change it. It has connexions with the scholastic view, which both Boyle and Locke were attacking, that every sensation represents to us a real quality of objects. The beginning of the direct attack on it is the question whether ideas in us and in objects resemble one another. In II.xxxi.2 Locke says "'Tis true, the Things producing in us these simple *Ideas*, are but few of them denominated by us, as if they were only the cause of them; but as if those *Ideas* were real Beings in them'.

By section 8 the time has come to dispense with the loose way of speaking and make the word 'idea' more precise. This involves distinguishing formally between ideas and qualities and eliminating the ambiguity by restricting the word 'idea' to mental entities. So we have

> Whatsoever the Mind perceives in it self, or is the immediate object of Perception, Thought, or Understanding, that I call *Idea*; and the Power to produce any *Idea* in our mind, I call *Quality* of the Subject wherein that power is. (II.viii.8.)

There immediately follows, as illustration, the passage about the snowball.

What have, up to now, been called 'ideas' are divided into two classes: thought of as in things they are to be called 'qualities' and thought of as in minds they are to be called 'ideas'; and if Locke sometimes, inadvertently or for brevity, slips into the old way of talking he warns us to remember that he is to be understood in the new way. If, on these occasions, he were speaking strictly he would not use 'red' and 'white' as if they were names of qualities but would instead give descriptions, if they were available, of the textures responsible for causing our ideas of red and white. In everyday discourse we are justified in saying that snowballs are cold and white but, as philosophers, we must be clear what this means and we must speak more precisely.

All this is supported by Locke's statement that

> *Flame* is denominated *Hot* and *Light*; *Snow White* and *Cold*; and *Manna White* and *Sweet*, from the *Ideas* they produce in us. Which Qualities are commonly thought to be the same in those Bodies, that those *Ideas* are in us .... (II.viii.16.)

That is, we call flame hot, and so on, transferring these names from our ideas to the objects because we think of the objects as having qualities resembling the ideas. It is a short step, often unnoticed, to using the word 'idea' both for what is in objects and for what is in us.

When Locke again describes the distinction between primary and secondary qualities, in II.viii.23, he says, in describing secondary qualities,

> Secondly, The Power that is in any Body, by Reason of its insensible primary Qualities, to operate after a peculiar manner on any of our Senses, and thereby produce in us the different Ideas of several Colours, Sounds, Smells, Tasts, etc. These are usually called sensible Qualities.

He has clearly said in the paragraph before that we can discover by observation the primary qualities of middle-sized objects so he does not mean to say, here, that all primary qualities are insensible, in contrast to secondary qualities, all of which are sensible. It might be objected that Locke's italics in the last-quoted passage constitute some evidence against my interpretation. I suggest, however, that in the phrase 'its insensible primary Qualities' the word 'insensible' is to be emphasized and so is left unitalicized in an italicized context; the insensible primary qualities are just the primary qualities of the individual corpuscles, whose patterns cause ideas of secondary qualities. We may take what are 'usually called sensible qualities' to be 'colours, sounds, smells, tastes, etc.,' which are ideas. Locke is, I suggest, objecting to this usual way of speaking since he has already said that these are not qualities. The argument goes on in section 24; this way of talking misleads people into thinking that ideas are qualities and that all ideas are real qualities. I think that he is again proposing a way of talking different from the usual way: colours, sounds, smells, tastes, etc., should not be called 'sensible qualities' but 'ideas of secondary qualities', which qualities really are qualities of bodies, though they are insensible because they are the fine superficial textures of bodies composed of corpuscles.

In sections 14 and 15, which deal with resemblance, I believe that Locke is, inter alia, contrasting what are usually called sensible qualities with what *he* calls secondary qualities. In section 14 he says

> What I have said concerning *Colours* and *Smells*, may be understood also of *Tastes* and *Sounds*, *and other the like sensible Qualities*; which, whatever reality we, by mistake attribute to them, are in truth nothing in the Objects themselves, but Powers to produce various Sensations in us, . . .

If I am correct, for Locke what the man in the street means by 'sensible qualities' must be secondary qualities *as sensed*, *i.e.*, ideas. When Locke in II.xxiii.9 and IV.iii.28, for example, appears to contradict this by talking of sensible secondary qualities I think he is using 'sensible' not in this vulgar sense but in the learned sense to mean 'able directly to cause sensations'.

Both Locke and Boyle were worried by the uncertain and conflicting ways in which the word 'quality' was commonly used at the time. Boyle says that he is not going to waste time enquiring into 'all the several significations of the word *quality*, which is used in such various senses, as to make it ambiguous enough . . .' (Boyle 2, p. 292.)

Locke from time to time speaks, with signs of unease, about vulgar ways of talking. In III.iv.16 he says

> . . . the general term *Quality*, in its ordinary acception, comprehends Colours, Sounds, Tastes, Smells, and tangible Qualities, with distinction from Extension, Number, Motion, Pleasure, and Pain, . . .

In II.xxxi.2, talking of our ordinary way of describing fire as light and hot, he says

> Such ways of speaking, though accommodated to the vulgar Notions, without which, one cannot be well understood; yet truly signify nothing, but those Powers, which are in Things, to excite certain Sensations or *Ideas* in us.

All this is connected with Locke's calling secondary qualities, in section 22, 'imputed qualities'. We never strictly perceive secondary qualities because they are textures responsible for our perceiving colours, smells, sounds and tastes. The textures fit to produce these ideas in us must be *imputed* to bodies on the basis of scientific investigation and inference. Primary or real qualities, on the other hand, we sometimes, at least, perceive as they really are in bodies.

Light is thrown on this by II.xxx.2, where Locke says that even though whiteness and coldness are not in snow yet these are 'real *Ideas* in us whereby we distinguish the Qualities that are really in things themselves' by being either 'constant effects' or 'exact resemblances' of those qualities. 'And thus' he says 'our simple *Ideas* are all real and true, because they answer and agree to those Powers of Things, which produce them in our Minds, that being all that is requisite to make them real, and not fictions at Pleasure'. Thus when Locke calls primary qualities 'real' and secondary qualities 'imputed' he is probably not contrasting real primary qualities with *fictional* secondary qualities but indicating something about the basis for attributing secondary qualities to objects.

Why, then does Locke call the powers of bodies to affect us 'secondary qualities immediately perceivable' and their powers to affect other bodies 'secondary qualities mediately perceivable'? Does this not conflict with my interpretation? I think it does not. Locke does not mean that some secondary qualities are perceivable in the way in which the shape and colour of a piece of porphyry are. He explains what he means in II.viii.26: secondary qualities immediately perceivable are those powers of bodies whereby they are fitted 'by immediately operating on our Bodies to produce several different *Ideas* in us' and secondary qualities mediately perceivable are those powers whereby they are fitted 'by operating on other Bodies, so to change their primary Qualities, as to render them capable of producing *Ideas* in us, different from what before they did'. The contrast is between immediate and mediate operation on our bodies of the corpuscles of external bodies.

NOTES AND REFERENCES

This is a considerably revised version of an earlier paper (1975). I am grateful, for helpful suggestions for improving it, to Professor John W. Yolton, Mrs. Janet R. Sanders and Mr. David Pugmire.

Works to which reference is made:

Alexander, Peter, (1) "Curley on Locke and Boyle", *Phil. Rev.* LXXXIII, 2 (April 1974)

—— (2) "Boyle and Locke on Primary and Secondary Qualities", *Ratio* XVI, 1 (June 1974)

Bennett, J., *Locke, Berkeley and Hume* (Oxford, 1971)

Boyle, Robert, (1) *The Origin of Forms and Qualities* in *Works* (London 1772), Vol. III.

—— (2) *Introduction to the History of Particular Qualities* in *Works* (London 1772) Vol. III.

Butler, R. J., "Substance Un-Locked", *Proc. Arist. Soc.* LXXIV, (1973–4).

Curley, E. M., "Locke, Boyle and the Distinction between Primary and Secondary Qualities', *Phil. Rev.* LXXXI, 4 (October 1971).

Kretzmann, Norman, "The Main Thesis of Locke's Semantic Theory", *Phil. Rev.* LXXVII, 2 (April 1968).

Locke, John, *An Essay Concerning Human Understanding* ed. Peter H. Nidditch (Oxford 1975). All references to the *Essay* are to this edition

XIV*—ON PUNISHING

by Alec Kassman[1]

"There is nothing worse than impunity."[2]

I THE TOPIC

Hans Kelsen, founder of the Vienna School of jurisprudence, erstwhile associate of the Vienna Circle, published in 1946 *Society and Nature*,[3] a book he described as a sociological inquiry, which he conducted mainly from secondary sources. In it he argued that for primitive man the principal category of explanation is in terms of wrong followed by retribution, both within society and in the realm of nature, for nature is regarded by primitive man as an extension of society. A version of this belief persisted among the ancient Greeks and was manifested in, for example, their stories of 'the spirit of the place', and even in the assertion of Heraclitus that the *Erinyes* keep the Sun in his courses.[4] The gradual abandonment of retribution as a category of explanation in nature is pointed by Archelaos with the development of the antithesis between *physis* (nature) and *nomos* (convention) and consequently separate categories of explanation of natural events and of social conduct. Ultimately a total reversal of the original primitive view of nature as an extension of society was effected by the Stoics who sought to establish society as a part of nature.

Alongside the foregoing developments in Greek thought, the Orphics and Pythagoreans agreed in teaching that it was part of the plan of a moral universe that all shall get their due deserts, that is to say, the virtuous shall prosper and the wicked shall not. Since, however, this manifestly does not occur in this World, it follows that this World is not all that there is: there must be another in which the moral principle does take effect. This view was adopted by Plato and expressly

---

* Meeting of the Aristotelian Society at 5/7, Tavistock Place, London W.C.1, on Monday, 16th May, 1977 at 7.30 p.m.

stated in the *Phaedo* (81B–82B), and clearly intended in the eschatological myths of the *Phaedo* (107C–114C) and the *Gorgias* (523A–527C), and also subsequently repeated by Jesus of Nazareth (*passim*).

What is especially significant about this is, I suggest, that the notion of basing a cosmology, and also the immortality of the soul, upon the 'deserts' principle, should be seriously considered and adopted, and not immediately derided as manifest rubbish. That Pythagoras and the Orphics, Plato and Jesus should all assert the same thesis does not, of course, make it true, but it does make it at least respectable.

Now that we have seen some of the loading that the 'deserts' principle can bear, we may look at it more closely, and the first thing to emphasis is that it is a dual principle:

bonis bona et malis mala.

In practice, the principle seems almost always to be considered by reference to the latter element—*malis mala*—and that for good reason: it is more dramatic and arresting, so that the problems are seen more nakedly. All the same, there appears to be no difference in principle between the two elements, and we may just as well ask *Cur bonis bona?* as *Cur malis mala?* and hope to gain as much enlightenment from the former as from the latter formulation. Only it doesn't seem to worry us so much. Why it doesn't is, I think, a fascinating question, but I shan't pursue it here. Just let us not forget that what we have to say about punishing the vicious should also be sayable, *mutatis mutandis*, about rewarding the virtuous in the absence of any special grounds for discriminating between the two cases.

Let us, then, turn to punishing and I want to ask first, what is it? Prof. Hart in his Presidential Address to this Society[5] criticises those who attempt to limit discussion by means of a definition, so I must make clear my claim that I am seeking not to limit discussion but to refine it. I think we shall find that, when we have looked closely at what punishing is, a number of questions, which formerly appeared to arise, in fact fall away as they have no purchase. Well, let's see.

I start with a leading authority on logic:

". . . There's the King's Messenger. He's in prison now, being punished: and the trial doesn't even begin until next Wednesday: and of course, the crime comes last of all."

"Suppose he never commits the crime?" said Alice.

"That would be all the better, wouldn't it?" the Queen said . . .

Alice felt there was no denying *that*.

"Of course it would be all the better," she said: "but it wouldn't be all the better his being punished."

"You're wrong *there*, at any rate," said the Queen: "were *you* ever punished?"

"Only for faults," said Alice.

"And you were all the better for it, I know!" the Queen said triumphantly.

"Yes, but then I *had* done the things I was punished for," said Alice; "that makes all the difference."

"But if you *hadn't* done them," the Queen said, "that would have been better still; better, and better, and better!" . . .

Alice was just beginning to say "There's a mistake somewhere—," when the Queen began screaming . . .[6]

1. Punishing is an activity which involves at least six *relata*: at time t' A (a sentient being) punishes B (a sentient being) by imposing upon B c (something disagreeable) in respect of d (some conduct or neglect by B) which occurred at an earlier time t. In order to clear the ground, I shall start with some preliminary observations upon some points which I take to be relatively clear and uncontroversial: and I need hardly add that the same schema will also represent rewarding: the difference is that, in rewarding, c is something pleasing.

2. A and B can be, and sometimes are, conflated—that is to say, it is intelligible that a man should punish himself.

3. A and B will be not lower than human agents. If we saw, say, a pack of dogs making things unpleasant for one of their number and we were told that they were punishing him for something he did last week, I think that we should find that incredible, for we will not attribute the concept of punishing

to any creatures lower than man. As to beings higher than man, we can conceive of gods' punishing one another: Homer and Hesiod have some intelligible accounts of this. We can also conceive of angels' punishing one another, and Milton's accounts of this are also intelligible. I am not sure about devils' punishing each other—it bears consideration. Still I shall arbitrarily exclude gods, angels and devils from the discussion in this paper, except in relation to Plato's myths.

4. Regarding the disagreeable quality of c, it is not necessary that either A or B should in fact find c disagreeable; what is necessary is that A should believe that B will find c disagreeable and B must know that A does believe it and is acting on that belief.

5. Both A and B must be aware that c is imposed in respect of d and each must know that the other is aware of it.

6. As it stands, the schema is too wide since it would include such things as revenge and vendetta, which lie outside the scope of punishment. I wish now to consider how punishing may be isolated and distinguished from those other activities.

II   THE PARTIES

Let us start by considering A, the punisher or agent.

(i) As mentioned above, A may be identical with B. That case raises a number of points of interest, but I propose to confine myself to cases where A and B are different from one another.

(ii) I think it is evident that A must be seen to be in some position of entitlement to impose c upon B. The obvious case is that of A's legal auhority to impose a legal punishment, but we can also entertain cases of *de facto* authority. For example, if a schoolboy recklessly throws a cricket ball through a neighbour's window, and the boy's father pays for the damage but, by way of punishment, deducts the cost of it from his son's pocket money, that is intelligible as punishment of the son. If, however, the neighbour simply compels the boy to hand over the cost of a new window, we cannot accept that as a case of punishment. I think that the difference lies in the status of father and of neighbour respectively, in relation to the boy. As things are in our society, the father *qua* father has authority to impose punishment, while the neighbour has not, so that the latter's action, prudent though it may be, cannot be accepted as punishment. The point that I am trying to make may be alternatively phrased as that punishing is a social activity of which the nature and quality are in part determined by the norms of each particular society. The relevance of these norms lies in establishing the authority of the punisher to act as such, and the competence of the punished to fill that rôle. This latter point I shall consider further below in relation to the status of the punished.

(iii) It is necessary that *A* should be some recognisable or definable person, either an actual human being or group of human beings, or else a legal or other social *persona*. Thus, in England, most crimes are punished by agents of 'the Crown' which is a corporation sole[7] and not any particular individual person who is the monarch at any one time. We also recognise that, for example, a limited company, a trade union, a university, or "the family" may properly be said to punish an offender in appropriate circumstances. Each of the first three is a legal *persona*; the fourth is not, but it can be identified in some cases as a social *persona*. What I am getting at here is to distinguish between a penalty seen to be exacted by an authorised human agent from some damage or injury caused by some unauthorized agency (for example, a rioting mob) or some non-human agency (for example, a falling golden cross; see Gibbon's account of the sack of Constantinople).

(iv) It is necessary that *A* should recognise himself as being a person (or *persona*) acting pursuant to and in accordance with the authority vested in him for the specific purpose of punishing. What is less clear is whether or not *B* should also recognise *A* as being a person (or *persona*) acting in that manner. Thus, in the time of the Protectorate, a Royalist supporter of the King in exile might well have found it impossible to recognise the authority of any of the courts in the realm sitting in the name of the Lord Protector. It is, I think quite a difficult question to decide whether such a Royalist could recognise a penalty imposed by any such Court as constituting a punishment, properly so called, or whether he would be bound to regard it as an act of some entirely different sort, for example, revenge, treason, or act of war. At least I think it is proper to say that in such a case the defendant, after understanding that the prosecution and judges genuinely believed themselves and claimed to be acting in accordance with legal authority, would accept that they would be seen by themselves and by their supporters as genuinely seeking and imposing punishment notwithstanding the defendant's inability to see their actions in that light. If, however, the defendant did not even understand what the claim of the judges was, then I think that he could not even grant that they were claiming or purporting to punish. I think, therefore, that the conclusion is that the punisher's claim in relation to his authority, must at least be understood by the punished, even if not granted by him.

Let us now look at B, the punished or recipient.

(A) As indicated above, it is necessary that B should have the competence to stand in the position of the punished. This involves a number of considerations. For example:

> (i) B must at least understand what the features of the situation are. If, owing to, say, infirmity of mind, or because B comes from some alien culture whose concepts, norms or mores do not include anything of this sort, he does not understand the complex of *relata* about him, then in such cases it is unintelligible to B to talk to him about his being punished, and so the proper minimal set of relationships fails to be established.
>
> (ii) B must at least see himself as answerable for d. Thus, if he has no recollection of d, or genuinely believes that d was performed by somebody else, once again a necessary element is missing from the basic relationships.

(B) B must be the knowing performer of c. This condition involves a number of far-reaching considerations explored in English law under a concept of *mens rea*. ('*Actus non facit reum nisi mens sit rea*', the agent does no evil unless his mind be evil.) It will not pursue the intricacies of this doctrine as that would take us too far away from the present inquiry. I think it suffices to say that it is recognised that B

must know what he is doing and intend to do it. This excludes such cases as hallucinatory action (for example, the man who thought he was butchering a pig and cut his victim's throat) and involuntary action (for example, the man who is thrown by centrifugal force out of a moving vehicle driven by another, and crushes a passer-by).

In this Section I have attempted, by eliciting features of the parties which I take to be relatively free from controversy, to clarify the basic conditions of conducting intelligible discourse concerning the concept of punishing. I now wish to turn to a different feature—namely the relation between d (the wrongful action) and c (the penalty).

III   THE ACTION AND THE PENALTY

It is, I think instructive to recall Plato's two myths of Tartarus, *Gorgias* 523A–527C and *Phaedo* 107C–114C, the import of both of which is roughly the same, that after death the souls of men appear before the judgment seat and are distinguished according to the lives they have led on earth —those who have lived well receiving their due reward; and those ill, their just punishment. Plato's purposes in introducing these two myths are different in the two dialogues, but yet in a way related. In the *Gorgias* he is concerned to establish that it is better, both morally and hedonically, to suffer injustice than to perform it, on the grounds of the respective effects of each upon man's immortal soul. In the *Phaedo* Plato's aim is to establish the immortality of the soul, and one of his considerations is that on this earth it is often the case that good is apparently penalised, while evil apparently rewarded; the principle of justice inherent in the universe requires that this evident imbalance be rectified by a more far-reaching and supra-temporal application of the principle of justice. For this purpose, the soul cannot be restricted to the spatio-temporal conditions of this sub-lunary world, but must have an existence beyond it. What is, I think particularly striking about these two myths is the power of the concept of justice which they incapsulate. In effect, one of Plato's theses is that the vision of injustice victorious is so outrageous that from its reversal stems the necessary consequence of the immortality of the soul. Now, as indicated above, what is significant here is not that critics accept or reject Plato's conclusions, but that his premiss, that justice requires the reward of the virtuous and punishment of the vicious, is nowhere dismissed as trumpery and foolish. At the heart of the matter lie the concepts of just reward and just punishment. Let us pause to consider just and unjust punishment.

As noticed above, the mere imposition of the penalty c does not *ipso facto* constitute an act of punishing; it might be private vengeance, self-help, or some other recognisable practice. The considerations outlined above in relation to the parties are intended to help us to distinguish between genuine punishment and some other procedure of the like nature. Our present inquiry, therefore, is not 'Is the imposition of this penalty a genuine punishment or something else?' but, 'Is the imposition of this penalty a reasonable or unreasonable punishment?' which presupposes that the former question has already been answered.

I think it is true to say that the question 'Is this punishment?' relates principally to the identity of A and of B. If there is something wrong there, then the imposition of the penalty is not genuine punishment. The question 'Is this punishment reasonable?' refers rather to the relation between penalty, c, and the conduct complained of, d. In brief, there must be some proportion or balance between them.

Anybody who has been concerned with the conduct of proceedings before a criminal tribunal, for example, a magistrate or a Crown Court, will know that it is an essential part of the preparation of an advocate's case on behalf of the defendant that he prepare a 'Plea in Mitigation', that is to say, on the assumption that the defendant will be found guilty, an address to the Court for use after the verdict, to persuade the bench that it would be just to impose a mild penalty.[8] The sort of thing that is so pleaded is that the prisoner was hitherto of unblemished character, that he lost his job through no fault of his own, that he has to maintain an invalid wife and several young children, that he was suddenly faced with an overwhelming temptation, that he has been full of remorse ever since, and so on. Now the point is that this sort of plea

is not only acceptable to the Court, it is expected as part of
the duty of the prisoner's advocate. That is to say, it is recognised that the severity of the sentence must properly be
tempered according to the moral obliquity of the defendant
in committing the act complained of—the less flagitious, the
lighter the sentence and, consequently, the more iniquitous
the heavier the sentence.

It is well known that in the English courts many sentences
upon convicted prisoners are determined in part by the manner of the conduct of their defence in court. Thus, judges are
more leniently inclined towards prisoners who plead Guilty
to the charge, than to those who plead Not Guilty and occupy
the time of the court upon a determination of guilt. Also,
bargains are frequently struck between prosecution and
defence, whereby the prisoner pleads guilty to a lesser charge
which is subject to a modest penalty, and the prosecution drop
the major charge which would carry a much more severe
penalty. What is striking about such cases is the indignation
which is, now and again, publicly expressed about them. The
ground of such indignation is that the courts ought not to
allow such extraneous and irrelevant considerations as the
convenience of the prosecution or the time of court proceedings to enter into a determination of the severity of a wrong-
doer's punishment, for that should be determined by the
principle of justice, and that principle is the one elicited by
the concept of the Plea in Mitigation.

Remorse
An habitual feature of the Plea in Mitigation is some
emphasis laid upon the prisoner's subsequent remorse after
committing his offence. That such a consideration should be
recognised without question as pertinent to the determination of sentence does indicate that the gravity of the offence
itself is not, and should not be, the only factor determining
the severity of the sentence. We have already seen that the
offender's previous criminal record, or lack of it, is an admissible consideration. Now, we introduce the further factor
of the offender's subsequent remorse as also pertinent. These
considerations demonstrate that the principle of justice in
punishment requires us to take into account the degree of

turpitude of the offender as a whole, that is to say, covering the period before his offence, the commission of his offence, and the period thereafter: that is to say, while the moral quality of the offence is a determining factor, it is so as part of the more general consideration of the moral quality of the offender *in toto*.

In the opening parts of this paper, I have attempted to show that the question whether or not the imposition of a sanction is a case of punishment for an earlier offence, is determined by the identity and status of each of the two parties, the punisher and the punished. In the third part, I have tried to show that the question, what sort of punishment ought reasonably to be imposed, is one of balance which is determined by the moral quality of the offender and his conduct complained of, so that the introduction of other considerations of a different nature is unreasonable and improper.

IV BOGUS AND UNJUST PUNISHMENT

Let us consider a miscarriage of justice, say, someone punished for somebody else's offence, for example, Captain Dreyfus sent to Devil's Island for another officer's treason. The question is, Is this punishment? If we assume the *bona fides* of the prosecution and of the Court Martial in that case (a difficult assumption!) then we can say that the judges claimed to be, and believed that they were, imposing a punishment; and certainly what happened to Captain Dreyfus as a result was as bad as any punishment could be. But what of Captain Dreyfus himself, and of the conspirators who concocted the false case against him? They all knew that one *relatum* was missing from the total schema, namely, the prior offence *c*, so that they could not properly talk of Captain Dreyfus's being punished but, in veridical discourse would have to use some such terms as 'persecuted', 'oppressed', 'victimised', or 'injured'. Although we do in practice talk loosely of, say, Captain Dreyfus's being punished for another man's treason, it is evident that that is an extension of the term, for the sake of convenience, to cover cases of bogus punishment, just as we might loosely say, "These banknotes are forged", when we mean that the documents are not banknotes at all and, therefore, properly ought not to be so called.

If, therefore, a man is 'punished' for an offence he did not commit, then that is not a case of unjust punishment but, rather, it is not a case of punishment at all. I think that one reason why we are inclined to talk of 'punishment' in such extended cases is partly because we are careless in our speech and partly because we are inclined to think that every bit of nastiness imposed on a man by the criminal courts must be a punishment, but that is not so. A magistrate may commit a man for trial and remand him in custody pending trial. That period of imprisonment is not strictly a punishment. Or consider the *peine forte et dure*, a form of torture introduced by the Statute of Westminster I, 1275. This followed the virtual abolition of trial by ordeal after the resolution of the Lateran Council of 1215. It then became necessary to induce persons accused of felony in the King's Courts to accept trial by jury, and to that end, they were required to plead either Guilty or Not Guilty before the Court. Now, if the accused were found guilty of felony, the penalty was death, but in addition, his goods would be forfeit to the Crown and his land to his feudal Lord, and that forfeiture could not happen if he refused to plead. The statutory procedure then was to press the accused under iron weights until he either consented to plead or died. Many men did so die, the last recorded case being as late as 1658, but it was not until 1772 that the *peine forte et dure* was abolished. Now it is important to realise that this form of torture was not deemed to be punishment at all but a mere procedural device to enable a plea from the accused to be recorded in court. The reason why it was not a punishment was the very fact that there was no antecedent offence proven to have been committed by the accused.

We may contrast with the foregoing cases such episodes as, say, the case of the Tolpuddle Martyrs. There, all the necessary ingredients were present and the acts complained of (administering unlawful oaths) were genuine offences known to the law. However, the enormity of the penalties, transportation, was so disproportionate to the technical nature of the legal offences that even at the time no serious attempt was made to justify them as acts of justice, or as anything other than acts of political expediency. Here, then, lies the explanation of the notion of unjust punishment: not in harassing a man for what he didn't do, but in unreasonably punishing him for what he did do, such unreasonableness taking the form of disproportionate severity of the punishment in relation to the moral quality of the offence.

It is claimed that the analysis up to this point has elicited the following features of punishing:

1. Punishing is a moral activity conducted in a social *milieu* by an authorised agent upon a competent recipient in respect of some antecedent conduct of an improper nature on the part of the recipient.

2. Punishing is justly conducted if, and only if, the severity or mildness of the penalty imposed bears some reasonable relation to the degree of moral obliquity or innocuousness of the offence and of the recipient's conduct in general.

3. The admission of considerations other than justice into the determination of the penalty imposed derogates from the justice of the punishing process.

It is hardly necessary to add that in relation to 2 above, it is no part of my purpose here to attempt to determine what is a reasonable and proper relation between penalty and offence. That difficult question has to be determined on every occasion by the appropriate agent, taking into account all the facts as they are known to him.

V   FURTHER CONSIDERATIONS

It follows from the foregoing that the questions what the act of punishing essentially is, and wherein, if anywhere, lies the justice of it, are to be determined by looking backwards in time at the offence complained of, and at the other conduct of the recipient. Consequently, any introduction of considerations of a forward-looking nature, as for example, the consequences upon the recipient, or upon the agent, or upon anybody else, is not pertinent to the nature of the punishing process or to its application, and will therefore, tend to conduce to injustice. This is not to say that in practice such considerations ought to be, or even can be, ignored. The effect, say, of sending an offender to prison in a certain case may perhaps be expected to have disastrous consequences upon his character, or upon the welfare of many persons dependent on him, so that a judge would quite properly take this consideration into account in determining a penalty. Nevertheless, this is not a matter of justice: it is a matter of social or political expediency, or simply of mercy. That is to say, justice is not the only consideration. An excessively mild sentence may be as unjust as an excessively severe one, and each may be expedient for one reason or another; and mercy is no less a virtue than justice, but it is not itself justice.

It further follows that such considerations as using the penalty to make the recipient a better man, or to scare him from doing the same sort of thing again, or to scare others from following his example, are in no way pertinent to a determination of the nature of the act of punishing or to its justice or injustice. All such forward-looking considerations as those, which we may conveniently lump together under the label 'utilitarian', point to ways in which the act of punishing can be, and often is, used for an entirely different purpose, just as a chisel may be used as a screwdriver, but using it as a screwdriver does not make it a screwdriver, or in any way deprive it of its character of chiselry. But we have seen that punishing is essentially a moral activity within a social *milieu*, namely, the redressing of the balance of justice. Consequently, all attempts to explain or justify, or recommend, or assess the justice of punishment by reference to utilitarian considerations may be set aside as basically immoral and unjust, and also as founded upon misconceptions of what punishment is, what is just punishment, and what may be an expedient use of it.

It further follows that to ask what is the justification of punishment, is to ask a misconceived question, for it raises the prior questions, what is the justification of morality, and what is the justification of society. It is not clear that these are intelligible questions, but even if they can be shown to be so it is clear that they cannot be approached by asking the subordinate question, what is the justification of punishment, but rather is the subordinate question to be approached by way of the fundamental ones. If, as I suspect, the antecedent questions are not genuine ones, then the subordinate question is not a genuine one either. And if the superior questions can be shown to be genuine questions, it does not follow that the subordinate question is a genuine one—and I think it is not, in any event, for reasons indicated above.

VI THE STATE AS PUNISHING AGENT

The State not only punishes but also conducts other activities which are *prima facie* like punishing, and we have already seen some examples of these. It is profitable to contrast punishing with some of the others as well. These others may be conveniently classified into peace-keeping activities and non-peace-keeping activities. Let us look at the latter first.

A. *Quasi-Penal non-peace-keeping State Activities*

These are quasi-punishing activities of the State which are not directly concerned with the preservation of peaceable order within the realm. They may again be sub-classified into those activities which are designed to secure some course of conduct from the recipient, and those activities which are not so designed. Let us consider the latter first.

1. *Quasi-Penal non-peace-keeping State Activities not designed to secure a course of conduct from the recipient*

The sort of thing that falls into this category is disagreeable conduct towards people for the sole reason that they are what they are, with no expectation or intention that they will become anything different—except dead. It includes, for example, ill-treatment of prisoners of war, persecution of people on the grounds of their religious beliefs, or on the grounds of their lineage. The treatment of such persons may be as bad as any punishment, and worse than most. The puzzlement arises when you ask the agent, What are you ill-treating them for? If he wants to answer in terms of punishment he can only say something like "I am punishing them for being enemy prisoners", "for being homoiousians", "for having one Jewish grandparent", or "for disbelieving the word of the Prophet". Now this sort of answer is not only shocking, it leaves us perplexed by reason of its conceptual confusion. The purportedly explanatory phrase explains nothing. It seems to be on about the same level of intelligibility as saying, "I am thrashing this dog because it is a labrador and not a spaniel". It is intelligible (even though disgusting) for a man to say "I hate prisoners of war and I am doing this to give vent to my hatred", whereas, it is not intelligible for him to say "I am punishing these people because they are prisoners of war". The vocabulary of punishing is wrong in this context because the recipients are suffering because of what they are and not because of what they have done.

2. *Quasi-Penal non-peace-keeping State Activities designed to secure future conduct*

These would include such activities as committing a man to a mental hospital to secure his adherence to the State's policy, or depriving a man of his livelihood to induce him to join a trade union, or holding a man in prison until he agrees to attend the established church. In none of these cases would the agent even claim that he was *punishing* the recipient; his claim would be, I imagine, that he was attempting to induce the recipient to mend his evil ways and to induce him to pursue a better way of life in future, or, even if that should fail, to dissuade others from following the recipient's example.

An interesting borderline case, which is not at all easy to classify, is provided by committal to prison for contempt of court. Contempt of court is a legal offence and it is usually manifested by failure to comply with an order of the court. Committal is indeed a punishment and is usually ordered by an angry judge who deems himself to be the object of contempt; nevertheless, the purpose of the committal order is to induce in the offender a right and proper appreciation of the authority and dignity of the court, and obedience to its wishes. The offender is committed to prison until such time as he 'purges his contempt', that is to say, until he obeys the order he had previously flouted and also files in court an affidavit containing an abject and diplomatic (and entirely insincere) apology for his previous failure. When all this has been done, the judge will very grandly declare that he is satisfied that the offender has purged his contempt, and thereupon set him at liberty. The case is anomalous because the nature and extent of the penalty imposed depends entirely upon what the offender does about it then and thereafter. The original contempt is the occasion for the committal order but it then falls out of consideration, and the offender's treatment is determined by the strength of mind, or obstinacy, with which he chooses to defy or submit to the authority of the court. The underlying theory, as indicated by the term 'purge his contempt', is that the offender has benefited from receiving some spiritual therapy, and thereby becomes a better man with a healthy attitude towards the court and the law. It is for this reason that agitation arises from time to time to reform the institution, since it is in practice, in most cases, a piece of coercive machinery disguised as punishment.

In this sub-section on Quasi-Penal State Activities of a non-peace-keeping nature, we have found reason to distinguish them from genuine punishment, either on the ground of the absence of any antecedent offence to which the penalty is directed, or else on the ground that whether or not there has been any such antecedent offence, the penalty imposed is designed to coerce the 'offender' or others into some future course of action, rather than to secure a just requital of his past conduct.

B. *Quasi-Penal State Activity of a Peace-Keeping Character*

Examples of this sort of thing would be commandeering private supplies, chattels or property for use in the restoration of peace during civil disturbances, conscription for military or other service to the State, confining a jury without food or heat until they reach a unanimous verdict, and so on. Once again, it is needless to state that the hardship and suffering caused to the recipient may be far greater than that occasioned by many punishments. Nevertheless, these are not cases of punishment because in no case is the recipient deemed to be guilty of any offence at all so that no justice is deemed to be visited upon him; he is simply deemed to be the victim of unavoidable State activity directed towards the superior end of establishing and maintaining the welfare of the State and its citizens by the preservation of public order and of institutions that conduce thereto. What is involved here is not justice but expediency and the public good to which the interests of the individual are necessarily subordinated.

Genuine Penal Activities of the State

The State's genuine penal activities are in effect, punishing by law, and that is a topic which will occupy the remainder of this paper.

VII   PUNISHING BY LAW

In Parts I–V of this paper I have argued that punishing is a moral activity, the restoration of justice in relation to wrong-doing, so that it is immoral to punish for some extraneous purpose, for example, to change the character of the evil-doer, or to discourage others from following his example. I now wish to consider one of the more dramatic and ritualistic forms of punishing, that is, punishing by law. But at the outset I should enter a number of caveats.

First, there is no one universal system of law, there is no such thing as 'the Law'; what we have are numerous different systems of law, more or less closely or distantly related to one another. There is only the system of law of this or that place, Country, Province, State, division and so on.

Secondly, although across the centuries, from the Stoics to the present day, attempts have been made to formulate 'Natural Law' as such a universal system, what has been presented under this rubric has been either a universalised system of a set of moral rules which especially commended themselves to the formulator (*e.g., audi et alteram partem*), or else the application and extrapolation of the rules of Roman Law (as, for example, by Grotius), or both. At best, 'Natural Law' may serve as a criterion of just law—but not as itself 'the law of the land' in any territory.

Thirdly, in general, references to 'the Law' signify the law of one's own country, and in this paper I do so use the term, that is, to signify English Law unless otherwise indicated either expressly or by the context.

In relation to punishing, two basic questions arise in law:

Q.1 : What is legally punishable?
Q.2 : What is legally a punishment?

As to Q.1, the short answer is 'crimes', of one sort or another, heinous or venial, dangerous or innocuous. To clarify this notion it may be helpful to contrast it with sin, with moral obliquity, and with injury.

In regard to sin, I take it that the essential element is that it bears the taint of unholiness, that it is an offence against God, so that what is a sin will depend upon the prevailing religious doctrines of some place, time and people, for example, praying in this or that way, eating this or that food, and also the more spectactular forms of wrong-doing. In a theocracy or an hieratocracy, pretty well all sins will be crimes, and all crimes sins.

In regard to moral obliquity, in general this will include most but perhaps not all sins. As a rule, moral obliquity will cover a wider scope than sin, but in a theocracy they may be expected to be virtually co-terminous.

Crimes will normally include most sins and many but not all immoral actions, and some crimes may be neither sinful nor immoral. There is no satisfactory short formula, but some essential elements are (i) breach or non-observance of a legal rule, (ii) the remedy is sought by the State and not by an individual, and (iii) the remedy is in the nature of a penalty.

An injury may be to the person or to property, and it is sometimes a sin, sometimes immoral, sometimes a crime, and sometimes none of those.

Sin is the province of the Canon Law; moral obliquity of no law; crime, of the criminal law; and injury—if a sin, of the Canon Law—if immoral, perhaps of the civil law of contract, tort and so on—if a crime, of the criminal law—and if none of those, perhaps of the civil law. Obviously, the foregoing schema is much too tidy, and there will, in practice, be much overlapping between the categories; still, in general we are able to recognise that in relation to crimes, the relevant law, the Criminal Law, lays down punishment, while in relation to injury (other than crimes) the relevant law, of contract, tort, and so on, is concerned with private remedy and protection of private rights and property.

In England, there are a few anomalous cases, but most of these, for example, the old Common Informer actions, have been largely removed, and we can recognise the clear distinction drawn above. This, however, was not always so, whether in England or elsewhere and I think that a brief glance at history may be instructive.

It will be recalled that the nations of Western Europe owe their origins to the drive from the East of the barbarian tribes who came as nomads, and over-ran the land following the collapse of Rome. These tribes in general retained their nomadic character until they were halted by such natural limits as sea and mountains, and then were compelled to settle on the land to which they were thus restricted. They were led by their Chiefs and more or less subordinate commanders and, when the land was settled, these became Kings and Barons. Following the spread of Christianity and the Holy Roman Empire, Pope and Emperor were added to the hierarchy and, by way of further complication, Patriarch and the Emperor of the East. (These last two are mentioned for completeness only, and will now be neglected.)

If we consider the four classes of rulers, Pope, Emperor, King, Barons, and remember that each class was attempting to establish its own ascendancy over, or independence of, the others, in social, political, religious and legal affairs, we see that in practice the Barons, having their forces on the spot, were best placed, and next best, the King. Between these two classes, Barons and King, there developed a contest for legal jurisdiction over land, tenants, and people—villeins, serfs and slaves. In the first instance, the settlement of local disputes and complaints would be the business of the Court of the Baron, and the story of legal history is the record of the slow and gradual extension of the King's jurisdiction, beyond the limits of his own feudal lands, at the expense of the Barons, and the development of the concept of the King's Peace through which this was effected, until his Peace covered his entire country. The purpose of all this juristic activity was 'compensation' in the wide sense of the old German tribes.[9]

The development described above was not without its financial aspect. Both Baron and King were concerned to pay their Judges, and to enlarge their own incomes, and this each of them effected through a system of percentage impost upon the value of each claim or dispute brought into his Court, and each established a system of sale of rights for an acknowledged scale of charges! Thus the extension of legal jurisdiction represented a combination of compensation and penalty for the litigant, and revenue for the Lord of the Court. Gradually, in the course of history, the King established his authority and that of his Courts, over the Barons and their Courts, and the development of the system of the King's Courts, by way of the King's Peace, led to the extension of his hegemony as feudal superior over the entire realm, and the spread of the King's Justice throughout the country, together with the correlated decline of the Barons' Courts.[10]

It is instructive to recall that, following the Norman Conquest, there was an interregnum between the death of one monarch and the accession of the next. During that period of no King there was no King's Peace, so that each man had to defend his own Peace, and the consequences to the public safety were calamitous. Eventually, Edward II succeeded to the throne *immediately* upon the death of Edward I, with no interregnum, and since then that precedent has always been followed, expressly to avoid any suspension of the King's Peace.[11]

Furthermore, in the interests of public order, the King was concerned not only to visit sanctions upon the commission of offences, but also to keep this office to himself in order to suppress the possible proliferation of offences and breaches of the peace through the operation of private recrimination and private execution of 'justice', for the victim of an offence may be as great a threat to the public peace and to the common weal, as the perpetrator. *A fortiori*, it falls to the King to secure the common weal against the incidence of private punishment effected not by wronged individuals but by concerted groups. For if and when the King, or the State, will not, or cannot, secure the execution of justice upon wrongdoers, then we see from history that this leads to the development of quasi-states within the State, each of them executing its own form of justice or vindictiveness in accordance with its own lights. Examples of this may be seen in the mediaeval armies of feudal retainers, the private armies of the sixteenth and seventeenth centuries, the bootleg gangs in the U.S.A. of the 1920s and 1930s, and the religious armies of Northern Ireland to-day. On the footing that *salus populi suprema lex*, these few examples indicate that not only is the State justified in claiming and exercising the power of the administration of justice but, in addition, it has a duty to do so, and is in dereliction of its duty when it allows crime to proceed unpunished. From this dereliction of duty flows the risk of civil strife and social disintegration.

The point of this foray into history is to bring out the importance of the concept of the King's Peace, and its preservation, and its emergence as a separate element in the development of the law, distinct from the safety of, and compensation for, individual citizens. In due course, the protection of the King's Peace became the province of the criminal law, while other branches of the law, land law, Common Law, Equity and so on, developed the system of remedies for the individual and his property. This division, in England, is illustrated by the establishment and development of the office of Justice of the Peace, which was a royal creation and a royal appointment.[12] But although the King's Peace is an English institution there is nothing particularly English or even Germanic about the replacement of private vengeance for private wrong ('*nemo me impune lacessit*') by the public administration of a system of criminal law. In relation to Roman Law, for example, Moyle writes:

> In such a social condition [*i.e.*, of social disharmony] the only mode in which a man who conceived himself wronged by another could obtain satisfaction was by taking the law, as it is said, into his own hands. A system of self-redress, in the form of private vengeance preceded everywhere the establishment of a regular judicature.[13]

From the process thus described we may see that the concept of crime has its origin in the notion of a breach of, or threat to, the King's Peace, that is to say, the welfare and safety of the realm. Here, then, is revealed the public aspect and the essential feature of the criminal law, namely, the preservation of public security. The foundation, then, of the criminal law lies in the maxim '*salus populi suprema lex*'. That this is not a mere relic dredged up out of antique history, but that it remains the principle of the criminal law in England, is illustrated by the recent case of *Gouriet* v. *Union of Post Office Workers and others*, Court of Appeal, 1977, reported in *The Times* during January 1977, especially 28th January 1977.[13a] See in particular the explanation by the Attorney General to the House of Commons in Parliamentary Report, *The Times*

28th January 1977, that he had decided, upon the facts dis-
closed in that case, that it would be wrong for him, as the
senior Law Officer of the Crown, to take any active steps to
prevent the intended commission of a crime because in his
view (mistaken as it turned out) the consequences of any such
steps on his part would be more damaging to the public
security than would the consequences of the intended crime.
While the Minister was criticised from various quarters, that
principle was not challenged.[13b]

Furthermore, it is as well to recognise that, in England at
least,[14] the criminal law is not negative in its effect upon the
individual citizen, but positive upon him. That is to say, the
citizen is not required merely to refrain from causing or
threatening damage to the common weal, but also actively to
secure it. Thus the citizen has at Common Law a right of
arrest in respect of certain offences committed in his presence,
and he is obliged to go to the aid of a police officer who calls
upon him to assist in the apprehension of a suspected person.
Since, therefore, the major sanction of the criminal law is
punishment, it follows that the purpose of legal punishment
is positively to impose upon the subject the active duty to
respect the law and maintain the (at present) Queen's Peace.

Furthermore, since punishment is an instrument whereby
the criminal law is made effective, it follows that, in law,
punishment is always tendentious. Consequently, from the
conclusion reached in Part III, it seems to follow that punishment in law is always immoral, or at best lies outside the
realms of morals. This last conclusion would be perfectly
acceptable to proponents of the Pure Theory of Law as developed by Hans Kelsen, for he argued that all law lies outside the realm of morals.[15] However, the Pure Theory of Law
is an entirely different kettle of fish from the discussion in
this paper, so I feel obliged to look at the question of the
relation of Law to Morals, thus thrown up.

VIII   LAW AND MORALS IN RELATION TO PUNISHING

We saw in Parts I to III that from the principle of 'deserts' it
follows that in morals it is wrong to punish in order to secure
some end or purpose other than punishment itself in relation

to wrong-doing. We also found reason to conclude in Part VII that in most contemporary systems of law punishment is imposed to achieve the purpose of the Criminal Law *i.e.*, the security of the realm. Does it therefore follow that either the process of legal punishment is altogether outside morals, or else it is immoral to enforce the Criminal Law?

The law relates principally to people and their interrelationships, and people are moral agents. I take that as axiomatic. The characteristic of moral agency inheres in people as such, and it is not a feature that can be assumed and discarded at will; for the very attempt to discard the characteristic would itself be a denial of one's own moral status and hence an immoral act. Consequently, in the prosecution of any human process all the parties concerned are will-nilly moral agents and their participation therein is *eo ipso* a moral activity, for better or for worse. From the nature of things, this is as true of a legal process as of any other form of human endeavour.

Let us consider the principle *salus populi suprema lex* which we found to lie at the root of the criminal law. It is not a principle *of* the law but a principle *about* the law, and is clearly a moral principle from which the law stems. Consequently, so long as that principle is effective in shaping the development and application of the law, so long and to that extent will the law itself give effect to a moral principle.

Furthermore, we saw in Part I that punishing is a social process. Consequently, the preservation of the social *milieu* in which it can occur is a precondition of its taking place, so that the principle upon which such preservation rests is both logically and morally prior to the principle of the performance of the social process.

Moreover, it is important to grasp that the two principles, the 'deserts' principle and *salus populi*, are not in theory antithetical but complementary. *Salus populi* is the ground for the State's taking over the whole process of juristic punishment, for the establishment and maintenance of its institutions rules and procedures, but it is not the ground for the imposition of this or that punishment in any particular case. This latter decision is the area of application of the 'deserts' principle. I am not saying, of course, that in every case of sentencing the 'deserts' principle is always properly applied, or even that it is always actually applied; in many cases it is not. My concern here is to show that the two principles do not constitute an antinomy, but rather an ordered pair. But here a further caveat is apposite.

In arguing away from the conclusion suggested in section VII that legal punishment is morally wrong, we must not be led to the opposite pole, that all legal action is morally right. The arguments above are designed only to show, in opposition to the Pure Theory of Law, that legal action does not lie outside the realm of morals, and that on that footing legal punishment is not necessarily morally wrong. But it does not follow that it is necessarily morally right—only that it can be. And it is a further consequence that legal punishment cannot be morally neutral, nor claim to be exempt from the application of moral judgment, and that such judgment cannot be a mere mechanical application of the conclusion reached in Part III.

What emerges, then, is that in law, as in morals, the important question to ask in relation to punishing is: what exactly is this activity? When that has been answered, it can be seen that the further question, what is its justification?, simply does not arise. Consequently, to ask if its justification be deterrence, retribution or reform, or some other characteristic or result, is to betray a failure to grasp the nature of the problem. Hence, to attempt to frame a penal policy upon lines determined by one or more of those allegedly justifying concepts, is not only downright immoral, it is conceptually confused.

IX CONCLUSIONS

In this paper I have been arguing a case for an account of punishment which is derived from the principle of justice elaborated by Plato in his two Tartarus myths, and epitomised by St. Paul in *Galatians* VI, 7: "Be not deceived; God is not mocked: for whatsoever a man soweth, that shall he also reap." The point that I hope to have established is that punishing is only punishing if it is recognisable to all parties that the penalty imposed represents the recipient's just deserts for his antecedent wrongful act, and if the procedure be conducted as a moral action within a social *milieu*. In most of these respects there is a converse analogy with reward, but there the social environment plays a less significant part, and it is hardly intelligible to talk of a man's rewarding himself.

The so-called utilitarian theories of punishment, the re-formative theory and the deterrent theory, are found to be unhelpful in eliciting the concept of punishment, fundamentally immoral, menacing to the social fabric, and confused in conception.[16]

It will be recalled that Ulpian formulated as his third principle of justice, the so-called *Lex Justitiae: suum cuique tribuere*, the same principle as that of the traditional morality put forward by Cephalus in Book I of the *Republic*. The case argued here is little more than an application of that principle, to render to each man his due, that is to say, for his person and belongings, respect; for his virtues, reward; for his sins, punishment.

NOTES

[1] I am very grateful to members of the Open University Philosophy Seminar in London who have politely and patiently listened to and criticised earlier drafts of this paper. I am deeply indebted to Dr. Trevor Saunders for letting me see his unpublished paper "Punishment in Greek Thought", and to Mr. R. F. Stalley for a copy of his unpublished paper "Plato's Theory of Punishment."

[2] I am pretty sure that this was an *apperçu* of Lord Acton, but unfortunately at the time of writing I have not been able to trace the reference. Anyway, whoever said it, I endorse it.

[3] Kegan Paul, Trench, Trubner, London, 1946.

[4] Frag. 94.

[5] "Prolegomenon to the Principles of Punishment", *Proc. Arist. Soc.* LX, 1959–60 pp. 1–26.

[6] L. Carroll, *Through the Looking-glass and What Alice Found There* (Macmillan, London 1871), Chapter V.

[7] But see Maitland, "The Crown as Corporation", 17 *Law Quarterly Review* (1901) pp. 131–146, repr. in *id.*, *Selected Essays* (Cambridge U.P. 1936), for a contrary view. Mrs. Janet Sanders kindly drew my attention to this reference.

[8] Not always easy: I once knew a very young barrister who was defending an aged sinner before the old Middlesex Sessions. The prisoner had been found guilty of house-breaking and his police record extended over thirty years; Preventive Detention seemed inevitable. The Judge look at learned Counsel: "Yes, Mr. So-and-so?"

"I would ask your Lordship to bear in mind that this man has gone straight for three months."

"Are you attempting to be frivolous?"

"By no means, m'lud."

[9] *Cf.* Tacitus, *Germania*, cap. XXI: "It is a duty among them to adopt the feuds as well as the friendships of a father or a kinsman. These feuds are not implacable; even homicide is expiated by the payment of a certain number of cattle and of sheep, and the satisfaction is accepted by the entire family, greatly to the advantage of the state, since feuds are dangerous in proportion to a people's freedom." (Trans. Church and Brodribb, Macmillan, 1877.)

[10] For a more extensive and partially documented account of this process see Robertson, *The History of the Reign of the Emperor Charles V*, Vol. I, *A View of the Progress of Society in Europe from the subversion of the Roman Empire to the Beginning of the Sixteenth Century* (London, 1769); also Hume, *The History of England*, Appendix II, "The Feudal and Anglo-Norman Government and Manners" (London 1761).

[11] See Pollock and Maitland, *The History of English Law before the Time of Edward I*, 2nd Edn. (Cambridge, 1898) Vol. I, pp. 521–2. I am grateful to Mrs. Janet Sanders for eliciting the pertinence of this point.

[12] See Beard, *The Office of Justice of the Peace in England in its Origin and Development* (New York, 1904).

[13] Moyle (ed.), *Imperatoris Iustiniani Institutionum Libri Quattuor*, 5th ed. (Oxford U.P. 1923) Excursus X, "The earlier history of Roman Civil Procedure", p. 629.

[13a] See *Weekly Law Reports* 1977, Part 7, 25th February, 1977 [1977] 2W.L.R. 310–347.

[13b] See also *Reg.* v. *Secretary of State for Home Department, Ex parte Hosenball* (C.A.), *per* Lord Denning M.R., *The Times* newspaper report 30th March, 1977 (not a criminal prosecution but an application for *certiorari* to set aside a deportation order on an alien): '. . . it was no ordinary case. It was a case in which national security was involved. When the state was in danger, our own cherished freedoms, and even the rules of natural justice had to take second place.' And 'The overriding supervision of the court remained whereby if it was a question of the minister or his advisers not having acted fairly, the courts could review their proceedings. If fairness came into play, the supervisory jurisdiction of the courts came into play to see that it was observed:' and 'Great as was the public interest in the freedom of the individual and doing justice to him, nevertheless in the last resort it must take second place to the security of the state.'

[14] And, I imagine, in most other countries within the same legal tradition.

[15] Out of his numerous and extensive writings, see *e.g.*, Kelsen, "The Pure Theory of Law" trans. C. H. Wilson, *Law Quarterly Review* 1934, 1935; also, for a synoptic summary of his contributions to jurisprudence, Lauterpacht, "Kelsen's Pure Science of Law" in Jennings (ed.), *Modern Theories of Law* (Oxford U.P. 1933).

[16] "I believe it to be quite one of the crowning wickednesses of this age that we have starved and chilled our faculty of indignation, and neither desire nor dare to punish crimes justly. We have taken up the benevolent idea, forsooth, that justice is to be preventive instead of vindictive . . . that we are to punish, not in anger, but in expediency . . . that we may frighten other people from committing the same fault. The beautiful theory of this non-vindictive justice is, that having convicted a man of a crime worthy of death, we entirely pardon the criminal, restore him to his place in our affection and esteem, and then hang him, not a malefactor, but as a scarecrow. That is the theory." John Ruskin, "The Relation of Art to Morals" Lect. III in *Lectures in Art* 1870, 2nd edn. (Oxford, 1875), p. 83.

XV*—GOD, GOOD AND EVIL

by Stephen R. L. Clark

My topics are the problem of evil and the supposed autonomy of ethics.[1] I wish to suggest that the discussion of these problems has often been vitiated by taking them separately, and that the former problem has at least as destructive an effect on rational humanism as it does on theism. I shall make use of Gnostic speculations, and of the Valentinian name for the world-archon, Ialdobaoth. I shall refer to my opponent, my *alter ego*, as Diabolus.

The phenomenal universe appears to contain physical and moral evils that would be signs of cruelty and injustice if they were laid to the charge of a will competent to avoid them. Efforts to mitigate these horrors, as being necessary but minor evils leading to, or consequent upon the possibility of, a supremely worthwhile state of being, rarely convince Diabolus. Perhaps a finite power could be excused for its hamfistedness or for the regrettable by-products of its well-meaning industry. An infinitely capable power, who has selected his own parameters, his own causal laws, his tools, his very ends, can hardly escape judgment by such appeals to 'happenstance', *force majeure* and ignorance. The phenomenal universe is not the sort of thing we would whole-heartedly compliment any Cosmic Engineer for having produced. To be sure: since that Engineer (if he exists at all) has cunningly endowed us with an unreasoning pleasure in our continued existence (thereby multiplying misery), we may be inclined to think that such existence defies gratitude. Any existence is so infinitely superior to non-entity that its Creator owes us nothing more. That may be the final and only answer to our complaints, that the potter does not argue with the pot. What we are, He made us, and our very complaints are by His courtesy. "For without Him who can enjoy his food, or who be anxious?" (*Ecclesiastes* 2.25 (N.E.B.)) But such resignation does not come by argument. Surely, Diabolus insists, a woman who knowingly con-

* Meeting of the Aristotelian Society at 5/7, Tavistock Place, London, W.C.1, on Monday 30th May 1977, at 7.30 p.m.

ceived a child destined for physical deformity, social ostracism, moral corruption would still be at fault even though that child itself has not been *wronged*? She has freely increased the sum of misery. What is the point of saying that she should not act so if the God of all gods Himself does it and is praised for doing so? Perhaps all creation involves risks (though the Omnicompetent should surely avoid most of them) and perhaps creation is nonetheless a "good thing", but there are degrees beyond which the wilful creation of suffering, whatever its attendant goods or opposing virtues, is simply incompatible with any will that we should normally praise. Moral goods, such as courage in the face of evil or forgiveness for the sin of cruelty, may require that there be evil (both physical and moral), but it is not clear that such virtues are more than *pis-allers*. As Aristotle remarked (*Nicomachean Ethics* X.1178b10f), we cannot properly attribute them to gods in a divine universe. Nor do we praise men who torment their children to cultivate their moral character, even if their predictions are correct (though in this we perhaps differ from our forefathers). Consider also William Blake's acid jest : "Pity would be no more if we did not make somebody poor" (*Songs of Experience*). And again: It is not wholly certain that the Omnicompetent could not cause there to be (what are clearly logical possibilities) beings who freely and invariably choose the right, despite temptations to err. It is admittedly also not certain that He could, for if we take time seriously at all even God can only create free beings who are *likely* not to sin: beings who are certain never to sin cannot be considered free agents. But in other contexts than the problem of free will theists have been less eager to claim clear knowledge of what self-contradiction is in the case of deity. All these traditional moves in the game are profoundly unconvincing to Diabolus.

My strategy is to accept the charge: the phenomenal universe is not such as we can easily imagine a decent creator's creating or sustaining. Any will that willed or was willing to accept the biosphere's multiple ingenuities of torture, or permitted the corruption and suffering of tyranny's victims in all ages, is not a will that we should normally consider good. If the Galactic Empire has observers on the Earth they are absolved of criminal responsibility only in so far as they are themselves subject to laws and generalities not of their own making. The God of religion, of course, is experienced in cult and meditation as being confronted by us as problems which He must solve under the rubric of general laws: as such He is presumably excusable. But it is an article of faith that He has posed Himself the problem, and Himself decrees those laws: the excuse wears rather thin.

Very well: the phenomenal universe is not worth sustaining. The attempt to argue otherwise is reminiscent of traditional anthropodicies: "There is much talk of the misery which we cause to the brute creation; but they are recompensed by existence. If they were not useful to man, and therefore protected by him, they would not be nearly so numerous" (Samuel Johnson: *Boswell's Life*, May 1776, p. 753). But as Boswell commented, there is a question whether the animals would accept existence on their present terms. If it is wrong for the Omnicompetent to sustain the world in misery, it is surely wrong for us to excuse ourselves by arguments which are that much less plausible by how much our powers are less (for it is not entirely true that our victims owe their lives to us, save in the sense that we have not yet taken them).[2]

This point has a very general significance: if the world is not such as can be decently sustained by one who has the power to do otherwise, then we cannot decently sustain it either. We cannot decently continue to cooperate in phenomenal existence. We ought to preach sterility, and seek ways of eliminating all conscious or sentient being. Professional philosophers, of course, have made their own compromises with the powers-that-be: their pupils may one day astonish us. The Gnostic philosophers were more consistent in their hostility. Only a savage, or at best a power just without mercy, could have made the world, and in denouncing that Creator they abjured his work. Copulation was evil just in that it was procreative, and their enemies accused them of promiscuity, *coitus interruptus*, abortion and the ceremonial eating of embryos. Gnostics (and Buddhists, who have a similarly low opinion of Brahma) are indeed less committed to a policy of genocide than Diabolus. For they suppose the world to be fundamentally mentalistic: material suicide will not release us from the Wheel—for that, if it is possible at all, a lengthier discipline is necessary. A materialistic Diabolus has an easy solution for his *ennui*. To be sure: even the Last War can only purge the Earth, and there may be millions of inhabited worlds still under the yoke. But if the undefined weight of those millions is to weaken our resolve to eliminate what evil we can it must cast all our projects into doubt. If it is not worth the bother of genocide, it is not worth the bother of continued living, for nothing we can do (on those terms) makes more than an infinitesimal difference.

Diabolus has a reply. The world is not such as can decently be sustained by one who can do better (as the Omnicompetent could). But we do not better the world by destroying it, or the awareness of it. The world is made of grain and chaff obscurely mixed: we have a duty to improve it, or at least not to make it worse. We do not have a duty to destroy it. By the same token, of course, the Creator was under no obligation to destroy the world He got when He created, only to create as good a world as He could. There then arises the question whether even the Omniscient can know the quality of merely imaginary worlds: perhaps He must create in order to know what the world He creates is like, and having created should sustain it till it can achieve its own felicity. I have no answer to this question, and will continue to accept that the world is not one that a decent Creator can easily be supposed to have created. Diabolus, at any rate, is (so far) permitted to live. But of course he is permitted to live only at the price of making the world better, or not making it worse. The Karamazovs agreed that they would not purchase universal felicity by torturing a baby to death (*Brothers Karamazov* V.4)—and doubtless they did well in this, for there is only one salesman who would offer such a bargain, and he is not noted for his fidelity. But our agents and our moralists regularly defend the torture of innocents for the sake of goods much less enticing than universal felicity. Flesh-foods, cosmetics, aspirins and indigestion tablets to alleviate the effects of nicotine-poisoning or over-eating are all purchased at the price of extreme suffering and deprivation on the part of our non-human cousins. If Ialdobaoth is condemned, like Soame Jenyns' celestial *voyeurs*, so also are we.[3] All spokesmen for Diabolus, and particularly those who make much of animal suffering, should seek to separate themselves from our millenial tyranny, so as not to make the world worse than they have to, and so as not to be like the God they hate. Gnostics and Buddhists often do so: I had not observed that modern spokesmen for Diabolus were so honourable. In condemning Ialdobaoth we condemn ourselves.

Diabolus may reply that his attack upon the Creator is, as it were, *ad hominem*. It is not that he disapproves, nor commits himself to avoidance of the moral evil he condemns, but merely that he denies such a being any title to the justice and compassion predicated of Him in the theistic tradition. But this response is clearly not in full accord with the moral seriousness of his original charge, and allows the apologist to evade the real point: that only the "good" are worthy of worship. Diabolus may also insist that his charge against Ialdobaoth is that He has occasioned animal suffering that is unnecessary to human welfare or even wholly unhelpful. Diabolus is therefore licensed to torture to obtain human advantage even while attacking Ialdobaoth for using torture for His own purposes. The fact remains that we too cause unnecessary suffering, even if Ialdobaoth could avoid more than we. Nor can I see why Ialdobaoth is not allowed to torture for His purposes if we are allowed to torture for ours. At the very least a Gestapo officer is in no very strong position to condemn Ialdobaoth, and neither is the rational humanist, unless he changes his ways.

Again, Diabolus may remark that it is not obviously true that just the same behaviour is required of a "good pantocrator" and a good man, any more than identically the same behaviour (except under the general description of "doing the right thing") is required of good young men and good old women. This is not to accept an account of theological language as uniquely analogical: simply to remember that "good" is not straightforwardly descriptive. It does not follow that because good men work to support their families good children must do likewise: our duties may be more specialised than that, and what is required of pantocrators may not be required of us. But of course, if Diabolus does insist on this, he leaves himself open to the reply that the duties of pantocrators cannot so easily be deduced from the duties of men.

Despite Descartes, we cannot properly conclude that a good pantocrator would not deceive us, nor that He would not hurt us. He may do both if He conceives it to be for the final good of His creatures and Himself, and there is no speedier, less hurtful way: and of that we cannot be certain.

Diabolus would be better advised to stick to Mill's challenge: "I will call no being good, who is not what I mean when I apply that epithet to my fellow creatures; and if such a being can sentence me to hell for not so calling him, to hell I will go" (Nelson Pike (ed.) *God and Evil* p.43). Mill's own criteria for goodness, of course, render it difficult to force the case against Ialdobaoth: utilitarian considerations and a respect for individual liberty may compel Ialdobaoth to allow passing evils. God can operate a utilitarian ethic too: indeed, it seems likely that only the Omniscient and Omnicompetent could do so. If His utilitarianism is unbearable, our own clumsy calculus had better be abandoned too. But Mill's challenge still stands as an inspiring defiance of the powers-that-be, a defiance that moralising philosophers are inclined to consider heroic. It is a challenge, however, with some odd features. A psycho-analyst friend of mine, perhaps more aware of the treacheries of the human heart, once wrote to me that he *hoped*, if there turned out to be a God, that he would have the courage to spit, as it were, in His face. He *hoped*: it may be that he only meant that he would be glad if he did, or was glad to think that he would, or would be glad to be sure that he was going to—though none of these paraphrases quite catches what is meant by "hoping". We do not have to accept Marcel's judgment that "hope is a desperate appeal to an ally who is Himself also Love" (*Being and Having* 17.3.1931) to agree that hope involves a partial conviction that something in the universe at least might be on one's side.[4] And if God is against us, who shall be for us? "*Who* durst defy th'Omnipotent to arms?" Or rather, who can? How exactly did Mill expect to defy that power which sustained his existence? To whom was my friend, half-consciously, appealing for help to stand firm? "Pray God that I may be granted grace to defy God to the very end!" And perhaps he will.

This is to emphasise the point I have already mentioned, that our complaints are by His courtesy. There is a curious lack of fit between the content of Diabolus's accusation and its existence. At its crudest the charge is that God is responsible for all that goes on, but in making the charge Diabolus presents himself as an independent agent over against God. But either there are independent agents or there are not: if there are, then God is not responsible for the evil they do; if there are not then Diobolus deceives himself, and should recognise that his hope (?) of being Prometheus is simply another act of God. In less crude forms, avoiding the pragmatic inanity of determinism, Diabolus' complaints are rather that God allows to His independent creatures more liberty than Diabolus would wish. Diabolus wants to be allowed to complain: he does not want others to be allowed to do what they want to do. The classical fear was that God was a tyrant (but if He is, He is too successful for any extrinsic judgment); the more modern, liberal slander is that He is a do-nothing. In short, we now complain not that He performs judgment, but that He exercises mercy (or at least delay). "O God, if only thou wouldst slay the wicked!" (Psalm 139.19): "but He is very patient with you, for it is not His will for any to be lost, but for all to come to repentance" (2 Peter 3.9). Those who call for judgment may find at last that it comes.

To put the same point slightly differently: Diabolus may say that God has indeed (by hypothesis) created us as independent agents, so that we may both accuse Him and ourselves work evil against His will. If we are so far independent of Him that we may sin, that is His fault, and we are entitled to say so. But the price of being able to complain is that we are also able to sin—that is, to take offence at the workings of God's providence. Would the world really be better if we disallowed such liberty?

A further oddity in Mill's defiance also harks back to an earlier point. When some sadistic moron shows a Jain extremist the manifold life he must destroy in drinking water, and that Jain at once defies the world to do its tawdry worst and foreswears food and drink thereafter our hearts do not beat high. We can hardly restrain our scorn for such "noble foolishness". What good does it do? Sensible people "accept the universe", and we murmur "God, they'd better". Even where unconventional conduct would cost us nothing, amateur and professional moralists constantly appeal to the fact that creatures commonly behave in a certain way to "prove" that we can have no moral duty to behave otherwise. If fish eat fish we are entitled to copy their example, even while proclaiming our own superiority to such exemplars. We oddly denounce the hypothetical Creator and His works at the same time as assuming that the world enshrines an adequate standard for our own behaviour. But why? Why is it noble to defy God, but merely silly to adopt other standards than, let alone to defy, the world? A storm is no greater an evil for being caused by an evil spirit (S. Johnson: Boswell's *Journal of a tour to the Hebrides* 16th August), though this may add a further, moral evil. If we should disobey and despise the will that perhaps occasions storms, disease and corruption, we should surely (at the least) take some pains not to act like that ourselves, and even to reject all profit from cooperation in such a sinister universe. If Mill was ready to reject all future felicity when offered him by a Creator Devil, why should he accept it so readily at the world's hands? If on the contrary we should make the best we can of what is offered us, what offence is there in joining the only, and celestial, game in town? Or is the point simply and discreditably that we do not expect our bluff to be called? God is bound to prefer our noble outspokenness to the cowardice of sycophantic churchmen (though I cannot see why He should therefore give us credit for what is His gift to us), or at least our fellow-men will be more impressed by those who pretend to call the Omnicompetent to court.

But whose court? "If only there were one to arbitrate between us" (*Job* 9.32). The Gnostic Adam took his lawsuit to the Great First Life (Mandaean GT 437: H. Jonas *The Gnostic Religion* p.88), and it was by the standard of eternity that the archons were judged. It is because we are, or there is something more than the archons, that we have an escape. It is because there is an unborn, an indestructible, as Gautama taught, that there is an exit from the Wheel. If there is not, whose court is it we call to?

Diabolus at once replies that ethics are autonomous, that they owe nothing to the dictates of a celestial Augustus, that they are supremely super-empirical. The laws of justice are binding even if they are never operative; the innocent are in the right even if they are never vindicated. Diabolus, rather oddly, is sometimes even inclined to think that ethics, to avoid vulgarity, must be empirically unsuccessful, even while denouncing God and His creation for not vindicating the oppressed. It is wrong that justice does not prosper, but it would also be wrong if it did. More circumspectly, Diabolus insists that there need be no actual court of appeal, no power in the world, that could successfully condemn Ialdobaoth; yet nonetheless Ialdobaoth is condemned *morally* in the hearts of all honourable men by the independent standards of right and wrong. That he cannot be brought to trial in the outer world is unfortunate, but at least we know what verdict would be given.

Philosophers have disagreed about the nature of these intuited standards. It is perhaps significant for my thesis that Platonism, one of the most determined attempts to depict them as eternal realities independent of phenomena and of the observing mind, was historically unstable: the Ideas ended up as the thoughts of God. It is, however, possible that some sort of Platonism could cope with the problems I shall raise. My principal quarrel, though, is with such modern spokesmen for Diabolus as are unlikely to appeal to such objective Ideas. Indeed, even if they did I suspect that my point would apply. For whatever the truth about objective morality our experience or intuition of morality is a matter of our own deep-seated preferences, antipathies, reasonings and feelings of respect. These either are themselves the content of ethics or our route to the ethical.

Even the Creator then must be judged by the deep-seated impulses and careful reasonings that He has implanted in us. We need no further court. But it is surely obvious that in condemning Him we cast doubt on our own ethical intuitions, unless these are held to come from Outside. The first move of any coherent Gnosticism is to adopt an ascetic renunciation of the desires of the flesh; the second is to brand the ethical law, in the Torah or in our own heart, as a further device of tyranny. The ascetic and antinomian modes of Gnosticism may alternate or even be conjoined in a sort of professional sado-masochism that practises, for example, promiscuity precisely insofar as it can be made repellent. A third move, of course, would be to reject even the reasonings that led to this or any other conclusion, and so to stand naked in the Void. If the Creator is evil (what we call "evil"), and there is no escape from His world, or at any rate no clear signpost to the exit, then as we cannot even count upon His keeping His threats and promises (C. S. Lewis *A Grief Observed* p.28) we no longer have any idea what to do for the best or what that best might be. Neither have we any coherent ground for thinking the Creator evil. That way lies madness.

My point is not a parochial one. Gnostics spoke of Ialdobaoth, but their systems could with equal cogency be outlined in purely materialistic terms. This universe of unpurposed force, greed, self-centredness and pain has accidently produced in the last few thousand years a species and a culture which professes, though it does not act upon, a liking for justice, compassion, logical rigour and so forth. Materialistic accounts of evolution have begun, though only begun, to devise detailed explanations for our having such preferences, both the ones that we share with all mammals or all primates and those that are peculiar to our species or culture. Of course the mere fact that there are such physical or sociological explanations for our thinking and feeling as we do does not of itself disprove or disallow those thoughts and feelings (though Diabolus sometimes assumes otherwise when dealing with religion). If evolutionary logic has produced beings who believe theses p, q, r, those very theses may still be true. But if evolutionary logic is a full explanation for our belief it is at least unnecessary to suppose our belief veridical unless we can independently show it to be true. But it can be shown to be true only, for us, by being shown to be evident (*i.e.*, believed) or to be logically dependent upon some other, evident belief. And the concept of logical dependency, as well as the variety of immediate beliefs have, by hypothesis, been generated in us (or we have been generated having them) through physical processes that have no relevance nor reference to the truth or metaphysical necessity of those concepts and beliefs. Our beliefs may be true, but we have no warrant for believing them: indeed we can no longer have any confidence in the notion of having or needing a ground for belief. From which it follows, if anything now does, that the whole materialistic account of

our history becomes, not obviously false, but simply unau-
thorised.

The situation might be saved by claiming that our beliefs
and our belief-forming systems have been selected for and
reinforced by past success, so that we have at least this much
reason to think them true, or at least to think materialism
coherent. I doubt if this works, both because of usual problems about inductive inference and because the story of our
past evolutionary success is itself on trial, but I am willing to
allow that our cognitive situation may not be beyond repair.
But our affective, and therefore our ethical, responses are
critically affected by Diabolus' system. When we come to believe of ourselves that we have certain affective preferences
only because of childhood indoctrination or genetic determinism we may continue to feel those preferences, but we are
almost bound to take them less seriously. We feel no com-
punction, and perhaps some enthusiasm, at educating ourselves out of them, and take no trouble to impose them on
others, save to the limited extent that by doing so we facilitate
our own satisfactions. So far my point is perhaps rather la-
boured: certainly the Laodicean tolerance currently popular,
as well as that inane morality that denounces those who seek
to persuade others to their own moral convictions, suggests
that many people have digested the implications of Diabolus'
creed. Morality, considered as binding upon oneself and
others, is confusedly considered illiberal. The confusion
should grow. For we are continuing to assess our moral preferences, or what were once our moral preferences, in terms of
other preferences which we have allowed to stand, such as a
wish for security, for human solidarity, for the survival of oneself and one's kind, for pleasure. But Diabolus' critique has
put other names on these passions: cowardice, racism, greed.
Pleasure is the bait in the scented trap of procreation, kinship
the outward sign of neo-Darwinian competition. In showing
the world to be depraved by the very standards we have come
to have, and in showing, admittedly rather sketchily, that our
standards are accidental products of just those depraved processes, he has cast doubt on our most basic preferences. There
is no reason to think that acting on them leads to anything we

might reasonably call good; there is no reason to take seriously our attitudes of respect, obedience, affection. It is not even that we are not *bound* to follow them, but may: rather, if we do follow them we are bound to consider the process of their begetting to be untrustworthy, or despicable. Morality is a superstition that has revealed its foundations to be quintessentially immoral. To love men is to hate the non-human; to seek pleasure is to propagate pain; to respect authority is to acquiesce in evil. It is not surprising that an uneasy relativism in ethics is often conjoined with a naive worship of natural processes: the same man may jeer at those who take morality so seriously as to act upon it to their own disadvantage and himself read moral lessons from the fact that creatures generally do behave in some way—"whatever is, is right", but without Pope's reason. This is not surprising: if we cannot force ourselves to believe that what happens is good we must be alienated from our own inclinations, unless we can invoke some transcendental standard and origin for our moral inclinations. How otherwise, in particular, can we take seriously the species-centred conceit that has begotten humanism? Men are my kind of creature? But this is to say only that our ancestors had certain preferences and antipathies: inter-racial antagonism may yet produce a number of hominid species— will members of one such species then be licensed to do as they please to members of another, just because their ancestors did? Those who think so are in no position to denounce Ialdobaoth, lest they thereby both condemn themselves and destroy the moral standing of their creed.

Diabolus may retort, once more, that his claim is only that the universe is such that its hypothetical Creator must have very different priorities and purposes from those which we associate with the good. "My ways are not your ways, says the Lord" (*Isaiah* 55.8), and Diabolus sardonically agrees. But this response misses his own moral seriousness in the charge and leaves it unclear why the theist must be puzzled. Plainly the pantocrator does not consider Himself bound by all the laws He proclaims to us: "*Thou* shalt not kill", but God reserves that privilege to Himself. "Vengeance is mine, says the Lord" (*Romans* 12.19). There are things that God does not allow us to do: it is hardly a surprise to find that He gives Himself more latitude. Certainly we cannot discover what we may do from an enquiry into what naturally happens, even if that is by God's providence. That there are miscarriages in pregnancy no more licenses embryonicide than murder is licensed by the fact of natural death.

On the other hand, "You shall be holy, for I the Lord your God am holy" (*Leviticus* 19.2). And again: "Be perfect, as your heavenly Father is perfect" (*Matthew* 5.48). We are commanded to be like Him, and if we are like Him we are being, and doing good. The problem of evil is precisely that not everything that naturally happens is the sort of thing that we could bring about and still hope to be called good. We are to be like God, but not always to act as He seems to. Some, but not all, natural processes are to be endorsed, and in endorsing them we accept God's judgment on ourselves and on the world. God's righteousness, *sedeq*, consists in the supreme consistency of His nature, and His consequent fidelity to the covenants formed between Himself and His creation (J. Pedersen, *Israel I-II* pp. 338f). These covenants require of us a perpetual remembrance that the world does not belong to us, and compassion particularly for the weak and defenceless: "rights" operate chiefly to protect those who are unable to negotiate contracts by their own power.

How are these points to be related to standard philosophical arguments, beginning from Plato's *Euthyphro*, for the autonomy of ethics? Must not even God's commands be obeyed only for non-moral reasons, out of fear or affection, unless they merely transmit moral obligation? To base one's conduct on messages from a celestial Augustus is surely to abandon morality. Such a god may, if he is of good character and sound moral judgment, command what is right, but it would still be right even if he commanded the opposite, and to do what he says only because he says it is to display moral myopia. Perhaps he may change his mind? Surely, to say that he is good must be more than to say he is self-consistent?

Such arguments are often repeated without due attention. It is worth asking Diabolus what reason he can imagine himself giving for saying that something commanded by God is in fact "wrong". "God tells us to love our enemies, but I think He's quite wrong." One who has invented all the things that

His creatures enjoy, and determines the causal laws that lead to enjoyment or its opposite, presumably gives better advice than Diabolus. Again, what good could we ever do by disobeying the Omnipotent? The good of not consenting to iniquity, perhaps (although the evil thing will still be done), but I have already pointed to our strange unwillingness to avoid such a consent in the case of natural event. And in any case, if a command is seriously experienced as iniquitous it cannot simultaneously be attributed to God, not because God is bound to obey an independent moral code, but because our perception of God's commands is precisely mediated in our serious moral convictions. Nor is it sensible to speak of "God's changing His mind", as if He were a creature subject to inconsistencies of judgment, mood and temper. It may be absurd to suppose that rape might be a moral duty; it is just as absurd to imagine God's suddenly commanding it, and hardly surprising that one absurdity follows from another. What of Abraham and Isaac? Well, what of them? Abraham did not kill his son, but he incurred no moral guilt at all by seeking to do so (how else should he save his son alive?), nor can any intelligible charge be made out against the Creator either for threatening Isaac's life or requiring Abraham to be His agent. Or if one can, it presumably also stands against all moral systems that require that personal or parental ties be subordinated to civic or universal justice.

Diabolus may be induced to agree that those acts commanded by God and those acts that are morally obligatory both are and must be identical, but he will still insist that these properties are distinct. If an act is right we have a reason to perform it which is quite independent of God's demanding it. Theistic moralists lend support to this point by claiming that their own particular version of God's commandments is the sole route to personal and social welfare. If it is, then it would be good even if *per impossibile* God did not demand it, and it remains good even if God does not exist at all.

It is not in fact obvious to me that anything can be morally good or obligatory in the absence of God. We can imagine that we might desire things even in a godless universe (though the careful imagination of such a universe must surely tend to make us think our desires futile), but such good (*i.e.*, desired) things might not then be in any sense morally good, such as should be required of all moral agents. It seems not unlikely to me that moral obligations are literally owed to someone or to Someone, just as legal obligations are. If philosophers can interpret the rules of justice as those which ignorant participants-to-be would accept, I do not think it impossible that moral laws should similarly be interpreted as those dictates which an omniscient and impartially benevolent judge would deliver, if he existed. What motive we could have for doing what such a fiction suggests I do not know, and it should at least perturb Diabolus that if he accepts such an analysis as valid he comes close to acknowledging that God must at least be possible—and if possible, then necessary (by the Ontological Argument in its valid second form).

But it is enough for my purposes to claim, not that being obligatory and being God's command are the very same thing (even if the atheist fails to draw the proper conclusion from his superstitious respect for moral obligation), but only that it is God who makes things to be obligatory, just as He makes things to be facts. For whenever Diabolus pretends to be judging God's commands and finding them (at best) in accordance with moral goodness, he forgets what was a major plank of his argument with respect to the problem of evil: namely, that it is the Creator who selects and sustains the causal laws governing or describing events. If justice, charity and compassion pay it is because He has decreed that they should. If they excite an immediate respect in us it is because He has made us so. Such reasonings are not, therefore, independent of God's will, but rather constitute (part of) the promulgation of that will. "It is surely wicked deliberately to inflict pain unnecessarily because of the nature of pain, and not primarily because God decreed that it should be" (A. C. Ewing in I. Ramsey (ed.) *The Problem of Evil* p.42). But by hypothesis it is God that envisaged our sense of physiological damage (which He also envisaged) as being *pain*, a thing that all with any will in the matter must in the first instance seek to escape. In creating it as such He has declared it an evil. Every other motive for being just, or suggested analysis of what it is to be good, depends upon God's creative activity, if He exists at all.

The atheist of course may experience moral demands upon

him, though if I am right he is likely to take such natural impulses less and less seriously (and thereby lose any standing in
the charge against Ialdobaoth). The theist cannot suppose
that he has any independent, authoritative standards against
which to judge God's judgements or His mighty acts. If he
turns rebel, his "heroic defiance" of the Creator come down
at last to the self-alienating cry of "Evil, be thou my good",
the attempt to be as far as possible (*i.e.*, as far as God allows)
what oneself most hates. Only the most extreme of moralists(?)
can really find this sort of sado-masochism attractive. Certainly Diabolus cannot, on these terms, make much of a case
against Ialdobaoth.

The paradox to which I am pointing is just this: that only
if we can conceive that some natural processes and impulses
are divinely created, can we find any sure ground from which
to pass judgment on other natural processes. If everything that
happens is good, there is no charge against the Creator. But
if everything that happens is bad, there can also be no charge
against Him; nor yet can there be if everything happens
merely by nature. An archon, such as Ialdobaoth, can be
judged and condemned by the Standards of the Great First
Life, sparks from which still inhabit his world. If, as seems
likely, we cannot draw any clear line between the action of
those sparks and the action of natural law, we must allow that
there is a closer link between the Great First Life and the
phenomenal world than the Gnostics thought. What we cannot do is to denounce the Creator and simultaneously deny
the existence of a world independent of His. Nor, I think, can
we maintain any conviction of moral seriousness if we allow
the problem of evil to dissuade us from theism. Moral atheism,
rational humanism are simply superstitions, and Diabolus,
in raising the problem of evil against God, demonstrates only
that his heart is more religious than his head.

My claim as a theist is that Goodness is God: that is, that
there is an actual and not merely a possible satisfaction of all
desire in the enjoyment of an eternal life that is both the final
end and ,beyond all expectation, the first cause of the phenomenal world. I have not sought to explain how, perhaps by our
own hubristic or adventurous choice, the Great First Life is
now so strangely manifested. My point has been that the pro-

blem of evil is not a problem only for theists, and is therefore
no particular refutation of theism. My final point is concerned
also with epistemology.

Marcion went further even than most Gnostics in declaring
that nature was corrupt beyond redemption. For him all our
nature is of the Dark, and the transcendent Light has revealed
itself at one point only in all cosmic history, in the teaching of
the Lord Jesus Christ. The God and Father of Jesus is utterly
alien to our nature, and to the world we inhabit. Action in
accord with His commands can earn us no temporal advantage nor psychological assurance. Here even more than in
other Gnostic systems pragmatic success and truth are fiercely
divided. The Marcionite is in the same case as victims of
Lehrer's Googols or Unger's mad scientist: for all "practical"
purposes he inhabits a phenomenal world that is wholly spurious, and truth is wholly metaphysical. As far as experience
goes, his "truth" is a fantasy realm in which he can evade the
pressing claims of ordinary "reality". The standard answers
to sceptical arguments are implicitly Pyrrhonian, not to say
Pyrrhic, to the effect that we need only consider the consistency of phenomena, need not answer transcendental questions about the epistemological status of our experience, have
no apparent hope of discerning the "truth" and therefore no
need of such a category. Maybe the "truth" was shown, by the
Googols' carelessness, to a solitary and seeming lunatic, but
that sort of truth is useless to us. What matters is that we
should live agreeably with our friends, or those we find it
agreeable to suppose friends, in ready ignorance of transcendental doubt. Even that ghostly counterpart of the phenomenal world, namely the material universe, should not be taken
too seriously: we can only think our concerns important if we
forget the physical conditioning that makes us take them so
and the enormities of time and space that dwarf any serious
utilitarian concern. If we are truly limited to non-transcen-
dental life—whereas even the Marcionite hoped for post-
mortem felicity—then we shall make the best of our own
phenomenal, and fabulous, world. But in so doing Diabolus
loses all right to inveigh against the credulity and forgetful-
ness of religious believers. If God does not exist, why not
deceive ourselves? Only the religious believer can think it

obligatory to seek the truth, even the truth that God does *not* exist, just as it is only the religious believer that can denounce the world's injustice.

I end with a parable. We have woken, let us suppose, to find ourselves driving down a motor-way we did not build nor remember entering. At intervals we pass the wrecks of burnt-out cars and hear the screams of burning babies. We learn the costs to animals, to human families that must accompany the building and maintenance of such a road, all that we may achieve a temporary destination that much more speedily. There are no exits, only service stations, and our only escape (if any) is by death. What shall we do? Bury the risk, the knowledge of agony, in comfortable amnesia? Become an ambulance-driver till despair sets in? Fantasise some future felicity in which the dead, the maimed are "casualties, fallen on the field of honour" (Teilhard de Chardin *Human Energy* p.50)? Crash the barrier? It is hardly surprising that in comfortable times and classes amnesia is the preferred option. As that possibility grows more remote it will also not be surprising if the religious solution, in Gnostic or in Catholic form, comes to seem our salvation. "Men are asleep, they awaken at their death".[5] What other hope is there? What honest faith is possible without that hope?

NOTES

[1] I am grateful to the Philosophical Society of the University of Stirling for criticism of an earlier draft.

[2] See my *The Moral Status of Animals* (Oxford, 1977), pp.42ff for an elaboration of this point.

[3] *Free enquiry into the nature and origin of evil* (1757); see also Samuel Johnson's review in *Collected Works* (1787), vol.X, pp.220ff.

[4] Ramchandra Gandhi has made a similar point in *The Availability of Religious Ideas*, pp.49f.

[5] Attributed to Mohammed by Ibn Arabi: H. Corbin, *Creative Imagination in the Sufism of Ibn Arabi*, p.208.

XVI—GILBERT RYLE

by G. E. L. Owen

When Gilbert Ryle died, swiftly and cleanly as would be expected of him, he left work in progress. Some consisted in comments on manuscripts sent him and left neatly ordered; John Mabbott says that after going through Ryle's papers he wrote twenty letters to such correspondents—to the United States and Canada, Australia, Germany and Italy and France, Israel and Pakistan, Mexico and the Armenian Republic of the Soviet Union, conveying his comments and the news of his death. Ryle was assiduous in maintaining such philosophical traffic. It took some toll, perhaps, in the later years of his editing of *Mind*. (There was allegedly a Discussion Note that he thought should be published partly because, written from the Far East, it made so many references to different papers in *Mind*; but it turned out that the papers were from one issue and no doubt from one copy.) He went willingly to speak to philosophical conferences where most speakers were what he cheerfully grouped on return as "the continentals", and he enjoyed such occasions as that on which he and Urmson were due to give consecutive lectures in Europe and were introduced by "This is Mr. Urmson, whose work we know well, and this is Professor Waynflete, with whose writings we are of course equally familiar".

He left other work in progress. There was a paper on Plato's *Meno* ready for delivery to the Cambridge B Club in October, but here too he was still reviewing it: his last postcard to me in the summer carried some radically new proposals to be incorporated. (The postcard ended with a characteristic note to my wife: "Tell Sally not to try to remember what I asked her to tell you".) And on his final walking-tour with John Mabbott he was still exercised by the question why the *Meno* is some twenty pages shorter and the *Gorgias* some twenty longer than what he took to be the standard length for dialogues of their group. Just because they were counter-examples to a favourite thesis of his about the public delivery of such works, he could not let them alone or be content with his current solutions. Plato had held his interest since the 1930s. In 1939 he published a paper on the *Parmenides* which initiated a revolution in the philosophical interpretation of Plato's later work. (Yet he said to me in 1949 that no serious notice had been taken of it in its first ten years.) The same interest issued in other papers, in almost countless letters and drafts exchanged with colleagues, and then in two very different later works: the book *Plato's Progress*, which successfully teased non-philosophical historians on their own ground, and the exegesis of Plato which he contributed to Paul Edwards' *Encyclopaedia of Philosophy* and which rivals in importance and outdoes in scope those early papers on the *Parmenides*. Aristotle too he admired: in his reminiscences at the 500th meeting of the Oxford Philosophical Society he sketched the prehistory of *The Concept of Mind* and said that, as against a Husserlian phenomenology, he had been "fairly clear that what was wanted was a Nicomacheanized *De Anima*". But for as long as I knew him the greater and more constant stimulus was Plato. He proposed that one should dine with Aristotle, but then serenade Plato. For one whose musical sense matched that of the Old Lady of Breen, this was uncommon devotion.

When Stuart Hampshire wrote his admirable memoir of Austin for these *Proceedings* in 1960 the need was different. There were indeed seminal papers of Austin in print; but nothing comparable in range, either of time or of theme, with Ryle's books and collected papers. Hampshire's diagnoses had to await proof by the publication of Austin's lectures—and were proved. Hampshire wrote, partly, for those not in the know. Ryle's works have now been, as Austin's were only coming to be, combed and carded to the point where it is small part of this writer's duty to add another extended philosophical critique, even if there were space. Austin's methods in teaching and argument were pretty well known in 1960, but often in caricature and by hearsay. Ryle's, by dint of many graduate classes in Oxford and equally by his frequent appearances in many parts of the world where he took philosophy to be going on, are widely familiar. The number and geographical diversity of those who have heard him and find him unforgettable, whether they argued with him or not, are astonishing. So I write for those in the know, and my first job is to try to add things they may not know.

In the later 1930s two fairly jealously guarded groups of senior philosophers were meeting in Oxford. One, inaugurated some ten years earlier, included Ryle, Mabbott, Price and Hardie and at different times C. S. Lewis, Kneale and Cox. It met fortnightly for dinner and discussion and was formally disbanded some forty years after its inception. The younger group began later and dissolved earlier. It included Austin, Berlin, Hampshire, Ayer, Hart and Grice. Its weekly meetings were continued and enlarged after the war, and carried on after the loss of Austin by Paul Grice until he left Oxford. There was no overlap, or only the most occasional and contingent, in the membership of these groups. Their motivations were different. The earlier set had found the philosophy faculty at Oxford peopled with seniors who had been too old for service in the first war. Ryle said "Paton and Collingwood were the main, though not quite the only, chronological intermediaries to survive and return to Oxford from that war". But by the 1920s Russell's work, and even the *Tractatus* (if only in the charming King James translation), were known and prized by the younger men. There was no Vienna behind them, as there was behind the group that started in the 1930s. The seniors prized Moore, not for his published accounts of analysis or of perception, but for his indefatigable and unstubborn readiness to argue at Joint Sessions; and they found the same unstubborn provocativeness in Prichard. But the air was stale, and they opened windows.

One window which took some time to open but whose opening was, I believe, mainly due to the senior group was the Oxford B.Phil. In his Memorial Lecture for Ryle John Mabbott generously called him the inventor of the B.Phil. degree. Ryle sometimes said that it was a joint invention of the two of them. I am allowed to say something more of this. One, and probably the, principal impulse to the long and fruitful conversations between the two which issued in Ryle's construction and public advocacy of the new degree was Mabbott's lasting dissatisfaction with the postgraduate instruction in philosophy at Oxford of which he, but not Ryle, had had first-hand consumer's experience. No such instruction was specially engineered for graduates, save the attention of one supervisor in a special field which was unlikely to promote and likely to preclude philosophical debate with other graduates. Ryle's moves to redress this situation came after he returned to take up the Waynflete Chair in 1945, and they were systematically rehearsed to Mabbott. But the structure of the Degree was Ryle's, with its inventive combination of a thesis that was not to be a premature tome, with written examinations in subjects chosen from a range of other philosophers and philosophical fields. (There is small need to stress the difference from the conventional requirement of other universities, notably American, to take preliminary examinations *before* being allowed to proceed to the tome.) The inclusion of a paper on a Chosen Authority was Ryle's idea, and the choice of the Authorities was his: Plato, Aristotle and Kant were each to stand for one, but the Empiricists for instance represented only one choice. And the public advocacy was his, perhaps most notably in a letter to the Oxford Magazine in November 1946. It is worth quoting: "A man who has done distinguished work in Greats or P.P.E. can look for systematic advanced instruction in philosophy neither to Oxford nor to any other British University. Nor can a graduate from another Honours School get philosophical training outside the Final Honour School curricula . . . We want, therefore, to create a graduate philosophy School, the students in which are qualified to tackle contemporary philosophical theory and scholarship, and to get a wider and deeper knowledge of past philosophers than can be demanded in Final Honour Schools". After marking this project off from the B.Litt. he adds, almost as an afterthought, "We ought also to provide advanced training not only to our own graduates, but also to graduates from other Universities." He can hardly have foreseen the great strength of Americans and Australians, Canadians and other energetic nationals that characterized the B.Phil. classes once they were well under way in the 1950s.

The remarkable organization of classes and supervision that marked the subsequent stages of the B.Phil. was not very evident in its early years. But I recall some weekly sessions in 1949, held before the publication of *The Concept of Mind*, at which Ryle read parts of the forthcoming book for half an hour or so, then stopped and lit a pipe to initiate discussion. It was a fairly small group, and Hart and Cross were there; later, and I think rightly, it became the exception and not the rule to admit the senior establishment to B.Phil. classes. But Ryle's answers to any member took the same form: not the silencing epigrams sometimes ascribed to him but, as usual, pithy examples that the interlocutor had to accommodate or take leave to meditate.

This was the style of discusion with which his juniors became familiar. Sometimes indeed he talked in laconic paragraphs and not laconic sentences or phrases. Sometimes these even began with "Ah, I don't believe . . .". But the "that"-clause that followed "believe" was never a résumé of the interlocutor's thesis but a reminder of some larger debatable assumption behind that thesis. With him the conversation did not stop, there was no Q.E.D. in philosophy, the lapidary sentences were not lapidary stones; so even epistolary discussions were never concluded. One soon learnt that if two of his pages evoked a one-page reply that was in turn likely to evoke two pages or more, and not a sentence of them dispensable. (One of his replies to me finished "Sorry I haven't had time to make this shorter", and it would have been an unimmersed Japanese paper flower if he had.)

Karl Britton once divided a subset of philosophers into those who wished to write as they spoke and those who wished to speak as they wrote. To Ryle, I imagine, the question never presented itself. His grandfather, the Bishop of Liverpool, who wrote *Knots Untied* (not a bad title for *Dilemmas*), said "In style and comparison I have studied so far as possible to be plain and pointed and to choose what an old divine calls 'picked and packed' words". Ryle wrote and spoke in that family tradition.

In 1949 we juniors had pirated copies of the *Blue* and *Brown Books* in our hands; but we did not think Ryle's methods much indebted to Wittgenstein, even though both proceeded by "the assembling of reminders" and not by would-be proofs. It was not just that Ryle allowed himself "since" and "consequently"; but that was part of it, for he was patently ready to argue, often with a becoming immodesty, and on the evidence we could not envisage a direct argument with Wittgenstein using "No, because . . .". (What

Austin would have appreciatively called "a good bang-about".)

At any rate it is this readiness for argument that dissolves an unreal dilemma sometimes derived from Ryle's determination to maintain philosophy by personal interventions around the world. At least since his 1937 paper on "Taking Sides in Philosophy" he was implacably opposed to cults and sects in his subject. He prized his friendship with Wittgenstein but deplored the Cambridge adulation that he thought Wittgenstein tolerated or even encouraged. Neither of the two Oxford groups I have named came near to a cult, though perhaps the later came nearer. Yet inevitably Ryle himself became and knew he was becoming something of a cult figure, just because his own convictions on how to do and not to do philosophy were so deeply held and so widely and winningly presented. But where another man's students might unworthily ape even his tones and gestures of perplexity, Ryle was not aped. Savingly, he would have laughed at the attempt.

In his later years in Oxford he worked to establish a philosophical centre, with its own building and library, and succeeded; but he did not see the present splendid results himself. There is a room now dedicated to him. There are generations of philosophers dedicated, in the only ways he would have prized, to him.

XVII—DAVID POLE

by Ronald Ashby

Dr. David Pole, Lecturer in Philosophy at King's College London since 1955, died on the night of 28th–29th April, 1977, at the age of 53. He regularly attended the meetings of the Aristotelian Society in London and its annual Joint Sessions at various Universities throughout the country. His frequent contributions to the discussions at these meetings, and the papers he read before the Society and published in its *Proceedings* and *Supplementary Volumes*, gained for him the high respect of a very wide circle of philosophers.

From the early 1950's until the end of his life he maintained a keen interest in an extremely wide range of philosophical topics. He also gained a clear insight into the importance and contemporary significance of the philosophical writings of classical antiquity. He frequently attended meetings at the Institute of Classical Studies in London, and, although he was not a Greek scholar, he was so familiar with the translations of the works of Plato and Aristotle, and with the numerous commentaries on them, that he often made positive contributions with the accuracy of his remarks.

He wrote two books, *The Later Philosophy of Wittgenstein* and *Conditions of Rational Inquiry*. The first of these had the motivation and the merit of being the first attempt by a professional philosopher to introduce the general reader, by exposition and criticism, to the later writings of Wittgenstein. This attempt was regarded adversely by some specialists when the later works of Wittgenstein became better known, but throughout this controversy David Pole maintained, as in all his work, a high standard of intellectual honesty, a commitment to argumentation, and a recognition of fair and legitimate criticism. In his second book he developed his special interest in the relations between evaluation in ethics and in other forms of rational enquiry. Throughout his philosophical work he was mainly concerned with the problems of Aesthetics, Ethics and Axiology, and the concept of Rationality. From all his work he selected twenty-one papers and reviews, five of which have not at the present time been published, and

in a private communication expressed the wish that if anyone
were to undertake the publication of a collection of his writings, the contents should be taken from his selection. Of
these twenty-one papers and reviews, there are five on the
visual arts, four on literature and literary criticism, four on
ethics and values, and eight on various other topics. The last
weeks of his life were devoted to completing a paper entitled
"Relativism and Reason".

His close colleagues and friends will remember his keen
aesthetic responses, his idiosyncratic recitation of the many
passages of literature he knew by heart, and his ability to
carry on a conversation playfully in the metre of the poets he
most admired. In his private life he suffered immensely from
what he regarded as certain intellectual handicaps and from
several emotional incapacities and deprivations. His own experience of unhappiness and suffering gave him a remarkable
understanding of the unhappiness of others. His sympathy for
other individuals gained him the lasting affection of many
colleagues, students and other close friends. He had little
awareness of how much he was respected and loved, and no
anticipation at all of how much he will be missed by everyone
who knew him well. A memorial service for him was held on
25th May in the Gibbs Church of St. Mary-le-Strand, whose
architecture he loved so much, and where he spent the last
reflective moments of his life.

LIST OF OFFICERS AND MEMBERS FOR THE
NINETY-NINTH SESSION 1977–1978

THE COUNCIL

PRESIDENT
PROF. D. W. HAMLYN

VICE-PRESIDENTS

PROF. H. H. PRICE, M.A., B.Sc. (President, 1943–44).
PROF. R. B. BRAITHWAITE, M.A. (President, 1946–47).
PROF. W. KNEALE, M.A. (President, 1949–50).
PROF. J. WISDOM, M.A. (President, 1950–51).
PROF. SIR A. J. AYER, M.A. (President 1951–52).
PROF. DOROTHY EMMET, M.A. (President, 1953–54).
PROF. J. N. FINDLAY, M.A., PH.D. (President, 1955–56).
PROF. R. I. AARON, M.A., D. PHIL. (President, 1957–58).
PROF. SIR KARL POPPER, M.A., PH.D., LL.D.,D.LIT. (President, 1958–59).
PROF. H. L. A. HART, M.A. (President, 1959–60).
PROF. H. D. LEWIS, M.A., B.LIT. (President, 1962–63).
PROF. SIR ISAIAH BERLIN, M.A. (President, 1963–64).
PROF. W. H. WALSH, M.A. (President, 1964–65).
PROF. RUTH SAW, B.A., PH.D. (President, 1965–66).
PROF. S. KORNER, M.A., PH.D. (President, 1966–67).
PROF. RICHARD WOLLHEIM, M.A. (President, 1967–68).
PROF. D. J. O'CONNOR, M.A., PH.D. (President, 1968–69).
PROF. P. F. STRAWSON, M.A. (President, 1969–70).
PROF. W. B. GALLIE, M.A., B.LIT. (President, 1970–71)
MRS. MARTHA KNEALE, M.A. (President, 1971–72).
PROF. R. M. HARE, M.A. (President, 1972–73).
PROF. C. H. WHITELEY, M.A., PH.D. (President, 1973–74).
PROF. D. D. RAPHAEL, D.PHIL, M.A. (President, 1974–75).
MR. A. M. QUINTON, M.A. (President, 1975–76).
PROF. D. M. MACKINNON, M.A. (President, 1976–77).

HONORARY SECRETARY AND EDITOR
MR. ALEC KASSMAN
31, West Heath Drive, London, NW11 7QG.

HONORARY TREASURER
MR. OLIVER STUTCHBURY
45, South Street, Eastbourne, E. Sussex, BN21 4UT.

EXECUTIVE COMMITTEE

PROF. D. D. RAPHAEL, 1975.   MISS H. ISHIGURO, 1976.
MR. R. SCRUTON, 1975.   PROF. D. M. MACKINNON, 1977.
MR. A. M. QUINTON, 1976.   MR. P. FOULKES, 1977.

NORTH AMERICAN REPRESENTATIVE
PROF. K. KOLENDA
Dept. of Philosophy, Rice University, Houston, Texas, 77001, U.S.A.

AUDITORS
MESSRS. TANNER, JAFFER & CO.,
34, Thornhill Rise, Mile Oak, Sussex, BN4 2YN.

HONORARY MEMBERS

Mr. R. J. BARTLETT, 51 Warrington Road, Harrow, Middx.
Prof. H. H. PRICE, *Vice-President*, Hillside, 69 Jack Straws Lane, Oxford OX3 0DW.
Prof. R. B. BRAITHWAITE, *Vice-President*, King's College, Cambridge, CB2 1ST.
Mrs. M. MACE, 105 Roebuck House, Stag Place, London, S.W.1.
Prof. L. A. REID, 50 Rotherwick Road, London, N.W.11.
Mrs. B. ACTON, 5 Abbotsford Park, Edinburgh, 10.
*Prof. B. BLANSHARD, 4 St. Ronan Terrace, New Haven, 11. Conn., USA.
Sir GEORGE S. DUNNETT, Basings Cottage, Cowden, Kent.

MEMBERS

Elected

‡1932　Prof. R. I. AARON, *Vice-President*, Garth Celyn, St. David's Road, Aberystwyth, Wales.

1975　C. ABRAHAM, 42, Lisburne Road, London, NW3 2NR.

§1948　Prof. J. L. ACKRILL, Brasenose College, Oxford.

§1935　Prof. ELOF AKESSON, Skolradsvägen, 9, S-223 67 Lund, Sweden.

1959　Prof. V. C. ALDRICH, Dept. of Philosophy, University of North Carolina, Chapel Hill, North Carolina 27514, U.S.A.

§1945　Prof. P. ALEXANDER, Dept. of Philosophy, The University, Bristol 8.

*1966　Prof. D. J. ALLAN, 83 Bainton Road, Oxford.

*1966　HAROLD J. ALLEN, Dept. Phil., Adelphi Univ., Garden City L.I., New York 11830, U.S.A.

*†1975　Prof. W. P. ALSTON, Dept. of Philosophy, University of Illinois, Urbana, Ill. 81801, U.S.A.

1972　J. E. J. ALTHAM, Gonville and Caius College, Cambridge, CB2 1TA.

‡1969　D. J. C. ANGLUIN, Dept. of Sociology, The Polytechnic of North London, Ladbroke House, Highbury Grove, London, N5 2AD.

*†1971　Miss J. ANNAS, St. Hugh's College, Oxford.

‡1956　Prof. G. E. M. ANSCOMBE, 3 Richmond Road, Cambridge.

*†1969　SANSANDRO ARCOLEO, Via F. Sivori 1/18, 16134 Genova, Italy.

*†1960　Prof. PALL S. ARDAL, Department of Philosophy, Queen's University, Kingston, Ontario, Canada.

*†1969　Prof. D. M. ARMSTRONG, Dept. of Philosophy, Sydney University, Sydney, N.S.W. 2006, Australia.

1955　R. ASHBY, 14 Knoll Court, Farquhar Road, London, S.E.19.

1977　Miss P. A. ASHBOLT (P2), 43 Upham Park Road, Chiswick, W.4.

†1957　Prof. R. F. ATKINSON, Dept. of Philosophy, University of York, Heslington, York.

1976　GEORGE AUGUSTITHIS, 33 Ioannou Theologou, Zografu, Athens, Greece.

1967　Mrs. J. AUSTIN, St. Hilda's College, Oxford.

1976　Prof. S. AXINN, Dept. of Philosophy, Temple University, College of Liberal Arts, Philadelphia, Penn. 19122, USA.

1933　Prof. Sir ALFRED AYER, *Vice-President*, New College, Oxford.

1964　M. R. AYERS, Wadham College, Oxford.

1949　Prof. K. E. BAIER, University of Pittsburg, Faculty of Arts & Sciences, Dept. of Philosophy, Pittsburg, PA15260 USA.

*1966　E. BAKER, "The Bays", Kings Road, Southminster, Essex.

*1974　T. R. BALDWIN, Dept. of Philosophy, University of York, Heslington, York, YO1 5DD.

1972　G. B. BALLESTER, Linacre College, Oxford.

‡1960　J. R. BAMBROUGH, St. John's College, Cambridge.

1966　Prof. F. RIVETTI-BARBO, Via Pietro Mascagni, No. 2, 20122 Milan, Italy.

275

Elected
‡1960 M. J. W. BARKER, Danby Lodge, 239 West Ella Road, W. Ella, East Yorkshire.
‡1969 J. BARNES, Oriel College, Oxford.
1944 Prof. W. H. F. BARNES, 7, Great Stuart Street, Edinburgh, EH3 7TP.
*1962 Father CYRIL BARRETT, S. J., University of Warwick, Coventry.
1969 Mrs. E. J. C. BAXENDALE, 114 Petersburg Road, Edgeley, Stockport, Cheshire.
1975 A. BAXTER, Many Trees, Packhorse Road, Bessels Green, Sevenoaks, Kent, TN13 2QP.
1968 R. W. BEARDSMORE, Bryn Awel, Star, Gaerwen, Isle of Anglesey, Gwynedd.
1961 R. A. BECHER, 6 Weech Road, London, N.W.6.
1956 E. BEDFORD, Dept. of Philosophy, University of Edinburgh, David Hume Tower, George Square, Edinburgh 8.
1955 W. BEDNAROWSKI, 31 College Bounds, Old Aberdeen.
§1974 MARTIN BELL, Dept. of Philosophy, University of York, Heslington, York.
†1975 ANDREW BELSEY, Dept. of Philosophy, University College, Cardiff, CF1 1XL.
§1959 S. J. BENN, Inst. of Advanced Studies, Australian National University, P.O. Box. 4, Canberra A.C.T. 2600, Australia.
*†1957 Prof. J. F. BENNETT, Dept. of Philosophy, University of British Columbia, Vancouver 8, B.C., Canada.
‡1963 Prof. J. H. BENSON, Dept. of Philosophy, Bowland College, Bailrigg, Lancaster.
§1970 Mrs. F. BERENSON, 13 Lansdowne, 9/10 Carlton Drive, Putney, London S.W.15.
1937 Prof. Sir ISAIAH BERLIN, *Vice-President*, All Souls College, Oxford.
1945 U. R. BHATTACHARYYA, 103 Rash Behari Avenue, Calcutta 20, India.
1956 PETER BINDLEY, 11 Leinster Road, Muswell Hill N.10.
‡1955 Prof. G. H. BIRD, Dept. of Philosophy, The University of Stirling, Stirling.
1935 Prof. MAX BLACK, 408 Highland Road, Ithaca, New York, U.S.A.
1971 ROBERT K. BLACK, Dept. of Philosophy, The University of Nottingham, University Park, Nottingham NG7 2RD.
‡1974 S. BLACKBURN, Pembroke College, Oxford.
*1961 Miss MARGARET A. BODEN, The University of Sussex, School of Social Studies, Brighton BN1 9QN.
‡1974 Mrs. A. V. BOFF (24/3/75).
§1975 D. E. BOLTON, 3 Kenley Close, Bexley, Kent.
*†1970 E. J. BOND, 4226 Bath Road, Kingston, Ontaria, Canada.
*1965 W. L. BONNEY, Dept. of Philosophy, University of Sydney, Australia.
1974 C. V. BORST, Dept. of Philosophy, University of Keele, Newcastle, Staffs, ST5 5BG.
1972 DAVID BOSTOCK, Merton College, Oxford.
1969 Miss SOPHIE BOTROS (14/4/74).
1956 Prof. T. B. BOTTIMORE, Office of the Arts Deans, Arts Building, University of Sussex, Falmer, Brighton, Sussex.
§1972 Prof. K. BOUDOURIS, 5 Simonidou Str. Kalamaki, Athens 357.
1976 G. BOURNE, Faculty of Arts, The Open University, Walton Hall, Milton Keynes, Bucks.
§1975 JOHN BOUSFIELD, Eliot College, Faculty of Humanities, University, Canterbury, Kent.
1972 M. HARRISON BOYLE, 32 Roseneath Road, South Clapham, London SW11 6AH.
‡1967 D. D. C. BRAINE, Dept. of Logic, King's College, Old Aberdeen, Scotland.
1933 Mrs. M. M. BRAITHWAITE, 11 Millington Road, Cambridge.

Elected

*†1970   E. P. BRANDON, St. Mary's College, The Park, Cheltenham, GL50 2RH.

1976   R. W. BRIDGETT, 11 Margaret Avenue, Trentham, Stoke-on-Trent, ST4 1ND (P3).

1975   T. BRISTOL, London House, Mecklenburgh Square, London WC1.

‡1937   Prof K. W. BRITTON, Horthope, Millfield Road, Riding Mill, Northumberland.

1969   A. BROADIE, Dept. of Moral Philosophy, The University, Glasgow W.2.

*1971   F. BROADIE, Dept. of Philosophy, The University of Edinburgh, David Hume Tower, George Square, Edinburgh 8.

1952   D. G. BROWN, Dept. of Philosophy, University of British Columbia, Vancouver, Canada.

§1977   IAN D. BROWN, Residents Clerks Quarters, c/o 056 Ministry of Defence, Whitehall, London S.W.1.

*†1949   N. J. BROWN, Dept. of Philosophy, Queen's University, Kingston, Ontario, Canada.

§1954   ROBERT BROWN, Dept. of Social Philosophy, Australian National University, Canberra, A.C.T., Australia.

1962   S. C. BROWN, 42 Park Road, New Barnet, Herts.

1967   Prof. J. E. BROWLES (14/4/74).

1963   Miss NADINE BRUMMER (14/4/74).

†1974   P. D. BRUNNING, 38 Elsworthy Road, London N.W.3.

§1948   J. A. BRUNTON, University College, Cathays Park, Cardiff.

*†1974   CHRISTOPHER BRYANT, Dept. of Moral Philosophy, The University, St. Andrews, Fife.

1976   Mrs. MOIRA BRYANT, 54 Pelham Road, Clavering, Saffron Walden, Essex (P.5).

1966   GERD BUCHDAHL, 11 Brookside, Cambridge.

1948   ROGER BUCK (14/4/74).

1962   T. E. BURKE, Dept. of Philosophy, The University, Reading.

‡1964   M. F. BURNYEAT, 203 Highbury Quadrant, London N5 2TE.

§1975   P. A. BYRNE, Dept. of Philosophy of Religion, University of London, Kings College, Strand, London WC2R 2LS.

*1969   Mrs. EVA H. CADWALLADER, Department of Philosophy, Westminster College, New Wilmington, Pa. 16142, U.S.A.

1951   Prof. J. M. CAMERON, St. Michael's College, University of Toronto, Toronto 5, Ontario, Canada.

*†1974   Dr. RICHARD CAMPBELL, Dept. of Philosophy, S.G.S., Australian National University, Box 4, P.O., Canberra, A.C.T., Australia 2600.

1964   T. D. CAMPBELL, Dept. of Philosophy, University of Stirling, Stirling FK9 4LA, Scotland.

*†1974   STEWART CANDLISH, Dept. of Philosophy, University of Western Australia, Nedlands 6009, Western Australia.

†1975   A. D. CARSTAIRS, 12 Blenheim Road, London W4 1UA.

1975   T. CARVER, Dept. of Political Theory and Institutions, Roxby Buildings, P.O. Box 147, The University, Liverpool, L69 3BX.

‡1957   Miss EVA CASSIRER, 1 Berlin 33, Wildpfad 28, West Germany.

*†1967   Prof. HECTOR-NERI CASTANEDA, 224 Martha Street, Bloomington, IN47401 USA.

§1971   Mrs. S. C. DE CASTELL-JUNGHERTZ, 70 Hilfield Road, W. Hampstead, London N.W.6.

1946   Prof. A. P. CAVENDISH, Dept. of Philosophy, St. David's College, Lampeter, Cards., Wales.

*1970   J. H. CHANDLER, Philosophy Dept., University of Adelaide, Adelaide, South Australia, 5001.

1976   Mrs. L. M. CHANEY, 24 Wilmar Close, Uxbridge, Mx. (U3).

Elected
*†1959 Prof. V. C. CHAPPELL, Dept. of Philosophy, University of Massachusetts, Amherst, Mass. 01002, U.S.A.
§1966 Mrs. A. CHARLTON, Lee Hall Wark, Hexham, Northumberland.
1963 Prof. E. L. CHERBONNIER, 843 Prospect Avenue, Hartford, Connecticut, 06105, U.S.A.
1974 C. M. CHERRY, Eliot College, The University, Canterbury, Kent.
1958 Prof. N. CHOMSKY, Dept. of Linguists & Philosophy, Cambridge, Mass. 02139, U.S.A.
1958 Prof. W. A. CHRISTIAN (14876).
1974 Prof. F. CIOFFI, Dept of Philosophy, University of Essex, Colchester. CO3 3SQ.
§1975 A. W. CLARE, 105 Monks Orchard Road, Beckenham, Kent BR3 3BX.
§1963 M. CLARK, Dept. of Philosophy, The University, Nottingham NG7 2RD.
§ Mrs. M. CLEAR, 33 Egmont Road, Sutton, Surrey, SM2 5JR.
§1975 STEPHEN R. L. CLARK, 9 Clarence Drive, Glasgow G12 9QL.
1976 P. COATES, 15a Pembridge Crescent, London, W11 3DX.
D. A. COCKBURN, Dept. of Philosophy, University College of Swansea, Singleton Park, Swansea BA2 8PP.
*1970 Prof. A. B. CODY, Dept. of Philosophy, San Jose State College, San Jose, California, 95114, U.S.A.
1975 J. COFMAN-NICORESTI, 18 Lord Roberts Avenue, Leigh-on-Sea, Essex.
1961 Mrs. B. M. COHEN, Dept. of Philosophy, The University of Surrey, Guildford, Surrey.
1976 Mrs. CYNTHIA B. COHEN, 3935 Penberton, Ann Arbor, Michigan, 48105, U.S.A.
1963 G. A. COHEN, Dept. of Philosophy, University College, Gower Street, W.C.1.
*1959 JOSEPH J. COHEN, 150 West End Avenue, Apt. 25F, New York 10023, U.S.A.
§1948 L. JONATHAN COHEN, The Queen's College, Oxford.
‡1968 M. COHEN, Dept. of Philosophy, University College of North Wales, Bangor.
*†1972 SHELDON M. COHEN, Department of Philosophy, University of Tennessee, Knoxville, Tenn. 37916. U.S.A.
§1975 A. R. COLCLOUGH, 65 Winchendon Road, Teddington, Middx.
1971 Mrs. DIANE J. COLLINSON, Peekmill, Ivybridge, Devon, PL21 0LA.
1975 D. E. COOPER, School of Humanities and Social Sciences, Dept. of Philosophy, Guildford, Surrey.
1959 N. COOPER, 2 Minto Place, Dundee, Scotland, DD2 1BR.
1946 Prof. F. C. COPLESTON, S.J., 11 Cavendish Square, London, W1M 0AN.
1972 Prof. STEVEN CORD, 580 N. 6 Street, Indiana, Pa. 15701, U.S.A.
1976 M. CORRADO, Dept. of Philosophy, Ohio University, Athens, Ohio.
1976 PAUL CORNYETZ, 257 Central Park West, New York, NY.10020, USA.
1961 S. COVAL, Dept. of Philosophy, University of British Columbia, Vancouver 8, B.E. Columbia.
*1946 SYBIL M. CRANE, 2 Britannia Square, Worcester.
§1973 Prof. J. M. B. CRAWFORD, Common Room, Middle Temple Lane, Middle Temple, E.C.4.
1953 CAMPBELL CROCKET, The Spyglass, Apt. 520, 1600 Thomson Hghts. Dr., Cincinnati, Ohio 45223, U.S.A.
1948 I. M. CROMBIE, Wadham College, Oxford.
§1976 Prof. JOHN CRONQUIST, Dept. of Philosophy, California State University, Fullerton, California 92634 U.S.A.
‡1941 Prof. R. C. CROSS, The University, Aberdeen.
‡1963 C. R. A. CUNLIFFE, 29 Riverdale Gardens, Twickenham.
1954 Mrs. F. K. CUTLER, Bramley College, Sandy Lane, Bearsted, Kent.

278

Elected

§1975 MELVIN T. DALGARNO, 16 College Bounds, Aberdeen.

1977 R. M. J. DAMMANN, University of Sussex School of European Studies, Arts Building, Falmer, Brighton, Sussex BN1 9QN.

§1975 J. P. DANCY, Dept. of Philosophy, University of Keele, Keele, Staffs. ST5 5BG.

1976 D. J. DAVIES, 9 Brodorian Drive, Cwmryddy, Ceirw, Morriston, Swansea, SA6 6LP.

1948 J. P. DE C. DAY, Dept. of Philosophy, University of Keele, Keele, Staffordshire.

‡1965 R. F. DEARDEN, 49, Wattleton Road, Beaconsfield, Bucks, HP9 1RY.

*1969 Prof. CORNELIUS DE DEUGD, "Ravesteyn", Bourmalsen, Holland.

§1971 M. A. B. DEGENHARDT, Stockwell College, Rochester Avenue, Bromley, Kent.

†1973 COUNT LYSANDER DE GRANDY, Glen Eyre Hall, Bassett, Southampton, SO9 2QN.

§1975 N. J. H. DENT, Dept. of Philosophy, University of York, Heslington, York YO1 5DD.

1947 Prof. PHILIP DEVAUX (18.1.77).

*†1957 Prof. P. DIAMONDOPOULOS, Brandeis University, Waltham, Mass. 02154, U.S.A.

1962 Miss CORA DIAMOND, Dept. of Philosophy, The University of Virginia, 1512, Jefferson Park Avenue, Charlottesville, Virginia 22901, U.S.A.

1970 Prof. MALCOLM L. DIAMOND, Flat 7, 25 Lowndes Square, London SW1 9HE.

1975 R. DIETZ, 8 Fieldend, Waldergrave Park, Twickenham, Middx. TW1 4TF.

1974 K. J. DILLON, 31b Tanza Road, Hampstead, London N.W.3.

1955 ILHAM DILMAN, Dept. of Philosophy, University College of Swansea, South Wales.

*†1965 K. DIXON, Dept. of Sociology, Simon Fraser University, Burnaby B.C., Canada, V5A 156.

‡1952 A. H. DONAGAN, 1453 East Park Place, Chicago, Illinois 60637, U.S.A.

§1952 WILLIS DONEY, Dept. of Philosophy, Dartmouth College, Hanover, New Hampshire, U.S.A.

1968 NIGEL DOWER, Dept. of Logic and Moral Philosophy, Univ. of Aberdeen, King's College, Old Aberdeen.

§1961 Prof. R. S. DOWNIE, Dept. of Moral Philosophy, The University, Glasgow W.2.

1955 P. DOWNING, c/o Messrs. Turner, Peacock, 1 Raymond Buildings, Gray's Inn, London WC1R 5RJ.

†1969 B. S. DRASAR, London School of Hygiene and Tropical Medicine, Keppel Street (Gower Street), London W.C.1.

†1952 W. H. DRAY, Dept. of Philosophy, Trent University, Peterborough, Ontario, Canada.

1967 Prof. D. P. DRYER, Room 819, 215 Huron Street, University of Toronto, Toronto 5, Canada.

1951 M. DUMMETT, All Souls College, Oxford.

*†1967 Prof. ELMER H. DUNCAN, Baylor University, Dept. of Philosophy, Waco, Texas 76703, U.S.A.

‡1938 Prof. ALISTAIR R. C. DUNCAN, Queen's University, Kingston, Ontario, Canada.

1972 A. P. DURHAM, Philosophy Department, UCLA Los Angeles, Calif. 90024, U.S.A.

*1950 R. G. DURRANT, Dept. of Philosophy, University of Otago, Dunedin, New Zealand.

1964 D. J. DUTHIE, 35 Holmesdale Road, London N.6.

‡1970 JOHN L. DWYER, c/o Faculty of Law, University of Warwick, Coventry, Warwickshire, CB4 7AL.

Elected

†1970 J. C. DYBIKOWSKI, Dept. of Philosophy, University of British Columbia, Vancouver 8, B.C., Canada.

1971 Prof. W. EASTMAN, Dept. of Philosophy, Univ. of Alberta, Edmonton 7, Canada.

1969 Mrs. D. M. D. EDGINGTON, Dept. of Philosophy, Birkbeck College, Malet Street, London, W.C.1.

‡1958 Prof. R. EDGLEY, The University of Sussex, Arts Building, Falmer, Brighton, Sussex BN1 9QN.

§1974 MICHAEL EDWARDS, 134 Colney Hatch Lane, Muswell Hill, London, N10 1ER.

1956 Miss D. H. ELDERTON, 15 Wren Street, W.C.1.

1966 Prof. R. K. ELLIOTT, 12 Coppice Road, Moseley, Birmingham B13 9DD.

1934 Prof. DOROTHY EMMET, *Vice-President*, 11 Millington Road, Cambridge.

1956 ELLIS C. EVANS, 102 Woodhead Road, Holmbridge, Huddersfield.

1971 GARETH EVANS, University College, Oxford.

§1974 J. D. G. EVANS, Sidney Sussex College, Cambridge CB2 3HU.

*†1946 Prof. J. L. EVANS, The Dingle, Danybryn Avenue, Radyr, nr. Cardiff.

1958 H. S. EVELING, Dept. of Philosophy, David Hume Tower, George Square, Edinburgh 8.

§1953 J. EVENDEN, "Milton", 8 St. John's Avenue, Burgess Hill, Sussex.

*1968 NICHOLAS EVERITT, University of East Anglia School of Social Studies, University Plain, Norwich NOR 88C.

*1974 B. FALK, Dept. of Philosophy, University of Birmingham, Birmingham 15.

‡1971 E. J. FARGE, 12 Tanza Road, Hampstead, London, N.W.3.

1947 B. A. FARRELL, Corpus Christi College, Oxford.

*†1976 JOEL FEINBERG, The Rockefeller University, 1230 York Avenue, New York, N.Y. 10021, U.S.A.

1974 L. FIELDS, Department of Philosophy, The University, Dundee, Scotland.

*1948 Prof. J. N. FINDLAY, *Vice-President*, Department of Philosophy, Boston University, 232 Bay State Road, Boston, Mass. 02215 U.S.A.

1963 Miss M. FINNEGAN, Dept. of Politics, Alfred Marshall Buildings, 40 Berkeley Square, Bristol 8.

‡1975 D. R. FISHER, 23 Twining Avenue, Twickenham, Middx. TW2 5LL.

*1976 Prof. JOSEPH FLANAGAN, S.J., Chairman, Dept. of Philosophy, Boston College, Chestnut Hill, Mass. 02167, U.S.A.

†1952 Prof. A. G. N. FLEW, Dept. of Philosophy, The University, Reading, RG6 2AA.

1948 Mrs. P. R. FOOT, 15 Walton Street, Oxford.

1954 P. FOULKES, 24 Granville Park, London, S.E.13.

*1968 D. L. FOWLER, Dept. of Philosophy, The University of Trondheim, College of Arts & Sciences, 7000 Trondheim, Norway.

*†1970 WILLIAM H. FREIDMAN, V.C.U. Philosophy Dept., Richmond, Va. 23220, U.S.A.

†1967 Prof. PIERRE C. FRUCHON, Les Cjenets, Residence du Poutet, 33 Pessac, France.

§1936 Prof. E. J. FURLONG, 9 Trinity College, Dublin, Eire.

1973 Miss SUZI GABLIK, 5 Westmoreland Street, London W.1.

1976 C. GABRIEL, Challoner Crescent, London W14 (P2).

§1966 J. W. GALBRAITH, Woodlans Top Flat, Kilcreggan, Scotland, G84 0HQ.

280

Elected

1968 ROGER D. GALLIE, Dept. of Philosophy, The University, Leicester.
1937 Prof. W. B. GALLIE, *Vice-President*, Peterhouse, Cambridge.
1950 P. L. GARDINER, Magdalen College, Oxford.
1963 J. GARLAND, 30 Moore Street, S.W.3.
§1968 R. T. GARNER, Dept. of Philosophy, Ohio State University, 216 North Oval Drive, Columbus, Ohio 43210, U.S.A.
‡1972 Mrs. G. D. V. GARTHWAITE, 40 Sandy Bank Avenue, Rothwell, Leeds LS26 oER.
§1971 P. GASCOIGNE, 15, Marlborough Buildings, Bath, Avon, BA1 2LY.
1968 Mrs. NANCY GAYER, 1 Durham Terrace, London W.2.
*1948 Prof. QUENTIN B. GIBSON, Dept. of Philosophy, S.G.S., Australian National Univ., Canberra A.C.T., Australia.
§1975 A. J. GILMOUR, 316 Alexander Park Road, London, N.22.
‡1959 P. GOCHET, 78 Boulevard Louis Schmict, 1040 Brussels, Belgium.
1969 P. A. GOLDSBURY, Commonwealth Hall, Cartwright Gardens, London WC1H 9EB.
1970 J. GONLEY, 12 Gardenia Avenue, Luton, Beds.
1962 PHILIP GORDIS, 1 West 81st Street, Apartment 4DB, New York City New York 10024, U.S.A.
1951 D. R. GORDON, Dept. of Philosophy, University of Strathclyde, Livingstone Tower, 26 Richmond Street, Glasgow, G1 1XH.
1956 J. C. B. GOSLING, St. Edmund Hall, Oxford.
1975 KEITH GRAHAM, Dept. of Philosophy, The University of Bristol, Wills Memorial Building, Queens Road, Bristol, BS8 1RJ.
*1946 Prof C. K. GRANT, Philosophy Dept., The University, Durham.
1976 E. A. GRANT, 9 The Heights, 97 Frognal, London N.W.3.
1964 E. P. C. GREENE, 63F High Street, Oxford.
*†1969 Prof. HAROLD GREENSTEIN, 71 West Avenue, Brockport, New York 14420, U.S.A.
1976 Miss D. GREENWOOD, 15 Ballist Quay, London, S.E.10.
1956 Miss M. GREENWOOD, 66 Cliff Road, Leeds 6.
§1969 T. GREENWOOD, Dept. of Logic, University of Glasgow, Glasgow W.2.
1957 H. GREVILLE, "Walden", Bury Road, Stanningfield, Bury St. Edmunds, Suffolk.
1956 Prof. A. P. GRIFFITHS, Dept. of Philosophy, The University of Warwick, Coventry, Warwickshire.
†1975 L. J. GRIFFITHS, 33, Rickards Close, Long Ditton, Surbiton, Surrey.
*1968 B. GROSS (14/4/74).
*1964 H. R. J. GRUNER, Dept. of Philosophy, Sheffield University, Sheffield.
1976 ALEX B. GUNN, 24 Falkland Gardens, Edinburgh EH12 6UW.
1969 C. E. GUNTON, 33 South Drive, Brentwood, Essex.

§1974 Mrs. SUSAN HAACK, Dept. of Philosophy, University of Warwick, Coventry, Warcs, CV4 7AL.
1946 Prof. W. HAAS, The University, Manchester 13.
§1975 Miss A. HADJIPATERAS, 22 Abbey Lodge, Park Road, London N.W.8.
1965 V. HAKSAR, University of Edinburgh, Dept. of Philosophy, David Hume Tower, George Square, Edinburgh, EN8 9JK.
1962 J. C. HALL, 25 Hepburn Gardens, St. Andrews, Fife, Scotland, KY16 9DG.
†1972 Miss JANET HALL, 26 Wiberton Road, London S.E.26.
§1957 ROLAND HALL, Dept. of Philosophy, University of York, Heslington, Yorks.
1959 Prof. R. HALLER, Karl-Franzens-Universitat, Graz, Philosophischas. Institut, Heinrichstrasse 26/VI, A-8010 Graz, Austria.
‡1951 Prof. D. W. HAMLYN, *President*, 7 Burland Road, Brentwood, Essex.

Elected

1961   Miss A. HAMMOND, Flat 3, 33 Hampstead Hill Gardens, London N.W.3.

1937   STUART HAMPSHIRE, The Warden's Lodgings, Wadham College, Oxford.

1970   O. HANFLING, Linnets, Terry's Lane, Cookham, Maidenhead, Berks.

1959   R. ALISTAIR HANNAY, Institute of Philosophy, Niels Henrik Abels Vei 12, Blindern, Oslo 3, Norway.

*1945   J. B. HANSON-LOWE, c/o Mailing Section, Shell Sekiyu K.K., C.P.O. Box 1239, Tokyo, Japan.

§1947   Prof. R. M. HARE, *Vice-President*, Corpus Christi College, Oxford.

*1972   Prof. B. HARRIS, Eastern Kentucky University, College of Arts & Sciences Dept. of Philosophy, Richmond, Kentucky 40475, U.S.A.

1952   Prof. ERROL E. HARRIS, Dept. of Philosophy, North Western University, Evanston, Illinois, U.S.A.

‡1975   J. M. HARRIS, 62 Princes Street, St. Clements, Oxford.

1976   L. D. HARRIS, 75 Reading Road., Northolt, Mx. UB5 4PJ.

1962   ANDREW HARRISON, Dept. of Philosophy, The University, Bristol 8.

‡1962   Prof. B. J. HARRISON, School of English and American Studies, University of Sussex, Arts Building, Falmer, Brighton, Sussex.

‡1947   Prof. J. HARRISON, Dept. of Philosophy, The University, Nottingham NG7 2RD.

‡1971   T. R. HARRISON, King's College, Cambridge CB2 1ST.

†1946   Prof. H. L. A. HART, *Vice-President*, The Principal, Brasenose College, Oxford.

*†1975   W. D. HART, Dept. of Philosophy, University College London, Gower Street, London, WC1E 6BT.

1959   Miss L. C. HARVARD, The Old Rectory, Stock, Ingatestone, Essex.

§1973   H. H. HARVEY, Seafields, Blackgang, Ventnor, Isle of Wight.

1965   LAWRENCE HAWORTH, University of Waterloo, Dept. of Philosophy, Waterloo, Ontario, Canada.

1946   W. H. HAY, 39 Bagley Court, Madison, Wisconsin 53705, U.S.A.

§1977   Mrs. J. HEAL, Dept. of Philosophy, Armstrong Bldg., The University, Newcastle-upon-Tyne WE1 7RU.

*1946   Prof. P. L. HEATH, Dept. of Philosophy, University of Virginia, Charlottesville, U.S.A.

§1976   The Rev. B. L. HEBBLETHWAITE, Queen's College, Cambridge, CB3 9ET.

*1962   Prof. J. HEINTZ, Dept. of Philosophy, Faculty of Arts & Science, University of Calgary, Alberta, Canada T2N TN4.

*1967   PAUL HELM (14/4/74).

1968   M. HEMPOLINSKI (14/4/74).

*1958   Prof. G. P. HENDERSON, Dept. of Philosophy, The University, Dundee, Scotland.

1975   Miss P. A. HENDRA, 52 Glenloch Road, Hampstead, London, NW3.

†1969   Prof. D. HENRICH, Philosophisches Seminar, Der Universitat, 69 Heidelberg 1, Marsiliusplatz 1, West Germany.

1955   Prof. R. W. HEPBURN, Dept. of Philosophy, University of Edinburgh, David Hume Tower, George Square, Edinburgh 8.

1956   Miss M. B. HESSE, Whipple Museum, Free School Lane, Cambridge.

1949   T. J. O. HICKEY, 23 Lloyd Square, London, W.C.1.

‡1965   Prof. DAVID C. HICKS, Dept. of Theology, King's College, Old Aberdeen, Scotland, AB9 2UB.

‡1972   R. C. HICKS, Walcot, North Walls, Chichester, Sussex, PO19 1DB.

‡1974   GEOFFREY J. C. HIGGS, Birkbeck College, Dept. of Philosophy, 14 Gower Street, London W.C.1.

‡1966   Mrs. CORINNE HILL, 47 High Street, Hinxton, Saffron Walden, Essex.

Elected

‡1968   Mrs. RUTH HILLYER, Prior's Field, Godalming, Surrey GU7 2RH.
†1949   JOHN R. HILTON, Hope Cottage, Nash Hill, Lacock, Wilts.
†*1959   Prof. J. HINTIKKA, Institute of Philosophy, Unioninkatu, 40B, 00170, Helsinki 17, Finland.
‡1972   R. T. HINTON, 38 Regency Square, Brighton BN 2FT.
1964   E. HIRSCHMANN, 9 Limes Avenue N.12.
*†1961   Prof. P. H. HIRST, University of Cambridge, Department of Education, 17 Brookside, Cambridge CB2 1JG.
1954   Prof. R. J. HIRST, 179 Maxwell Drive, Glasgow, G41 5AE.
*1960   Prof. R. HOCKING, Madison, New Hampshire 03849, U.S.A.
*†1960   ROBERT HOFFMAN, 9, Wycomb Place, Coram, New York, 11727, U.S.A.
*1964   Prof. L. C. HOLBOROW, Dept. of Philosophy, University of Queensland, St. Lucia, 4067, Queensland, Australia.
§1950   Prof. R. F. HOLLAND, Dept. of Philosophy, The University of Leeds, Leeds 2.
§1968   L. A. HOLLINGS, Flat 1, 123, Ditchling Rise, Brighton, BN1 4QP.
1967   MARTIN HOLLIS, School of Social Studies, Dept. of Philosophy, University of East Anglia, Norwich.
*†1944   E. R. HOLMES, 84 Commercial Road, Bulwell, Nottingham.
†1962   T. HONDERICH, Dept. of Philosophy, University College, Gower Street, London, W.C.1.
1974   JAMES HOPKINS, King's College, Strand, London, W.C.2.
1975   Miss JANE M. HOWARTH, Dept. of Philosophy, University of Lancaster, Lancaster, Lancs.
*1968   W. D. HUDSON, Dept. of Philosophy, The University, Exeter.
1946   Prof. G. E. HUGHES, Dept. of Philosophy, Victoria University of Wellington, P.O. Box 196, Wellington, New Zealand.
1970   G. J. HUGHES, Heythrop College, 11 Cavendish Square, London, W1M 0AN.
1976   Mrs. K. M. HUGHES, 433 Felixstowe Road, Ipswich, Suffolk, IP3 9BQ.
1964   W. H. HUGHES, Wellington College, University of Guelph, Ontario, Canada.
1959   P. HUGHESDEN, 107 Corringham Road, London, N.W.11.
*1976   Prof. R. T. HULL, Dept. of Philosophy, State University of York at Buffalo, Baldy Hall, Buffalo, New York 14260, U.S.A.
1959   I. HUNT, University of Sussex, Falmer, Sussex.
1952   G. B. B. HUNTER, Dept. of Logic and Metaphysics, The University, St. Andrews, Fife, Scotland.
†1975   F. J. HURST, 27 Nilverton Avenue, Sunderland, Tyne & Wear.

‡1968   D. E. IDONIBOYE, School of Humanities, Dept. of Philosophy, University of Lagos, Lagos, Nigeria.
*1963   M. P. IRELAND, Dept. of Philosophy, School of Social Studies, University of Sussex. Brighton BN1 9QN.
1960   Miss HIDE ISHIGURO, Dept. of Philosophy, University College, Gower Street, London, W.C.1.
§1975   TARIQ ISMAIL, 103 South Hill Park, London N.W.3.
†1972   Prof. NANDINI R. IYER, Dept. of Philosophy, University of California, Santa Barbara, California, 93106, U.S.A.

*†1967   Mrs. J. M. JACK, Somerville College, Oxford OX2 6HD.
1958   A. C. JACKSON, Monash University, Victoria, Australia.
§1955   R. B. JACKSON, The Cottage, 9c, The Grove, London, N6 6JU.
1975   N. JARDINE, Whipple Museum of the History of Science, Dept. of History & Philosophy of Science, Free School Lane, Cambridge CB2 3RH.

Elected

1965   J. J. JENKINS, Dept. of Moral Philosophy, David Hume Tower, George Square, Edinburgh 8.

1936   Prof. T. E. JESSOP, The University, Hull.

‡1970   H. JOHANNESSEN, Department of Philosophy, University of Trondheim, Trondheim, Norway.

*†1957   Prof. A. H. JOHNSON, Dept. of Philosophy, The University of Western Ontario, London, Ontario, Canada.

§1958   O. R. JONES, Dept. of Philosophy, University College of Wales, Aberystwyth.

‡1964   P. H. JONES, Dept. of Philosophy, University of Edinburgh, David Hume Tower, George Square, Edinburgh 8.

1964   R. T. JONES, 3 Tungate Crescent, Cringleford, Norwich.

‡1955   Z. A. JORDAN, Dept. of Sociology and Anthropology, Carleton. University, Ottawa 1, Canada.

*†1967   W. D. JOSKE, Dept. of Philosophy, University of Tasmania, G.P.O. Box 252, Hobart 7001, Tasmania, Australia.

1969   N. S. JUNANKAR, 25 Welldon Crescent, Middlesex. HA1 1QP.

1973   H. KAMP, Dept. of Philosophy, Bedford College, Regents Park, London NW1.

1954   A. A. KASSMAN, Hon. Secretary & Editor, 31 West Heath Drive, London, NW11 7QG.

*1970   B. P. P. KEANEY, Dept. of Philosophy, University of Cape Town, Private Bag, Rondebosche, Cape Province, Republic of South Africa.

†1969   Mrs. GILLIAN KEENE, 38 Kidbrooke Gardens, London S.E.3.

‡1976   Miss P. D. KEFALAS, 4a Balgores Square, Gidea Park, Romford, Essex.

*†1963   Prof. C. W. KEGLEY, 7115 Mensa Verdi Way, Bakersfield, California, 93369, U.S.A.

1963   Prof. J. KEMP, Dept. of Moral Philosophy, The University, Leicester.

§1975   G. B. KESSLER, Flat 14, Ridgmount Gardens, London, W.C.1.

‡1971   Miss S. KHIN ZAW, 4 Devereux Road, London, S.W.11.

§1976   M. T. KHLENTZOS, 11 Denslowe Drive, San Francisco, California, 94132, U.S.A.

*1966   Prof. HOWARD E. KIEFER, State University College at Brockport, Brockport, New York, 14420, U.S.A.

*†1968   Prof. W. J. KILGORE, Dept. of Philosophy, Baylor University, Waco, Texas 76709, U.S.A.

1966   Miss E. F. KINGDOM, Institute of Extension Studies, 1 Abercromby Square, P.O. Box 147, Liverpool, L69 3BX.

*1969   Rev. Dr. F. T. KINGSTON, Canterbury College, University of Windsor, Windsor, Ontario, Canada.

†1967   ROBERT KIRK, Dept. of Philosophy, The University, Nottingham, NG7 2RD.

1960   C. A. KIRWAN, Exeter College, Oxford.

§1975   Miss ASTRID KJARGAARD, Universitetslektor Ternevej 43, 5000 Odense, Denmark.

‡1968   STANLEY S. KLEINBERG, Dept. of Philosophy, The University, Stirling, Scotland.

*†1937   Mrs. M. KNEALE, Vice-President, 4 Bridge End, Grassington, Nr. Skipton, N. Yorks,. BD23 5NH.

*1933   Prof. W. KNEALE, Vice-President, 4 Bridge End, Grassington, Nr. Skipton, N. Yorks., BD23 5NH.

1946   G. KNEEBONE, Bedford College, Regent's Park, N.W.1.

§1976   D. R. KNOWLES, Dept. of Moral Philosophy, University Glasgow, Glasgow W.2.

*†1973   Prof. K. KOLENDA, North American Representative, Dept. of Philosophy, Rice University, Houston, Texas, 77001, U.S.A.

Elected

§1946 Prof. S. KORNER, Vice-President, Philosophy Dept., The University, Bristol 8.

†1975 Prof. JULIUS KOVESI, c/o 5 Richmond Hill, Bath, BA1 5QT.

1970 Miss ANASTASIA KUCHARSKI, 209 Spring Avenue, Arlington, Mass., 02174. U.S.A.

1969 GERHARD H. KUSOLITSCH, 27 Highlands Heath, Portsmouth Road, London, S.W.15.

§1954 A. R. LACEY, Bedford College, London, N.W.1.

1975 L. LAGDEN, 12 Rutland Gardens, Harringay, London N4.

‡1976 A. C. LAMBERT, 2 Shaw Court, Ninehams Road, Caterham, Surrey CR3 5LL.

1974 Mrs. J. F. LAMBERT, 31 Finchams Close, Linton, Cambridge, CB1 6ND.

1968 S. G. LANGFORD, Dept. of Philosophy, Queen's Buildings, The University, Exeter.

‡1936 Prof. J. A. LAUWERYS, 167 Perry Vale, Forest Hill, London SE23.

φ1967 REYNOLD J. LAWRIE, 14 Chalcot Crescent, London N.W.1.

†1968 J. G. M. LAWS, 81 Alderney Street, London, S.W.1.

1948 Prof. M. LAZEROWITZ, Newhall Road, Conway, Mass. 01341, U.S.A.

1955 Prof. C. LEJEWSKI, Dept. of Philosophy, University of Manchester, Manchester 13.

*1956 RAMON M. LEMOS, Dept. of Philosophy, University of Miami, Coral Gables, Florida, U.S.A.

1976 Dr. A. G. LEWIS, Flat 33, 125 Park Road, London NW8 7JB.

*1964 H. A. LEWIS, Philosophy Dept., University of Leeds, Leeds 2.

§1938 Prof. H. D. LEWIS, Vice-President, 1 Normandy Park, Normandy, nr. Guildford, Surrey.

*1967 Mrs. J. H. LEWIS, 2 Lanark Court, Glen Waverley, Melbourne, Victoria 3150, Australia.

1973 P. B. LEWIS, Dept. of Philosophy, University of Edinburgh, David Hume Tower, George Square, Edinburgh.

1937 CASIMIR LEWY, 49 De Freville Avenue, Cambridge.

*1947 W. VON LEYDEN, 5 Pimlico, Durham.

*1961 A. T. W. LIDDELL, The Warden's Lodging, Whiteknights Hall, Upper Redlands Road, Reading RG1 5JN.

§1971 Prof. DAVID LIEBER, 305 El Camino, Beverly Hills, California 90212, U.S.A.

*1972 J. LIPNER, The Divinity School, St. John's Street, Cambridge, CB2 1TW.

§1965 J. E. LLEWELYN, Dept. of Philosophy, David Hume Tower, George Square, Edinburgh 8.

‡1954 Prof. A. C. LLOYD, The University, Liverpool 3.

1964 D. I. LLOYD, Stockwell College of Education, The Old Palace, Rochester Avenue, Bromley, Kent, BR1 3DH.

1959 V. G. LOKARE, Dept. of Clinical Psychology, West Park Hospital, Epsom, Surrey.

§1969 Prof. ANTHONY A. LONG, School of Classics, Abercromby Square, P.O. Box 147, Liverpool, L69 3BX.

*1973 J. ALLEN LONG III, 1 Fossfield Road, Midsomer Norton, Bath, BA3 4AS.

1956 P. LONG, Dept. of Philosophy, The University, Leeds 2.

1955 J. LUCAS, Merton College, Oxford.

1968 DAVID LUDLOW, 4 Torrington Court, Westwood Hill, Sydenham, London, S.E.26.

§1970 A. J. LYON, The City University, St. John Street, London, E.C.1.

*1970 Prof. DAVID LYONS, Cornell University, The Sage School of Philosophy, Goldwin Smith Hall, Ithaca, New York 14850.

1973 W. E. LYONS, Dept. of Moral Philosophy, The University, Glasgow, W.2.

Elected

§1969   D. A. LLOYD-THOMAS, Dept. of Philosophy, Bedford College, Regent's Park, NW1 4NS.

*1956   J. MACADAMS, Trent University, Peterborough, Ontario, Canada.

†1973   Prof. D. N. MACCORMICK, Dept. of Public Law, The Univ. of Edinburgh, Old College, Edinburgh EH8 97L.

1964   Miss O. A. MACDONALD, Dept, of Theology, The University, Bristol 8.

*1970   J. J. MACINTOSH, Dept. of Philosophy, University of Calgary, Calgary, Alta, Canada.

1955   Prof. A. MACINTYRE, Dean's Office, College of Liberal Arts, Boston University, Boston, Mass., 02215, U.S.A.

‡1971   J. L. MACKIE, University College, Oxford.

1945   Prof. D. M. MACKINNON, *President*, Corpus Christi College, Cambridge.

*†1967   Prof. P. T. MACKENZIE, R.R.5 Saskatoon, Saskatchewan, Canada.

1965   A. M. MACLEOD, Cartwright Point, Kingston, Ontario, Canada.

1937   D. G. MACNABB, Worpleway, Tompsets Bank, Forest Row, E. Sussex.

1951   Mrs. JEAN M. MACPHERSON, Clunebeg, Drumnadrochit, Inverness-shire.

§1972   B. MAGEE, 12 Falkland House, Marloes Road, London, W8 5LF.

§1973   W. J. MAGINNIS, 178 Finaghy Road South, Belfast, BT10 oDH.

†1976   T. A. MAGNELL, New College, Oxford OX1 3BN. (P.2)

*†1975   G. A. MALINES, Dept. of Philosophy, Queensland University, Brisbane, Australia.

1975   P. D. MANNICK, "Byways", Boarhills by St. Andrews, Fife, Scotland (P.3).

‡1951   Prof. A. R. MANSER, The University, Southampton.

1968   Miss P. MARCUS, 60 Pilgrim's Lane, London, N.W.3.

1961   Miss R. H. MARCUS, Dept. of Philosophy, Yale University, New Haven, Connecticut, 06520.

1967   K. A. MARKHAM, Dept. of Applied Psychology, UWIST, Llwyn-y-Grant Road, Penlan, Cardiff CF3 7JX.

§1975   ROGER MARPLES, Kastelle Cottage, Old Road, Buckland, Surrey RH3 7OV.

§1967   G. D. MARSHALL, Dept. of Philosophy, University of Melbourne, Parkville, 3052, Australia.

†1969   Miss S. E. MARSHALL, Dept. of Philosophy, University of Stirling, Scotland.

1957   R. P. MARTIN, British Council, 10 Spring Gardens, London, SW1A 2BN.

1949   B. M. MASANI, 120 Simrole Road, MHOW, M.P. India.

1975   R. V. MASON, Brewery Cottage, Southstoke, Nr. Bath.

§1953   Prof. WALLACE I. MATSON, Dept. of Philosophy, University of California, Berkeley, California 94720, U.S.A.

*1975   E. MATTHEWS, Dept. of Logic, University of Aberdeen, King's College, Old Aberdeen, AB9 2UB.

§1954   Miss G. M. MATTHEWS, St. Anne's College, Oxford.

‡1933   Mrs. C. MAUND, Springs Farm, Fittleworth, Sussex.

*1969   Prof. T. C. MAYBERRY, Dept. of Philosophy, University of Toledo, Toledo, Ohio 43606, U.S.A.

1971   D. G. MAYERS, University College, Durham.

1963   Miss S. MAYLETT, 5 Clyro Court, 93 Tollington Park, Finsbury Park, London, N.4.

§1952   Prof. B. MAYO, Dept. of Philosophy, The University, St. Andrews, Scotland.

‡1947   W. MAYS, Dept. of Philosophy, The University, Manchester 13.

§1975   Miss P. McAULIFFE, Dept. of Philosophy, University of Stirling, Stirling, FK9 4LA.

286

Elected

1974 DAVID J. McCANN, 42 Victoria Road, Swindon SN1 3AY.

*†1965 Prof. H. J. McCLOSKEY, Philosophy Department, School of Humanities, La Trobe University, Bundoora, Victoria, Australia, 3083.

*1976 S. McCREADY, University of Nigeria, Nsukka, Nigeria.

1967 J. H. McDOWELL, University College, Oxford.

§1973 GRAHAM JAMES McFEE, Dept. of Philosophy, East Sussex College of Higher Education, Denton Road, Eastbourne, Sussex BN20 7SR.

1975 I. G. McFETRIDGE, Dept. of Philosophy, Birkbeck College, Malet Street, London, C1E 7HX.

1975 C. McGINN, Dept. of Philosophy, University College of London, Gower Street, London, WC1E 6BT.

1968 R. S. McGOWAN, Dept. of Philosophy, The University, Leicester.

1966 C. J. McKNIGHT, Dept. of Philosophy, The Queen's University, Belfast, N. Ireland.

*†1967 R. M. McLAUGHLIN, Macquarie University, Dept. of Philosophy, North Ryde, N.S.W., Australia, 2113.

*1969 Prof. J. B. McMINN, Department of Philosophy, P.O. Box 6287, University of Alabama, College of Arts and Sciences, Alabama 35486.

*1973 DAVID A. McNAUGHTON, Dept. of Philosophy, Keele, University, Staffs, ST5 5BG.

‡1952 T. H. McPHERSON, Dept. of Philosophy, University College, P.O. Box 78, Cardiff, CF1 1XL.

§1967 DONALD A. McQUEEN, Dept. of Philosophy, The University, Nottingham.

§1955 Miss R. MEAGER, Birkbeck College, Dept. of Philosophy, Malet Street, London, W.C.1.

§1951 Prof. ABRAHAM MELDEN, Dept. of Philosophy, University of California, Irvine, California, 92664, U.S.A.

§1966 D. H. MELLOR, University of Cambridge, Faculty of Philosophy, Sidgwick Avenue, Cambridge CB3 9DA.

1958 Prof. J. MELOE, Institutt for Samfunnsvitenskap, Roald Amundsens Plass, 1, 9000 Tromso, Norge.

§1965 J. MELZACK, 32 Addisland Court, Holland Villas Road, London, W.14.

*1972 M. A. MENLOWE, Dept. of Moral Philosophy, King's College, University of Aberdeen, Aberdeen AB9 2UB.

§1975 PETER MEW, Dept. of Philosophy, Trinity College, Dublin 2.

*1976 B. E. MEYER, 830, Park Central Court, Indianapolis, Indiana, U.S.A. 46260.

1966 H. A. MEYNELL, Dept. of Philosophy & Theology, The University, Leeds.

*†1967 Mrs. J. MEYNELL, Dept. of Philosophy, The University, Leeds, LS2 9JT.

1975 Mrs. A. MICHAELSON, 75 Furscroft, George Street, London. W.1.

1949 G. C. J. MIDGLEY, Dept. of Philosophy, The University, Newcastle-upon-Tyne.

1972 Mrs. M. MIDGLEY, Dept. of Philosophy, The University, Newcastle-upon-Tyne.

‡1976 A. MILLAR, Dept. of Philosophy, University of Stirling, Stirling FK9 4LA.

§1959 D. E. MILLIGAN, 11 Trelawney Road, Bristol 6.

§1973 KEITH W. MILLS, 5 Hawthorn Crescent, Gilesgate Moor, Durham, DH1 1ED.

‡1969 E. P. MILLSTONE, First Floor Flat, 31, St. Michaels Place, Brighton, BN1 3FU.

§1949 Prof. BASIL MITCHELL, Oriel College, Oxford.

1954 D. MITCHELL, Worcester College, Oxford.

Elected
1953 J. S. MITCHELL, "South View", Potter's Heath Road, Welwyn, Herts.
1975 Miss SARAH MITCHELL, Dept. of Philosophy, Bedford College, Regents Park, London, N.W.1 (P.3).
1966 K. MITCHELLS, 1 Turner Close, London, N.W.11.
1970 Rev. R. MOLONEY, Heythrop College, 11/13 Cavendish Square, London W.1.
‡1962 J. A. MONCASTER, 3 York House, Kelvedon Road, Tiptree, Essex.
*1951 D. H. MONRO, Dept. of Philosophy, Monash University, Victoria, Australia.
‡1959 R. D. L. MONTAGUE, Dept. of Philosophy, The University, Leicester, LE1 7RH.
‡1952 ALAN MONTEFIORE, Balliol College, Oxford.
*† Prof. MARIO MONTUORI, The Italian Institute, 39 Belgrave Square, S.W.1.
1972 LAWRENCE MOONAN, 44 Knowsley House, Carslake Avenue, Bolton.
*1974 F. C. T. MOORE, Dept. of Philosophy, University of Birmingham, P.O. Box 363, Birmingham B15 2TT.
*1964 A. MORENO, Azcuénaga, 1877-1E, Buenos Aires, R. Argentina.
‡1960 G. MORICE, 46 Queen Street, Edinburgh 2, Scotland.
1976 Mrs. L. MORSE, 52 Priory Gardens, London N6 5QS.
1967 ALASTAIR MORRISON, Dept. of Politics, The University, Bristol.
1961 J. M. B. MOSS, 14 Northern Grove, Manchester M20 8WL.
*1965 Miss MARY MOTHERSILL, Dept. of Philosophy, Barnard College, Columbia University, New York, U.S.A.
1964 H. O. MOUNCE, Dept. of Philosophy, University College of Swansea, Singleton Park, Swansea, Wales.
*†1962 PHILIP MULLOCK, The School of Law, University of Pittsburgh, Pittsburgh, Pennsylvania 15213, U.S.A.
1958 Prof. M. K. MUNITZ, Marlborough Road, Scarborough, New York, 10510, U.S.A.
1969 DAVID MURRAY, Birkbeck College, 14 Gower Street, London W.C.1.
1976 Miss K. MURPHY, 4 Princess Gardens, Worpleston, Nr. Guildford, Surrey (S.2).

*1935 Prof. ERNEST NAGEL, Dept. of Philosophy, Columbia University, Broadway, New York, U.S.A.
*1969 MICHAEL NAISH, School of Education, Abercromby Square, The University, Liverpool 7.
†1967 Prof. H. NAKAMURA, Dept. of Philosophy, Chiba University, 33 1-Chome ya yoi-cho, Chiba, Japan.
‡1965 N. M. L. NATHAN, School of Social Studies, University of East Anglia, Univ. Plain, Norwich NOR 88C.
§1976 J. A. NAZARRO, 51 Beda Rd., Canton, Cardiff, Glam., Wales (P.3).
*†1966 Miss M. NESSER, Dept. of Philosophy, University of Natal, P.O. Box 1525, Durban, South Africa.
1961 K. NEUBERG, New College, Ivy House, North End Road, London N.W.11.
‡1956 J. G. H. NEWFIELD, School of Social Sciences, The Hatfield Polytechnic, P.O. Box 109, Hatfield, Herts.
‡1975 Rev. KENNETH NEWTON, The Parsonage, Chapel-of-Ease Road, St. David's, Bermuda.
1977 A. S. NICHOLLS, 20 Windermere Road, Wolverhampton NV6 9DW (S.2).
1959 Prof. P. H. NIDDITCH, Dept. of Philosophy, The University, Sheffield.
1977 R. J. NORMAN, Darwin College, Univ. of Kent, Canterbury, Kent.
1964 Prof. G. NUCHELMANS, Van Polanenpark 180, Wassenaar, Holland.

288

Elected

‡1943   Prof. D. J. O'CONNOR, *Vice-President*, Dept. of Philosophy, The University, Exeter.

1966   H. R. ODLUM, Burgh Cottage, Nr. Woodbridge, Suffolk.

1975   A. O'HEAR, Dept. of Philosophy, Univ. of Surrey, Guildford, Surrey, GU2 5XH.

*†1974   Prof. MASAHIRO OKA, Hiroshima Shirdo University, Japan.

*†1966   PATRICK G. O'KEEFE, 23 Liverpool Road, St. Albans, Herts.

1962   HAROLD OSBOURNE, 90A St. John's Wood High Street, London N.W.8.

*1966   C. OLSEN, Dept. of History & Philosophy, Ontario, Institute for Studies in Education, 252 Bloor Street West, Toronto, Ontario M5S 1V6.

§1962   LADY HELEN OPPENHEIMER, L'Aiguillon, Grouville, Jersey C.I.

‡1961   C. P. ORMELL, 19 Kenton Road, Reading R96 2LQ.

*1968   JACK ORNSTEIN, Dept. of Philosophy, Sir George Williams Campus, Concordia University 1455 de Maisonnevve Blvd West, Montreal, Quebec, Canada H3G 1M8.

†1969   I. C. ORR, 3 St. Giles Road, Camberwell, London SE5 FRL.

1956   BRIAN O'SHAUGHNESSY, 6 Oakhill Avenue, Hampstead, London N.W.3.

1970   DAVID E. OVER, Sunderland Polytechnic, Forster Building, Chester Road, Sunderland, SR1 3SD.

1952   Prof. G. E. L. OWEN, The Beeches, Lower Heyford, Oxford.

1962   H. P. OWEN, King's College, Strand, W.C.2.

*1969   EDGAR PAGE, Pembroke Lodge, 43 Chapmangate, Pocklington, York.

‡1974   F. G. PALMER, 12 Buckingham Close, Hampton, Middlesex, TW12 3JU.

‡1962   HUMPHREY PALMER, 82 Plymouth Road, Penarth, S. Glamorgan.

*†1972   DOMENICO PARISI, Via Iside, 12, Rome, Italy.

§1975   S. J. PARRY, 10 Barnsley Road, Thorpe Hesley, Rotherham, S. Yorks.

1961   M. F. PARTRIDGE, Dept. of Logic, King's College, Aberdeen.

‡1975   Prof. ALAN PASCH, 6910 Wake Forest Drive, College Park, Maryland 20740, U.S.A.

1971   B. PASKINS, King's College London, Strand, London W.C.2.

1976   A. PAPARODITIS, Flat 4, 11 Belsize Park, London, N.W.3 (P.2).

*1948   Prof. J. A. PASSMORE, Australian National University, Canberra, A.C.T.

1960   Miss MARGARET PATON, Dept. of Philosophy, David Hume Tower, George Square, Edinburgh 8.

1954   Prof. BERNARD PEACH, Dept. of Philosophy, Duke University, Durham N.C., U.S.A.

*†1970   The Rev. T. E. PEACOCK, Chemistry Dept., University of Queensland, St. Lucia, Queensland 4067, Australia.

1974   C. A. B. PEACOCKE, All Souls College, Oxford.

*†1948   D. PEARS, Christchurch, Oxford.

1958   DIETRICH PEETZ, Dept. of Philosophy, The University, Nottingham.

1974   C. W. P. PEHRSON, Hamels Lodge, Hamels Park, Buntingford, Herts.

1961   Prof. T. M. PENELHUM, Dept. of Philosophy, The University of Calgary, Alberta, Canada.

‡1967   Prof. L. R. PERRY (16.3.77).

§1946   Prof. R. S. PETERS, University of London, Institute of Education, Malet Street, London W.C.1.

1975   M. PETHERAM, 18 Spencer Walk, Rickmansworth, Herts.

1975   Miss A. PHILLIPS, Dept. of Philosophy, University College, Gower Street, London W.C.1 (P.3).

§1962   Prof. D. Z. PHILLIPS, Dept. of Philosophy, University College of Swansea, Singleton Park, Swansea.

Elected

*†1976   EDMOND L. PINCOFFS, Dept. of Philosophy, University of Texas, Austin, Texas 78712, U.S.A.

*1961   S. PLOWDEN, 69 Albert Street, London N.W.1.

1957   MICHAEL PODRO, 1 Provost Road, London N.W.3.

1962   LEONARDO POMPA, Dept. of Philosophy, David Hume Tower, George Square, Edinburgh EH8 9JX.

*1946   Prof. Sir KARL POPPER, *Vice-President*, Fallowfield, Manor Road, Penn, Bucks.

§1935   Prof. A. J. D. PORTEOUS, 8 Osmanston Road, Prenton, Birkenhead, Cheshire.

§1967   T. POTTS, Dept. of Philosophy, Leeds University, Leeds 2, Yorkshire.

‡1957   Miss BETTY POWELL, Dept. of Philosophy, The University, Exeter.

1968   W. K. PRESA (14/4/74).

1968   A. E. PRESTON, University of Exeter, Guild of Students, Devonshire House, Stocker Road, Exeter, Devon, EX4 4PZ.

§1976   A. W. PRICE, Dept. of Philosophy, Univ. of York, Heslington, York, YD1 5DD.

†1953   Prof. KINGSLEY PRICE, Dept. of Philosophy, The John Hopkins University, Baltimore 18, Maryland, U.S.A.

1973   A. C. PURTON, 8, Norwich Road, Chedgrave, Norwich, NR14 6HB.

1973   Miss E. M. PYBUS, Dept. of Moral Philosophy, The University, Glasgow, W.2.

1975   Mrs. T. M. PYBUS, 4 Harvey Gardens, Addison Road, Guildford, Surrey (U2).

‡1950   A. M. QUINTON, *Vice-President*, New College, Oxford.

*1968   J. DOUGLAS RABB, Dept. of Philosophy, Lakehead University, Thunder Bay, Ontario, Canada.

†1975   Professor R. D. RAMSDELL, c/o A. J. P. Taylor, 13 Mark's Crescent, London NW1.

*†1957   K. W. RANKIN, Dept. of Philosophy, University of Victoria, Victoria, B.C., Canada.

§1945   Prof. D. D. RAPHAEL, *Vice-President*, Imperial College of Science & Technology, Kensington, London, SW7 2AZ.

1971   M. SALMAN RASCHID (16.9.76).

1975   DAVID R. RAYNOR, Magdalen College, Oxford (P.4).

1976   Prof. L. M. READ, 8a Prince Albert Road, London NW1 7SR.

‡1968   Prof. A. J. RECK, Dept. of Philosophy, Tulane University, New Orleans, La 70118, U.S.A.

1938   R. T. H. REDPATH, 49 Madingley Road, Cambridge.

1947   D. A. REES, Jesus College, Oxford, OX1 3DW.

§1954   JOHN C. REES, Dept. of Politics, University College, Swansea.

1957   W. J. REES, 20 Bracken Edge, Leeds 8.

*1973   JOHN REEVE, 20 Raleigh Road, Richmond, Surrey.

‡1960   A. D. REID, Newbattle Abbey College, Dalkeith, Midlothian.

1972   Mrs. E. M. REID, Dept. of Philosophy, The University, Glasgow, W2.

*1966   Prof. NICHOLAS RESCHER, Dept. of Philosophy, University of Pittsburgh, Pittsburgh, Pennsylvania 15213, U.S.A.

†1959   R. RHEES, 5A Greville Place, London N.W.6.

1954   JOSEPH RHYMER, Notre Dame College of Education, Mount Pleasant, Liverpool L3 55P.

1972   A. RHYS-WILLIAMS, 35 Dorset Road, Forest Gate, London E7.

1961   H. P. RICKMAN, 4 Nancy Downs, Oxhey, Herts, WD1 4NF.

*1951   Prof. A. M. RITCHIE, Dept. of Arts, Newcastle University College, Tighe's Hill, 2N, N.S.W., Australia.

Elected

*1970 C. W. ROBBINS, Dept. of Philosophy, University of York, Heslington, York.

1968 Prof. GEORGE W. ROBERTS, Dept. of Philosophy, Duke University, Durham, North Carolina, U.S.A.

‡1963 T. A. ROBERTS, Dept. of Philosophy, University College of Wales, Aberystwyth.

*1948 Prof. C. D. ROLLINS, Philosophy Dept., The University of Connecticut, Storrs, Connecticut, 06268, U.S.A.

1977 Miss G. ROMNEY, St. Hugh's College, Oxford.

1971 SERGE RONDINONE, 2265 Grand Avenue, New York, N.Y. 10453, U.S.A.

†1971 Miss A. RORTY (22.1.77).

1976 C. J. ROSE, Flat 2, 78, Arthur Road, London S.W.19.

1968 F. ROSEN, 40 Priory Gardens, Highgate, London N.6.

‡1966 G. ROSS, 28, Welford Place, London SW19 5AJ.

1972 R. H. ROWSON, 52, Tonteg Close, Tonteg, Pontypridd, Glamorgan.

§1959 J. W. ROXBEE COX, 1 Rectory Barn, Halton, Lancaster, LA2 6LT.

*1971 DAVID-HILLEL RUBEN, 27, Bromley Road, London E.17.

§1968 Prof. W. M. RUDDICK, 110 Bleecker Street, New York, N.Y. 10012.

§1967 BEDE RUNDLE, Trinity College, Oxford.

*†1969 M. JACQUES RUYTINX, 5 Rue des Taxandres, Bruxelles, Belgium.

1976 R. C. P. Salter, 151 Kings Road, Westcliff-on-Sea. (S.3).

‡1977 Mrs. J. R. SANDERS, 33, Aldebert Terrace, London SW8 1BH.

1968 DAVID H. SANFORD, Dept. of Philosophy, Duke University, Durham, N. Carolina, 27708, U.S.A.

1976 C. SAUER, Moreland, Little Brickhill, Bucks. MK7 9LT (P.2).

1968 A. B. SAVILE, Dept. of Philosophy, Bedford College, Regent's Park, London N.W.1.

1962 Prof. R. L. SAW, *Vice-President*, 72 Grosvenor Avenue, Carshalton, Surrey.

§1967 EVA SCHAPER, Logic Dept., The University, Glasgow, W.2.

*1958 Prof. I. SCHEFFLER, Larsen Hall, Harvard University, Cambridge, Mass. 02138, U.S.A.

*1971 FREDERIC SCHICK, Dept. of Philosophy, Rutgers University, New Brunswick, N.J. 08903, U.S.A.

§1947 W. E. SCHLARTZKI, Dept. of Philosophy, University of Maryland, College Park, Maryland 20742, U.S.A.

1972 Prof. DANA S. SCOTT, Merton College, Oxford.

1966 Miss M. SCOTFORD-MORTON, Dept. of Sociology, University of Reading, Berks.

1970 R. V. SCRUTON, Dept. of Philosophy, Birkbeck College, Malet Street, London, W.C.1.

1959 J. R. SEARLE, Dept. of Philosophy, University of California, Berkeley 4, California 94720, U.S.A.

1976 Prof. D. SELIGMAN, Dept. of Philosophy, Northern Illinois University, De Calb, Illinois 60015, U.S.A.

‡1945 Prof. PAUL SELIGMAN, 48 Greenhill Drive, Thorold Ont. LV2 1W5.

1968 Miss ANNE SELLAR, Keynes College, The University of Kent, Canterbury, Kent.

‡1976 J. SERTIC, Dept. of Philosophy, American River College, Sacramento, California 95821, U.S.A.

*1956 A. SHALOM, McMaster University (Dept. of Philosophy), Hamilton, Ontario, Canada.

1975 Prof. F. A. SHAMSI, Islamic Research Institute, P.O. Box 1035. Islamabad, Pakistan.

‡1971 R. A. SHARPE, St. David's College, Lampeter, Cards.

1972 RABBI DANIEL MARK SHERBOK, University of Kent at Canterbury, Faculty of Humanities, Canterbury, Kent, CT2 7NX.

Elected

1975   Prof. R. A. SHINER, 1005-80 Avenue Edmonton, Alberta, Canada TG6 OR2.

§1970   J. M. SHORTER, Lincoln College, Oxford.

§1972   PETER J. SHOTT, 55 Frederick Avenue, Penkhull, Stoke-on-Trent, Staffordshire, ST4 7DY.

‡1951   Prof. F. N. SIBLEY, Dept. of Philosophy, University of Lancaster, Bowland College, Bailrigg, Lancaster.

§1969   Prof. B. A. SICHEL, 61 Duncan Road, Hemstead, New York 11550.

‡1962   J. W. SIM, Pine Cottage, Harfield Road, Sunbury-on-Thames, Middlesex.

1963   Prof. J. SILBER, Principal, Boston University, 147 Bay State Road, Boston, Mass. 02215, U.S.A.

1952   J. C. SIMOPOULOS, c/o The Librarian, St. Catherine's College, Oxford OX1 3UJ.

1970   R. W. SIMPSON, Dept. of Moral Philosophy, Kings College, Old Aberdeen, Aberdeen.

*†1952   Prof. MARCUS G. SINGER, 5185 Helen C. White Hall, University of Wisconsin, Madison, Wis 53706, U.S.A.

§1972   Miss D. J. D. SISSON, Dept. of Moral Philosophy, The University Glasgow, Glasgow G12 8QG.

§1969   R. A. SKILLICORN, Tan y Weirglodd, Clwt y Bont, Caernafon, Gwynedd, LL55 3DE.

‡1975   J. M. SKORUPSKI, Dept. of Philosophy, University College of Swansea, Singleton Park, Swansea, Glam., SA2 8PP.

1966   B. J. SMART, Dept. of Philosophy, University of Keele, Keele, Staffordshire, ST5 5BG.

1948   Prof. J. J. C. SMART, The Australian National University, Dept. of Philosophy, Research School of Social Sciences, PO Box 4, Canberra, ACT 3600, Australia.

§1969   Miss PATRICIA SMART, University of Surrey, Guildford, Surrey.

1956   Prof. R. N. SMART, Dept. of Religious Studies, Cartmel College, University of Lancaster, Bailrigg, Lancaster.

‡1958   COLIN SMITH, Dept. of French Studies, Faculty of Letters, University of Reading, Whiteknights Park, Reading, Berks.

1949   Prof. F. V. SMITH, University of Durham, Dept. of Psychology, Science Laboratories, South Road, Durham.

§1971   PETER SMITH, Dept. of Philosophy, University College of Wales, Aberystwyth.

‡1964   JAMES W. F. SOMERVILLE, Dept. of Philosophy, The University, Hull.

1967   R. SORABJI, 2 Dorlcote Road, Wandsworth Common, London S.W.18.

*†1972   A. W. SPARKES, Dept. of Philosophy, The University of Newcastle. N.S.W. 2308, Australia.

*1951   F. E. SPARSHOTT, Victoria College, Toronto 5, Ontario, Canada.

*†1970   Prof. S. F. SPICKER, 17, Longdane Road, West Hartford, Connecticut, 06117, U.S.A.

*1958   T. L. SPRIGGE, The University of Sussex, School of English & American Studies, Arts Building, Falmer, Brighton, Sussex BN1 9QN.

§1972   J. E. R. SQUIRES, 5 Drumcarrow Road, St. Andrews, Fife, Scotland.

1974   Miss H. S. STANILAND, Dept. of Philosophy & Classics, University of Nigeria Nsukka, Nigeria.

1966   M. STCHEDROFF, The Philosophy Dept., The Queen's University of Belfast 7, Northern Ireland.

1976   Mrs. B. L. STEELE, 34 Litchfield Way, Onslow Village, Guildford, Surrey.

*1958   Mrs. DOROTHY C. MACEDO DE STEFFENS, Rondeau, 669 Bahia Blanca, R. Argentina.

Elected

§1974   H. I. STEINER, Dept. of Government, University of Manchester, Manchester 13.

1964   AXEL STERN, Dept. of Philosophy, The University, Hull.

*1964   Prof. L. STERN, Dept. of Philosophy, Rutgers, The State University, New Brunswick, New Jersey, 08903, U.S.A.

*1965   G. G. L. STOCK, Dept. of Logic, King's College, Old Aberdeen, Aberdeen.

1953   S. J. STOLJAR, Institute of Advanced Studies, Australian National University, Canberra, Australia.

§1955   The Hon. COLIN STRANG, Dept. of Philosophy, The University, Newcastle-upon-Tyne NE1 7RU.

‡1947   Prof. P. F. STRAWSON, *Vice-President*, Magdalen College, Oxford.

1961   Prof. A. STROLL, Dept. of Philosophy, University of California, San Diego, U.S.A.

1959   Prof. W. STRZALWOWSKI, 207 Fulham Court, SW6 5PQ.

‡1950   OLIVER STUTCHBURY, *Hon. Treasurer*, 45, South Street, Eastbourne, E. Sussex, BN21 4UT.

§1966   S. R. SUTHERLAND, Dept. of Philosophy, University of Stirling, Stirling, Scotland.

‡1969   Mrs. A. M. SUTTON, 247 Avenue Albert 1st, B-1320, Genval, Belgium.

‡1961   Prof. R. G. SWINBURNE, Dept. of Philosophy, University of Keele. Keele, Staffs. ST5 5BG.

1963   M. K. TANNER, Corpus Christi College, Cambridge.

1976   Mrs. M. Y. TATHAM, 8 St. Michaels Road, Caterham-on-the-Hill, Surrey (P.2).

§1968   C. C. W. TAYLOR, Corpus Christi College, Oxford.

§1948   Prof. D. TAYLOR, Dept. of Philosophy, University of Otago, Box 56, Dunedin, New Zealand.

§1976   D. M. TAYLOR, Master Eliot College, Univ. of Kent at Canterbury, Kent, CT2 7NS.

1975   Mrs. E. G. TAYLOR, St. Annes College, Oxford.

*1975   E. H. TAYLOR, 2 Lowery Drive, Atherton, California 94025 U.S.A.

§1972   DAVID REX-TAYLOR, 1A Whitton Waye, Hounslow, Middlesex.

1970   Mrs. JENNY TEICHMANN, New Hall, Cambridge.

‡1968   Miss ELIZABETH TELFER, Dept. of Philosophy, University of Glasgow, Glasgow W.2.

§1969   Mrs. RACHEL TERRY, 74 Brook Drive, London SE11 4TS.

§1972   Prof. S. C. THAKUR, Department of Philosophy, The University of Surrey, Guildford, Surrey.

§1972   H. J. THIBAULT, All Hallows, Drumcondra, Dublin 9, Eire.

1960   D. O. THOMAS, Dept. of Philosophy, University College, Aberystwyth, Wales.

*†1966   Rev. J. C. THOMAS, Dept. of the Study of Religions, P.O. Box 66, The University, Legon, Accra, Ghana.

1975   Mrs. JANICE L. THOMAS, 4A Provost Road, London, NW3 3ST.

1945   L. E. THOMAS, Bodalwen, Merion Road, Bangor, Caerns. LL57 2BY.

1961   MANLEY THOMPSON, University of Chicago, Chicago 37, Illinois, U.S.A.

1975   H. THORPE, 2B Manor Park Road, London, N2 0SL.

1956   H. TINT (21.8.76).

1973   T. T. TOMINAGA, Dept. of Philosophy, University of Nevada, 4505 Maryland Parkway, Las Vegas, Nevada 89154, U.S.A.

1938   E. W. F. TOMLIN, Tall Trees, Morwenstow, Cornwall.

‡1972   ERIC TOMS, 9, Campsie Drive, Milngavie, Glasgow, G62 8HX.

1975   IAN M. TONOTHY, 20 Clarendon Gardens, London W9 1A2.

1965   Mrs. M. H. F. TOOMEY, Bard College, Annandale-on-Hudson, New York, U.S.A.

Elected
*1969   S. B. TORRANCE, Corpus Christi College, Oxford.
1948   STEPHEN TOULMIN (12.3.77).
1965   R. H. TRIGG, School of Philosophy, University of Warwick, Coventry, Warwickshire.
§1975   Mr. JUN'ICHI TSUCHIYA, Dept. of Philosophy, Kanazawa University, 1-1 Morunouchi, Kanazawa, 920, Japan.
1964   Prof. R. TSUESITA, (106) 1-5-22, Moto-Azabu, Minato-Ku, Tokyo, Japan.

1975   WILLIAM UNGLESS, 73 Holden Road, London, N12.
1939   J. O. URMSON, Corpus Christi College, Oxford.

1970   J. J. VALBERG, Dept. of Philosophy, University College London, Gower Street, London W.C.1.
§1976   A. J. D. VAN VESSEM, 102 Southfield Road, Oxford, OX1 1PA.
‡1974   Miss G. VAUGHAN, 44 Woodland Gardens, London N10 3UA.
1964   Prof. MICHALINA VAUGHAN, Dept. of Sociology, Cartmel College, Bailrigg, Lancs.
1952   Prof G. N. A. VESEY, Faculty of Arts, The Open University, Walton Hall, Milton Keynes, Bucks.
*1976   Professor GERALD VISION, Temple University, Philosophy Dept., Philadelphia, PA 19122, U.S.A.
1975   Professor GREGORY VLASTOS, Dept. of Philosophy, Princeton University, 1879 Hall, Princeton, New Jersey 08540, U.S.A.

†1975   G. I. WALL, 73 Ridge Road, London, N8 9NP.
1953   The Rev. Dr. N. E. WALLBANK, St. Peter's House, Oakley Crescent, City Road, E.C.1.
1965   J. D. B. WALKER, Dept. of Philosophy, McGill University, Montreal 2, Canada.
‡1950   Prof. W. H. WALSH, *Vice-President*, 19 Great Stuart Street, Edinburgh 3.
1964   R. S. WALTERS, School of Philosophy, University of New South Wales, P.O. Box 1 Kensington, N.S.W., Australia.
1972   Prof. G. N. WALTON, Department of Chemical Engineering, Imperial College, South Kensington, London S.W.7.
1971   K. A. WALTON, 940, Westbrook, Apt. 2, Perrysburg, Ohio, 43551, U.S.A.
1971   Revd. J. S. K. WARD, Trinity Hall, Cambridge.
*†1964   R. X. WARE, Dept. of Philosophy, University of Calgary, Calgary, Alberta, Canada.
§1969   MARTIN M. WARNER, School of Philosophy, University of Warwick, Coventry.
1949   G. J. WARNOCK, Principal, Hertford College, Oxford.
1971   Miss SARAH WATERLOW, Dept. of Philosophy, The University of Edinburgh, David Hume Tower, George Square, Edinburgh.
§1954   J. WATLING, Dept. of Philosophy, University College, Gower Street, W.C.1.
§1971   D. W. WATSON, Dept. of Moral Philosophy, The University, Glasgow, G12 8QQ.
*1967   SIK-YING WAUNG, 19A Repulse Bay Road, 10th Floor, Hong Kong.
1973   Miss GERALDINE WEBSTER, Dufferin House, 24 Dalrymple Crescent, Edinburgh 9.
*1973   Mrs. M. E. WEDDEN, 155 Ash Grove, Heston, Hounslow, Middlesex TW5 9DX.
1951   Prof. M. WEITZ, Dept. of Philosophy, Brandeis University, Waltham, Mass., U.S.A.
1977   MICHAEL WELBOURNE, Dept. of Philosophy, University of Bristol, Bristol BS8 1RJ.

Elected

1976 PHILIP L. WELLER, 67, Ambleside, Bodgrove, Aylesbury, Bucks. (P.1).

§1951 PAUL WELSH, Box 6846, College Station, Durham, N. Carolina, 27708, U.S.A.

§1977 A. K. P. WENSLEY, 301, New Kings Road, London SW6 URE.

*1969 D. J. WEST, Dept. of Philosophy, Acadia University, Wolfville, Nova Scotia, Canada.

1960 J. J. WHEATLEY, Dean of Graduate Studies, Simon Fraser University, Burnaby 2, British Columbia, Canada.

*1973 D. A. WHEWELL, Dept. of Philosophy, University of Durham, 50 Old Elvet, Durham.

§1962 Prof. A. R. WHITE, The University Hull.

*†1976 D. M. WHITE, Dept. of Politics, Monash University, Clayton 3168, Victoria, W. Australia.

1975 ROGER M. WHITE, Dept. of Philosophy, University of Leeds, Leeds.

1966 J. P. WHITE, Dept. of Philosophy, Inst. of Education, Malet Street, London W.C.1.

*1951 Prof. MORTON WHITE, The Institute for Advanced Study, Princeton, New Jersey, 08540, U.S.A.

‡1936 Prof. C. H. WHITELEY, Vice-President, Department of Philosophy, The University of Birmingham.

‡1962 Prof. D. WIGGINS, Dept. of Philosophy, Bedford College, Regent's Park, London N.W.1.

‡1960 GEORGE WIGHTMAN, 11 Bramham Gardens, London S.W.5.

1969 Y. WILKS, Dept. of Linguistics, University of Essex, Colchester, Essex.

1953 Prof. BERNARD WILLIAMS, King's College, Cambridge.

‡1961 C. J. F. WILLIAMS, Cluthaville, 1 Fossefield Road, Midsomer Norton, Bath, BA3 4AS.

§1976 S. WILLIAMS, 301, St. Margaret's Road, Twickenham, Middlesex.

1960 JOHN WILLIAMSON, Dept. of Philosophy, The University of Liverpool.

1976 G. A. WILLIS, 91, Bryans Leap, Burnopfield, Newcastle-on-Tyne (S.2).

1973 H. R. WILLS, Thomas Huxley College, Woodlands Avenue, Acton, London, W3 9DP.

1963 Mrs. S. WILSMORE, Willow House, Conduit Head Road, Cambridge.

*†1974 B. G. WILSON, 26661, Pepita Drive, Mission Viejo, California 92675, U.S.A.

1976 E. WILSON, 29 Heathend Road, Alsager, Stoke-on-Trent, Staffs.

1966 I. R. WILSON, Department of Philosophy, University of Stirling, Stirling, Scotland.

§1972 ROBERT D. WILSON, 86, Bramhall Lane South, Bramhall, Stockport, SK7 2EA, Cheshire.

‡1958 Prof. P. G. WINCH, Dept. of Philosophy, King's College, The Strand, London W.C.2.

1933 Prof. J. WISDOM, Vice-President, Colorado State University, Dept. of Philosophy, Fort Collins, Colorado, U.S.A.

*1932 Prof. J. O. WISDOM, Dept. of Philosophy, York University, Toronto, Ontario, Canada.

1951 Mrs. I. WISDOM, Flat 25 Hornton Court, London W.8.

1949 LORD WOLFENDEN, The White House, Westcott, Guildford Road, Nr. Dorking, Surrey.

1950 Prof. R. A. WOLLHEIM, Vice-President, Dept. of Philosophy, University College, Gower Street, London W.C.1.

1975 D. A. R. WOOD, University of W. Australia, Dept. of Philosophy, Nedlands, 6009, Australia.

1975 J. W. WOOD, Oriel College, Oxford.

§1948 OSCAR P. WOOD, Christ Church, Oxford.

§1958 M. WOODS, Brasenose College, Oxford.

1976 W. Woods, 8, Victoria Grove, Bideford, Devon.
1936 Prof. A. D. Woozley, 79a, Highbury New Park, London N5.
1976 D. Worrall, 1, Links View Road, Shirley, Croydon, Surrey CR0 8NB (S.3).
*1939 Mrs. L. E. G. Worsley, 167 Long Ashton Road, Nr. Bristol.
1970 A. C. H. Wright, 108 Derby Lodge, Wicklow Street, London, W.C.1.
1969 C. B. Wright, Dept. of Philosophy, The University of Exeter, Queen's Building, The Queen's Drive, Exeter.
†1975 C. J. G. Wright, All Souls College, Oxford.
‡1975 P. N. Wright, 29 Leaf Close, Northwood, Middlesex, HA6 2YY.

*1964 Rev. Michael Yanase, S.J., Faculty of Science and Technology, Sophia University, 7 Kioi-Cho, Chiyoda, Tokyo-ku, Japan.

1960 M. F. Zeidan, Faculty of Arts, Shatby, Alexandria, U.A.R.
*1968 Robert L. Zimmerman, Sarah Lawrence College, c/o Dept. of Philosophy, Bronxville, New York, 10708, U.S.A.
1976 A. Zuboff, 12, Belsize Park Gardens, London, NW3 4LD.